LEGENDARY LOCALS

OF

OAKLAND

CALIFORNIA

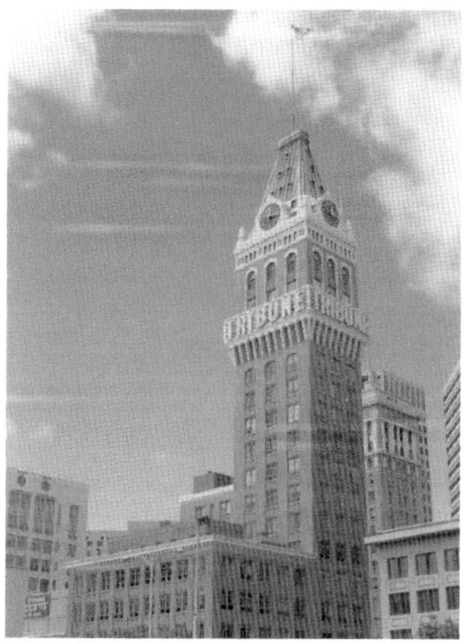

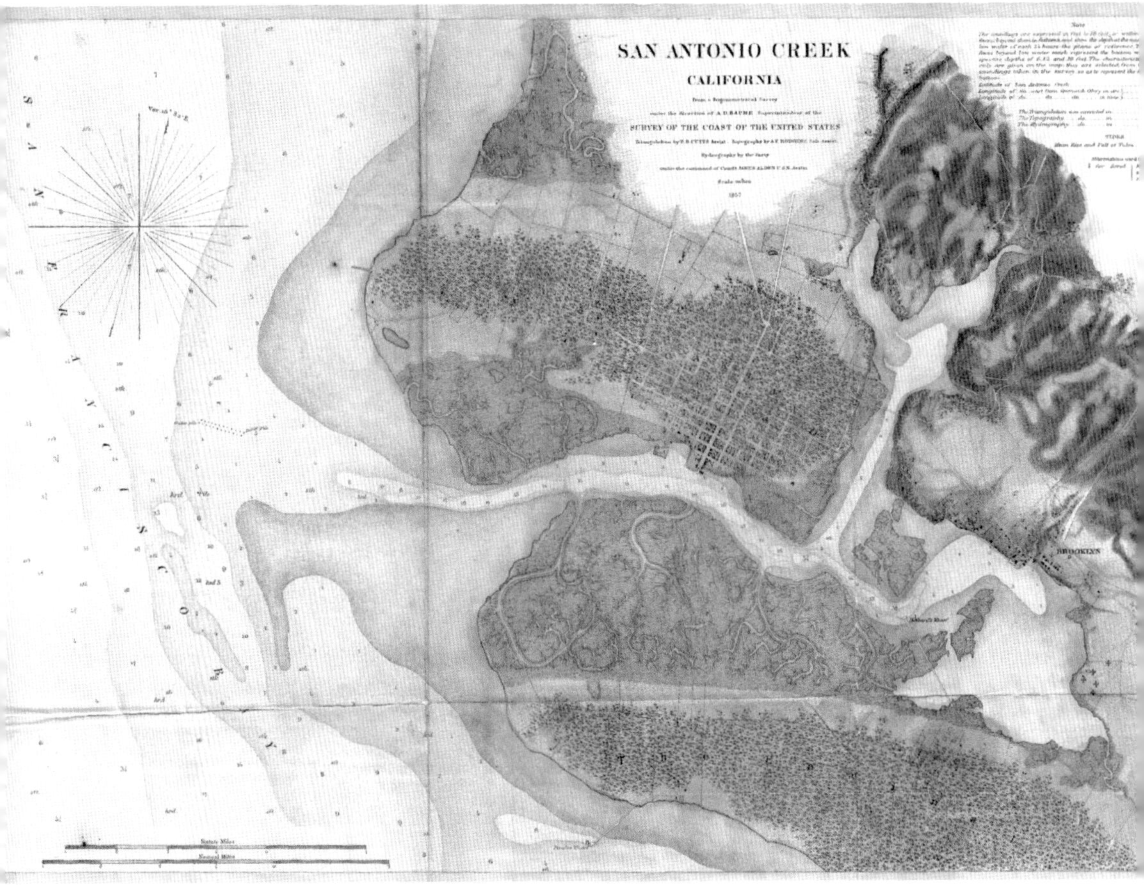

Oakland
This 1857 nautical chart shows Oakland just a few years after becoming a city in 1854. Although the landscape and coastline have changed, some landmarks like Broadway, Telegraph Avenue, and Twelfth Street are already visible. It is also much easier to see that Lake Merritt is actually a tidal slough connected to San Francisco Bay. (From United States Coast Survey, retrieved from Wikimedia Commons.)

Page 1: Tribune Tower
The *Oakland Tribune* has been part of Oakland since 1874 and the iconic Tribune Tower part of the skyline since 1923. The newspaper became part of the Alameda Newspaper Group in 1993 and moved out of the tower in 2007, but the tower and the newspaper are still very much a part of Oakland. (Author's collection.)

LEGENDARY LOCALS

OF

OAKLAND

CALIFORNIA

GENE ANDERSON

LEGENDARY LOCALS

ISBN 978-1-4671-0209-4

Legendary Locals is an imprint of Arcadia Publishing
Charleston, South Carolina

Printed in the United States of America

Library of Congress Control Number: 2014959796

For all general information, please contact Arcadia Publishing:
Telephone 843-853-2070
Fax 843-853-0044
E-mail sales@arcadiapublishing.com
For customer service and orders:
Toll-Free 1-888-313-2665

Visit us on the Internet at www.arcadiapublishing.com

Dedication

To my wife, Katarina Stenstedt, for her patience while I cycled and walked around Oakland collecting stories and taking pictures. And to the amazing people of Oakland who make it the great city that it is.

On the Front Cover: Clockwise from top left:
Artist and activist Favianna Rodriguez (author's collection; see page 94), musician Pete Escovedo (author's collection; see page 100), small business owner Tina "Tamale" Ramos (courtesy Paula Wirth; see page 124), whaling captain William Shorey (courtesy San Francisco Maritime National Historical Park Research Center; see page 32), politician Frank Ogawa (author's collection; see page 57), journalist Robert Maynard (courtesy Maynard Institute for Journalism Education; see page 66), astronomer Charles Burckhalter (courtesy Chabot Space & Science Center; see page 16), writer, poet, and art patron Gertrude Stein (courtesy Library of Congress; see page 20), Children's Hospital founder Mabel Weed (courtesy K. Bodding; see page 37).

On the Back Cover: From left to right:
Everett and Jones family, founders of Everett and Jones BBQ (courtesy Shirley Everett Dicko; see page 61), astronomer and teacher Kingsley Wightman (courtesy Chabot Space & Science Center; see page 106).

CONTENTS

Acknowledgments 6

Introduction 7

CHAPTER ONE Footsteps in the Past 9

CHAPTER TWO The Sunny Side of the Bay 15

CHAPTER THREE The City Beautiful 35

CHAPTER FOUR New Era, New Politics 53

CHAPTER FIVE Home Field 73

CHAPTER SIX Artists, Builders, and Makers 83

CHAPTER SEVEN Oakland Today 105

Bibliography 125

Index 126

ACKNOWLEDGMENTS

When I started on this book, it quickly became apparent that the biggest problem I faced was deciding who to include and who to leave out. There are so many interesting people who have shaped and are shaping Oakland that I could fill several books. I talked with authors, historians, politicians, business owners, friends, and family, and the more Oaklanders I talked to, the longer the list became. I have tried to include a cross-section with a few of the people of Oakland who made it the great city it is, but it is a long way from complete.

My first resource for people to include were the numerous books already written about Oakland and its people. I would like to thank Annalee Allen, Dennis Evanosky, William Gee Wong, Paul Brekke-Meisner, and the late Beth Bagwell, author of *Oakland: The Story of a City*.

I had another resource that wasn't available to these authors, the Oakland Wiki (www.oaklandwiki.org). This ever-growing online encyclopedia about Oakland allowed me to organize, research, and connect people in new ways. More than once, the Oakland Wiki also provided a way to connect with families of legendary locals and get photographs and facts that were not previously available. Thanks to Mike Detwiler, Lauren Briskin, Neal Parish, and the rest of the crew who contributed to the Oakland Wiki.

I would also like to thank some of the other historians in Oakland, including Betty Marvin of the Oakland Cultural Heritage Survey, Dorothy Lazard of the Oakland History Room at the Oakland Public Library, Randal Metz at Children's Fairyland, and Dave Hector of the Oakland Fire Department.

Finally, I would like to thank all the people I talked with about their own stories and the stories of their families, who provided photographs and information. You, too, are keepers of Oakland's history. The stories are theirs, but any errors in the book are mine.

INTRODUCTION

People in Oakland have a love for their home unlike any other. Show disrespect for "The Town," and most Oaklanders will spring to its defense. While some people will talk about the crime, the high cost of living, and too much development (or not enough), people in Oakland love their city.

Oakland incorporated as a town in 1852, largely through the efforts of Horace Carpentier. This came as a surprise to the residents of what had been the village of Contra Costa ("Opposite Shore"). However, Oakland's story begins long before the town was named for the oak trees that dotted the landscape. The Ohlone people lived around the San Francisco Bay when the Spanish started arriving in larger numbers in 1776. Alta California remained part of the Spanish empire until Mexico gained independence in 1821 and then was ceded to the United States in 1848 in the Mexican-American War.

The town of Oakland didn't spring from nothing; after the Ohlone were mostly gone, the four Peralta brothers received land that the Spanish crown had granted their father and had ranchos that covered the East Bay from San Leandro to Albany. Each built homes and other buildings, raised families, and hired laborers to work the ranchos. They leased some land to people like Moses Chase, the first American citizen to settle in what is now Oakland. Others settled on the land, legally or not, and many passed through on their way to the gold fields; the seeds were planted, and things began changing rapidly.

While natural forces like climate and earthquakes have shaped Oakland over the years, it has mostly been molded by the people who have called Oakland home. As soon as people settled in what is now Oakland, they began changing the shoreline, building wharves for shipping, filling in parts of the bay, and even damming San Antonio Slough to form Lake Merritt. San Francisco may have been a much bigger city with a natural port, but Oakland built wharves and dredged the estuary, and people lobbied to make Oakland the terminus of the first transcontinental railroad in 1869.

The railroad brought people from all over the country, and many of them settled here. Oakland grew and annexed other nearby towns. As with many coastal cities, World War II changed Oakland, and the postwar availability of automobiles and new freeways changed it more.

Oakland continues to change, sometimes to the consternation of those living here. While many people enjoy the influx of new restaurants and businesses, others are concerned about rising housing costs and existing residents being pushed out.

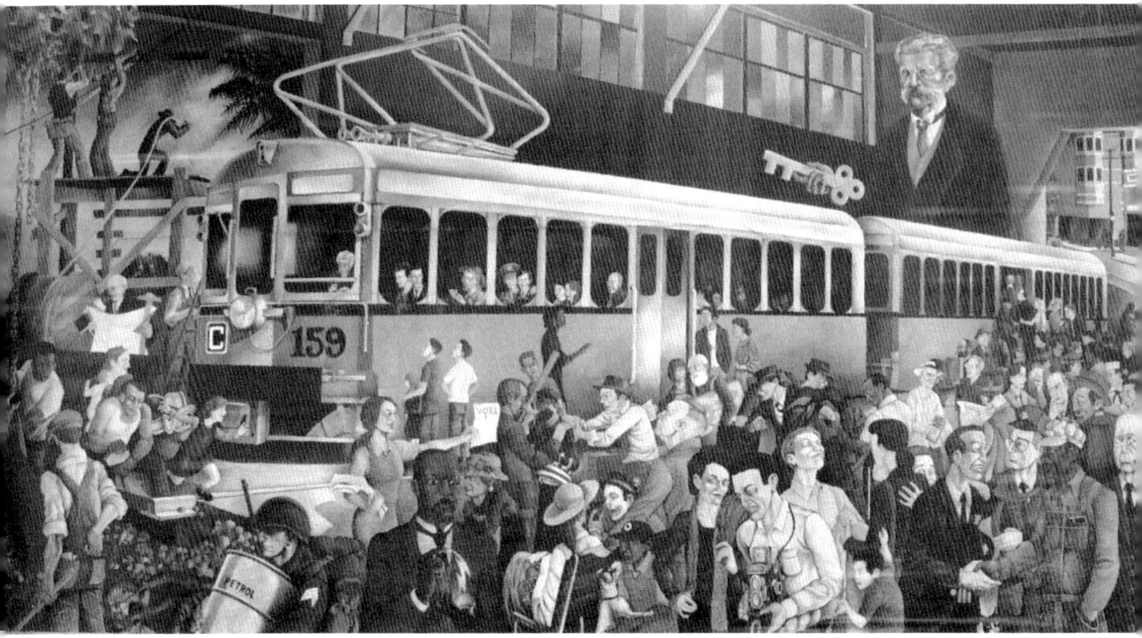

Key System Remembered
In the age of automobiles, it can be hard to remember that people used to get around Oakland mostly on foot and by streetcar. This mural by artist Rocky Rische-Baird commemorates the Key System, created in 1903. But things change; the last local streetcars ran in 1948, and the Key System shut down completely in 1960. This mural was destroyed in 2015. (Author's collection.)

CHAPTER ONE

Footsteps in the Past

The land is our gold.

—Luis María Peralta, to his sons

The Ohlone people were some of the first known residents of what is now Oakland. Long before Europeans arrived in the Bay Area in 1769, the Ohlone lived in small groups around the bay, hunting, fishing, and gathering. The land was dotted with oaks and other trees, and apart from fires that the Ohlone set to clear the underbrush and the occasional earthquake, the area changed very slowly for thousands of years.

Things began to change more quickly after 1776, when Juan Bautista de Anza led more than 300 Spanish and Afro-Latino settlers and soldiers from Spanish Mexico into California. Some were seeking a new life; Anza was seeking new lands for the king of Spain, and Fr. Pedro Font was seeking new converts for the church. Anza located sites for a mission in what is now San Jose and a mission and a presidio in what is now San Francisco. Once the missions were established, more people made the journey to settle in California.

Oakland's early history is similar to that of nearby San Francisco, but with some important differences. Both were home to groups of Ohlone people when the Anza expedition arrived. San Francisco with its presidio and mission received much more direct attention from the Spanish than Contra Costa (as the East Bay was then known), with one notable exception—the Spanish recognized the value of the towering redwoods in the hills of Oakland.

One member of Anza's expedition was 17-year-old Luis María Peralta, who came with his family. In 1820, after noted military service, Peralta was granted 44,800 acres by the Spanish crown. This land covered the East Bay from San Leandro to Albany. Peralta never lived on the land, but divided it between his four sons, telling them, "The land is our gold." It is worth noting that Peralta's land grant was from the shore to the crest of the hills, but the crown kept the harbor and the rights to the redwoods for itself.

The province of Alta California and the rest of Mexico became independent from Spain in 1821. By the time California became a state in 1850 and Oakland incorporated in 1852, disease and other factors had reduced the Ohlone population to 10 percent of its former size, settlers from all over were seeking their fortunes in the gold fields, and the time of the Spanish Californios was all but over.

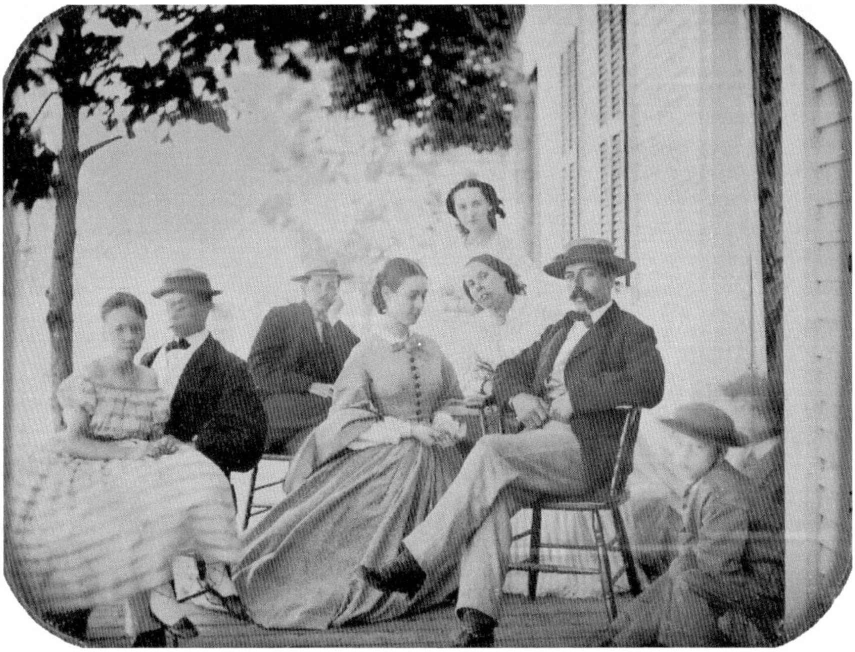

Last of the Californios

Antonio Peralta (seated on right, with various family members) and his brothers once owned most of the East Bay, including Oakland. Luis María Peralta divided his 44,800-acre Spanish land grant between Antonio and his three brothers—Hermenegildo Ignacio Peralta, José Domingo Peralta, and José Vicente Peralta—but they were not able to keep it. Squatters, legal battles (including with their five sisters, who were given cattle and an adobe in San Jose instead), dishonest lawyers, and taxes led to the Peraltas giving up all but a small fraction of their land.

The Italianate Victorian house where Antonio Peralta lived with his family beginning in 1870 is now the centerpiece of the Peralta Hacienda Historical Park. (Above, courtesy Friends of Peralta Hacienda Historical Park; below, author's collection.)

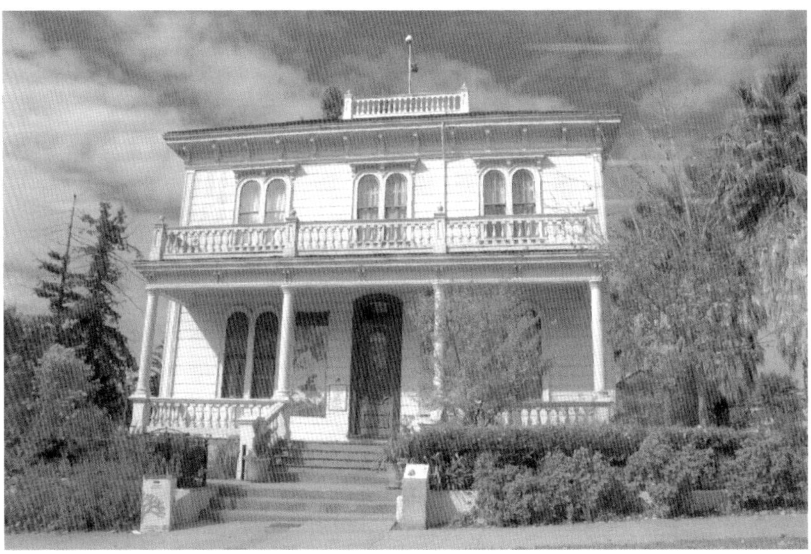

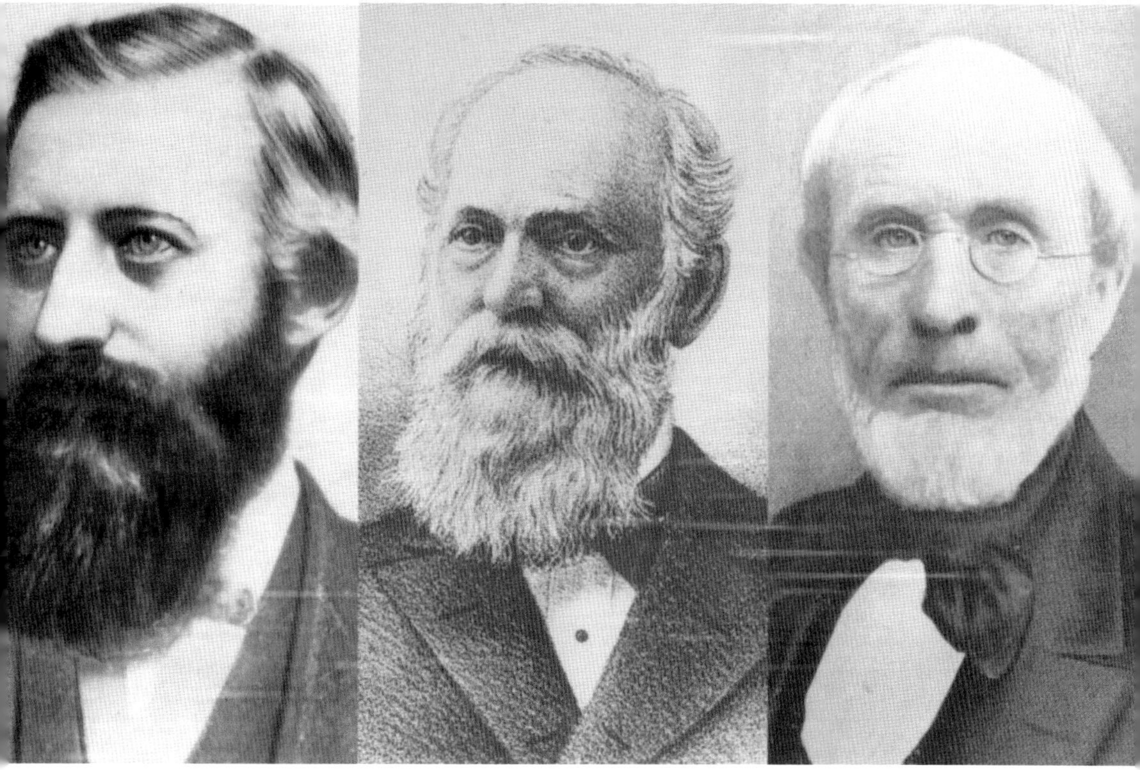

Founders or Scoundrels?

Some historians still debate the actions of Horace Carpentier, Edson Adams, and Andrew Moon (pictured here from left to right) and whether they intentionally defrauded the Peralta brothers of their land, but the result is the same. They leased land from Vicente Peralta and laid out much of what is now downtown Oakland before selling lots. The other Peralta brothers faced problems of their own and sold some of their land, giving some of it to Carpentier, who represented them in various legal proceedings. By the time the US Supreme Court finally ruled in favor of the Peraltas' claim in 1856, the land was covered with settlers and the Peraltas had lost all but a fraction of it.

Carpentier pushed forward the incorporation of Oakland as a town in 1852, much to the astonishment of the residents of the village that had been formerly known as Contra Costa. When Oakland became a city in 1854, Carpentier was elected the first mayor. This might otherwise be unremarkable, except there were more votes cast for him than there were voters in the nascent city.

Adams married Hannah Jayne, Oakland's first schoolteacher, and owned most of what is now the Adams Point neighborhood and Lakeside Park. Very little is known about Moon, except that he met Carpentier and Adams on the voyage west to California and was one of the town's first trustees. (Courtesy Oakland History Room, Oakland Public Library.)

Oakland's First Schoolteacher

Hannah Jayne was Oakland's first schoolteacher, working in a schoolhouse at Fifth and Clay Streets. She was the only public educator until January 1855, when officials decided it was too much work for one person and hired a principal, making Jayne his assistant. She gave up teaching after she married city founder Edson Adams later that year. (Courtesy Oakland History Room, Oakland Public Library.)

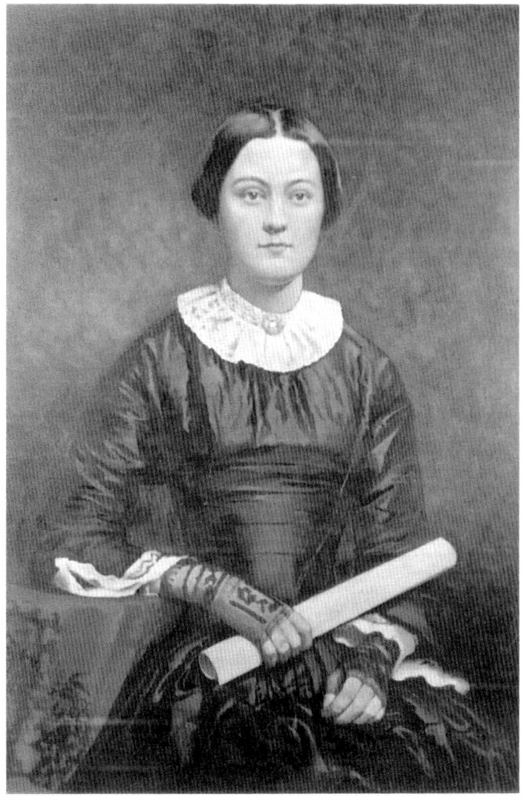

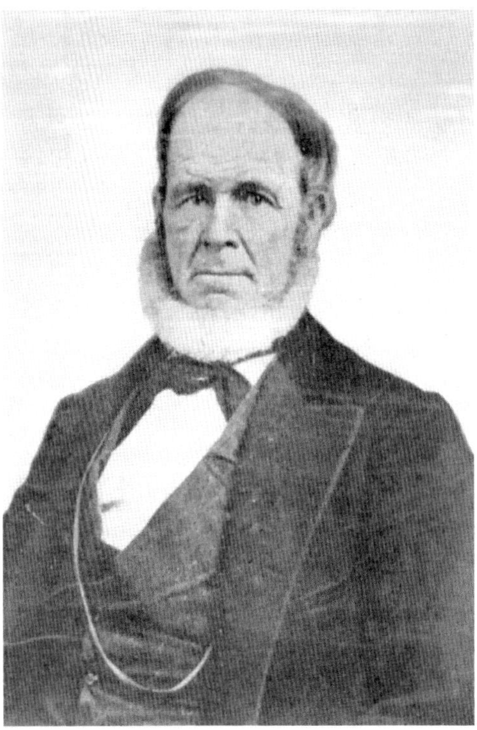

Father of Pacific Horticulture

Quaker and abolitionist Henderson Luelling was an early Oakland settler in what is now the Fruitvale district. He introduced varietal fruits to Oregon and later California and gave "Fruit Vale" its name. His care of the plants during the journey west to Oregon prompted his daughter to exclaim that he cared more about the trees than his family. (Courtesy Friends of Peralta Hacienda Historical Park.)

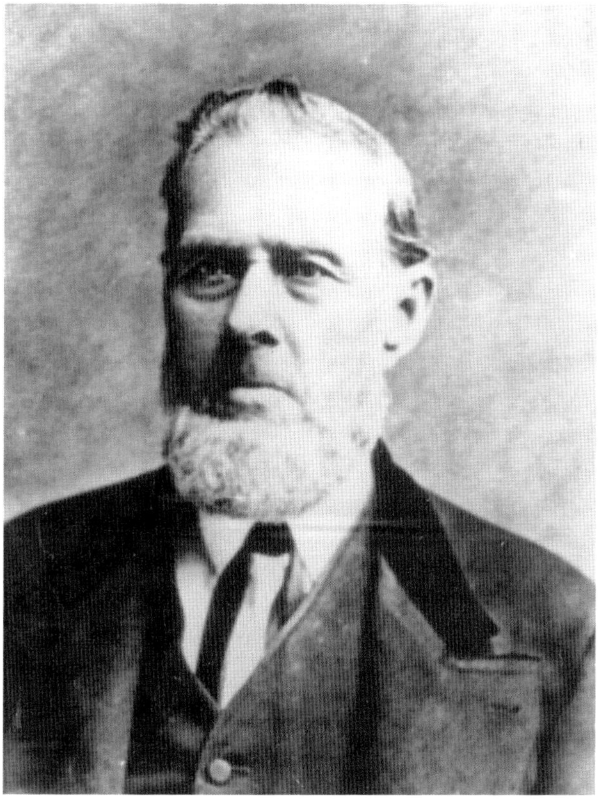

First American Settler in Oakland

Moses Chase was the first American citizen to settle in what is now Oakland. He came to California in 1849, hoping to make his fortune in the Gold Rush and to return to Boston to marry Mary Ellen Clinton. After his unsuccessful attempt at mining, he came to Oakland and, along with the Patten brothers, leased land from the Peraltas and founded the town of Clinton, named for his fiancée. Sadly, Clinton died before he returned. (Courtesy Oakland History Room, Oakland Public Library.)

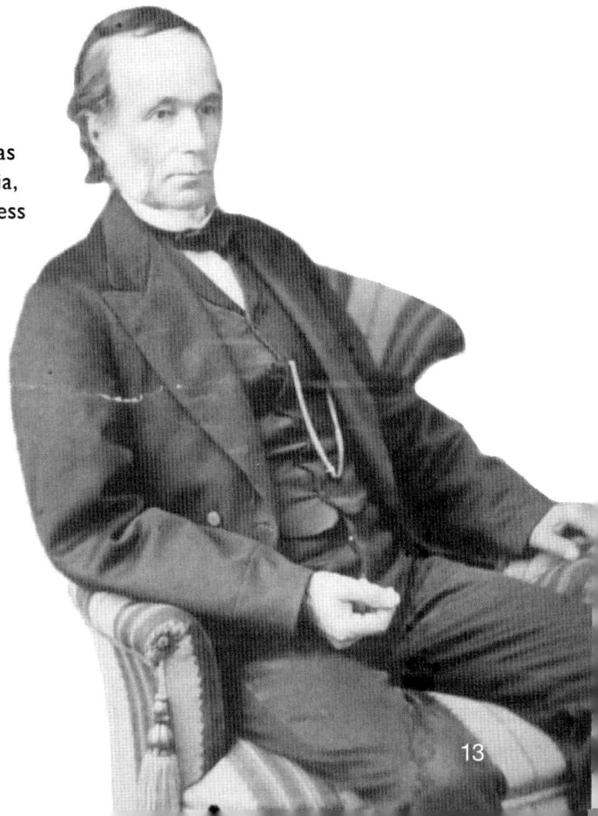

Founder of University of California

Rev. Henry Durant is probably best remembered as one of the founders of the University of California, and he served as its first president. What is less remembered is that the university started in Oakland as the Contra Costa Academy and later the College of California. It was merged into the new University of California in 1868 and was in Oakland until it moved to the new campus in Berkeley in 1873. Durant also served as the 16th mayor of Oakland. (Courtesy UC Berkeley Bancroft Library.)

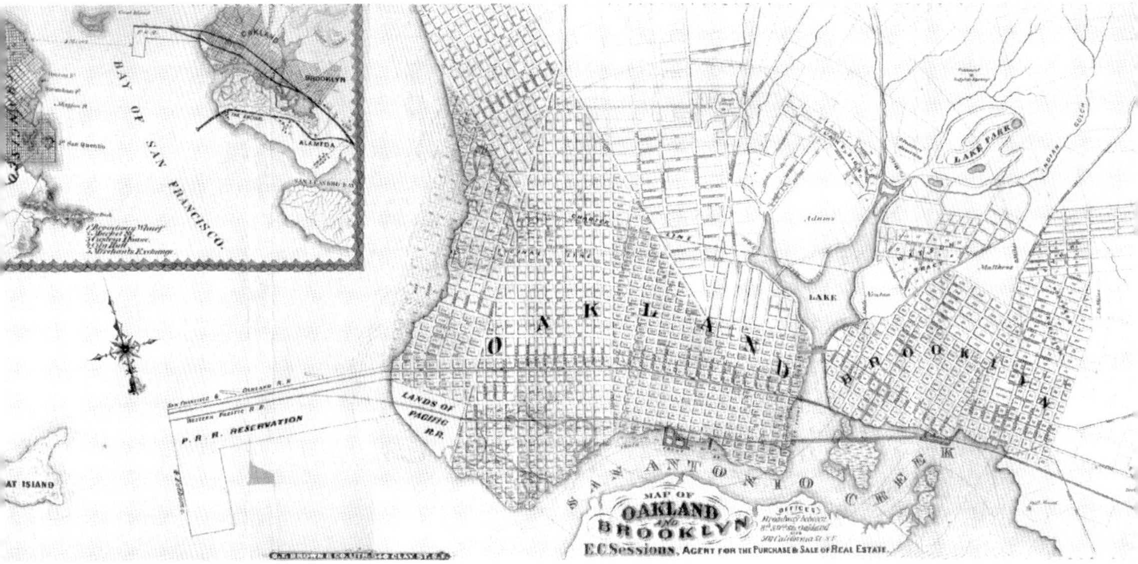

Don't Call it Brooklyn

One way to rile up some Oaklanders is to compare Oakland to Brooklyn, New York. But for a time, most of what is now Oakland was called Brooklyn. The name for the town of Brooklyn just east of Lake Merritt was suggested by county supervisor Thomas Eagar, who arrived in California in 1846 aboard the sailing ship *Brooklyn* with other Mormon settlers. Outside Oakland and Brooklyn, most of what is now Oakland was Brooklyn Township. Eagar later served in the state assembly. (Courtesy UC Berkeley Bancroft Library.)

CHAPTER TWO

The Sunny Side of the Bay

Even when the fog bank is high and envelops San Francisco in its humid embrace, Oakland almost invariably escapes it.

—*Information Concerning the Terminus of the Railroad System of the Pacific Coast*, 1871

Even in the time of the Spanish colonists, people recognized the weather was generally nicer on the Oakland side of the bay than in nearby San Francisco. Despite that, San Francisco grew much more quickly than Oakland, largely because of its presidio and mission, its deeper natural harbor, and the California Gold Rush that began in 1849. Treasure seekers came from all over the world to pursue fortunes in the gold fields of California. Some sailing crews even abandoned their ships to head to the gold country, leaving behind a forest of ship masts in the harbors.

San Francisco's population ballooned from about 1,000 in 1848 to 25,000 by the end of 1849, while a decade later in 1860, the city of Oakland's population was only a bit more than 1,500. The growth from the Gold Rush led to California's statehood in 1850 and the construction of Fort Point, beginning in 1851, to help secure the recent addition to the United States.

The rapid growth and steady changeover of population in San Francisco led to lawlessness, which drove some families to Oakland. Others moved because land and resources were more plentiful, and many because the weather was warmer and sunnier.

In the 1860s, the East Bay was sparsely populated, so while the great earthquake of 1868 on the Hayward Fault caused widespread damage, the death toll was relatively low. Still, it reminded people all around the bay that earthquakes were part of living in California.

Things changed more rapidly with the coming of the first transcontinental railroad in 1869. While San Francisco was a larger city, it was separated from points east by its namesake bay, so Oakland was the logical terminus for the railroad, and locals lobbied hard for it. While none of the "Big Four" of railroad fame lived in Oakland, Charles Crocker is buried in Mountain View Cemetery, and Leland Stanford's brother Josiah lived in what is now known as the Camron-Stanford House on the shore of Lake Merritt. Serving as a railroad terminus continued to impact Oakland for the next century, bringing people from all over the United States and later introducing the country to goods and ideas from California.

The single biggest event during this time was the 1906 San Francisco earthquake. The temblor was several times more powerful than the 1868 earthquake, and it was on the San Andreas Fault, which runs through the San Francisco Peninsula. In seconds, hundreds of people died and thousands were made homeless. The toll in Oakland was not nearly so bad, but water mains were broken and brick buildings and chimneys around the East Bay were damaged. An estimated 100,000–150,000 of the newly homeless of San Francisco came to the East Bay and doubled the population of Oakland in three days. Even as San Francisco rapidly rebuilt in the months and years following the quake, many of those people chose to stay in Oakland.

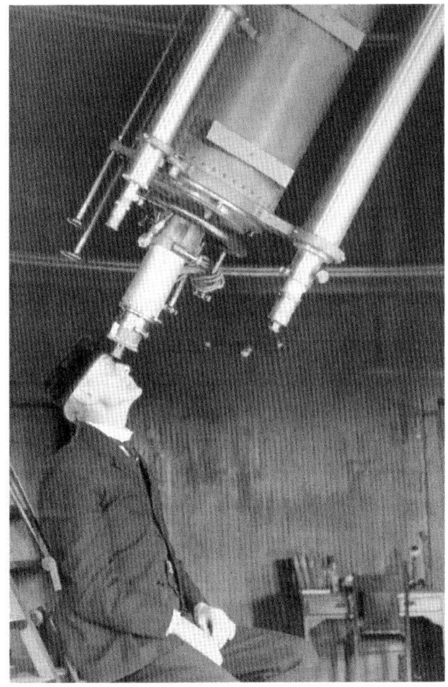

Teacher, Astronomer, Inventor

Charles Burckhalter was a teacher of astronomy and geography at Oakland High School and the first director of the Chabot Observatory. Due to increasing light pollution downtown, Burckhalter oversaw moving the observatory to its second location on Mountain Boulevard. Burckhalter also traveled the world, photographing solar eclipses. He invented an improved apparatus for photographing them. (Courtesy Chabot Space & Science Center.)

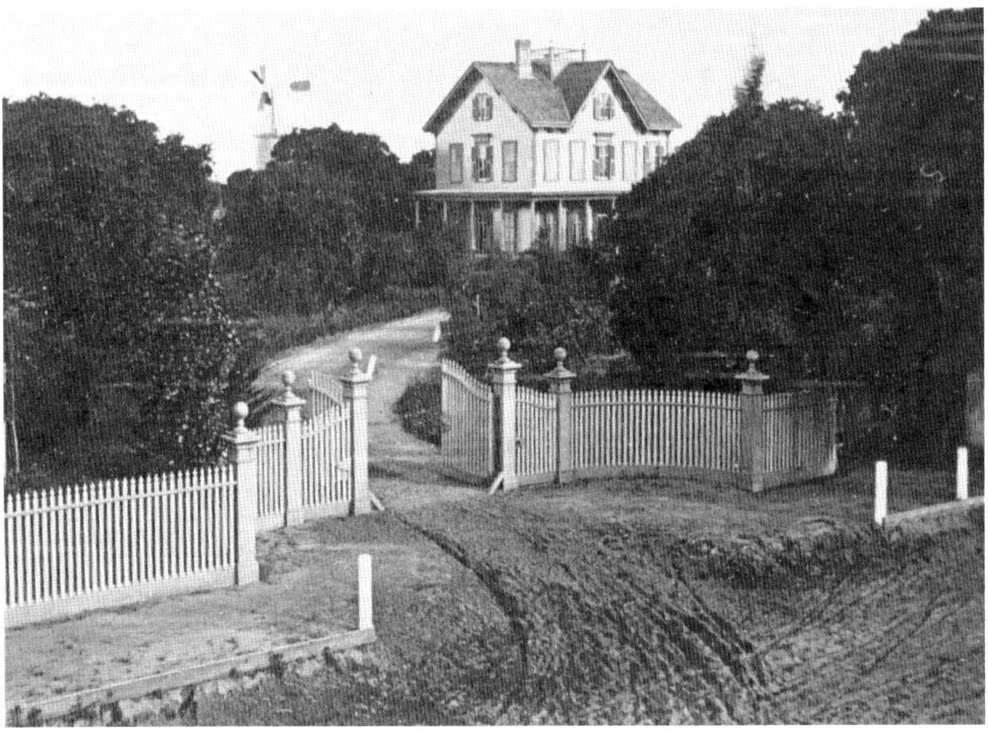

Namesakes of de Fremery Park

Dutch merchant James de Fremery and the daughter of a former slave, Virginie Therese de Fremery, were the heads of a wealthy family in West Oakland, where they lived in an 1864 Victorian home known as "The Grove" (pictured). Their son James Leon de Fremery sold the family estate to the City of Oakland to create de Fremery Park, though the family continued to live there until his death in 1911. (Courtesy Oakland History Room, Oakland Main Library.)

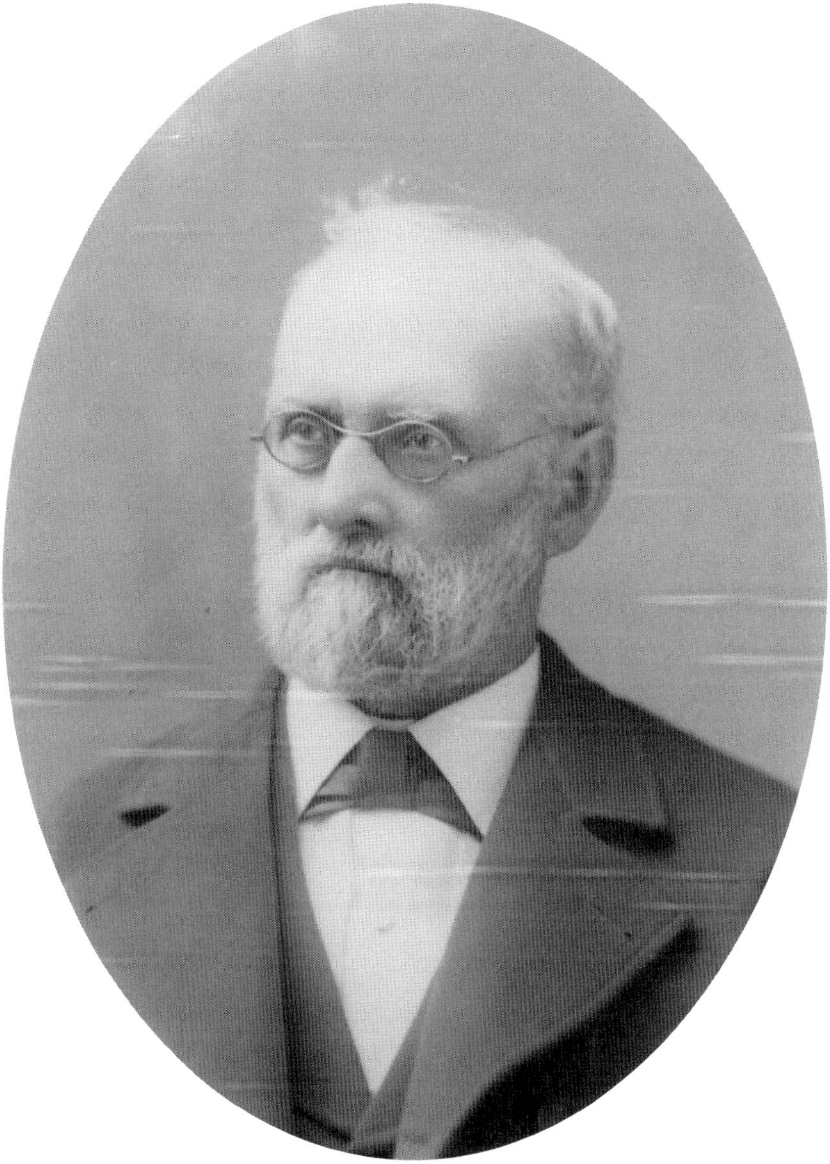

The Water King

Before Anthony Chabot started the Contra Costa Water Company in 1866 and piped the first water into Oakland, most of the city's water came from wells. But the growing population in the East Bay soon meant there was not enough, even after constructing Lake Temescal in 1868 and what is now known as Lake Chabot in 1870. Competition with William Dingee's Oakland Water Company was fierce, with each side sabotaging the other, but even after Dingee took control of the combined company, there was not enough water for the population. It took the East Bay Municipal Utility District to bring water from the Sierra Nevada in 1930.

Chabot also created water systems for San Francisco and San Jose, but is probably best remembered for donating money toward the first telescope in Oakland in 1883. After several moves and a major expansion in 2000, today the Chabot Space & Science Center in Redwood Regional Park is a world-class educational facility. (Courtesy Oakland History Room, Oakland Public Library.)

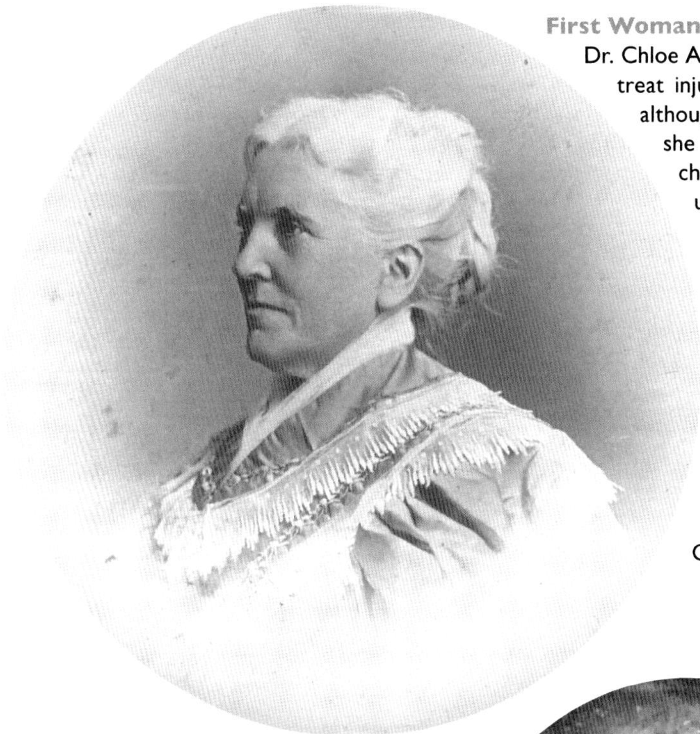

First Woman Doctor in Oakland

Dr. Chloe Annette Buckel volunteered to treat injured Civil War soldiers, and although she was a medical doctor, she was relegated to being in charge of the nurses. She set up six field hospitals and was in charge of the selection of Union Army nurses. In 1877, she became the first woman doctor in Oakland and, in 1878, the first woman admitted to the Alameda County Medical Association. Buckel also founded the local Agassiz Society and was active with the Ebell Society. (Courtesy Camron-Stanford House.)

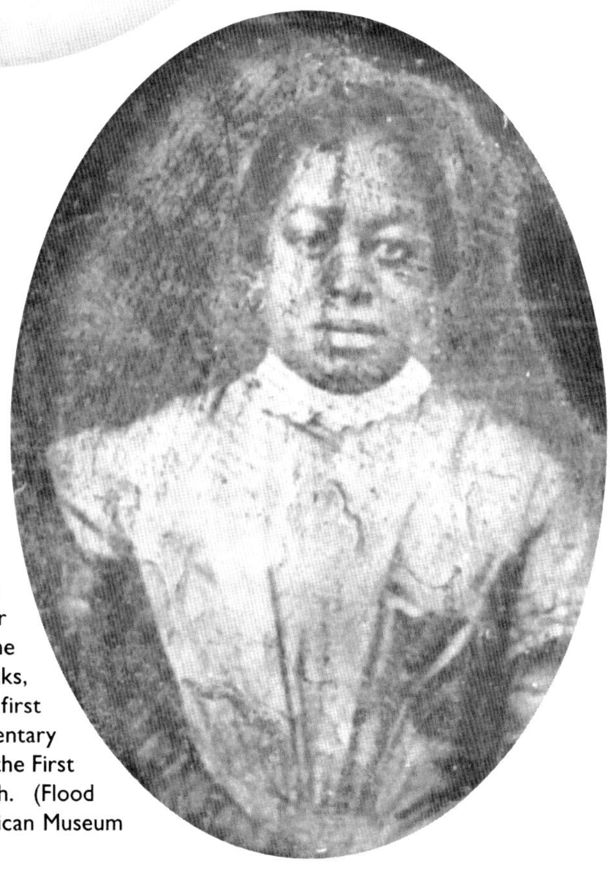

Teacher and Church Founder

When a school would not admit her son, Elizabeth Thorn Flood, pictured in this tintype portrait, opened a private school for black children. She and her husband, Isaac Flood, petitioned the Oakland School Board to admit blacks, and their daughter Lydia was the first black child to attend John Swett Elementary School. The Floods also helped found the First African Methodist Episcopal Church. (Flood Family Papers, courtesy African American Museum & Library at Oakland.)

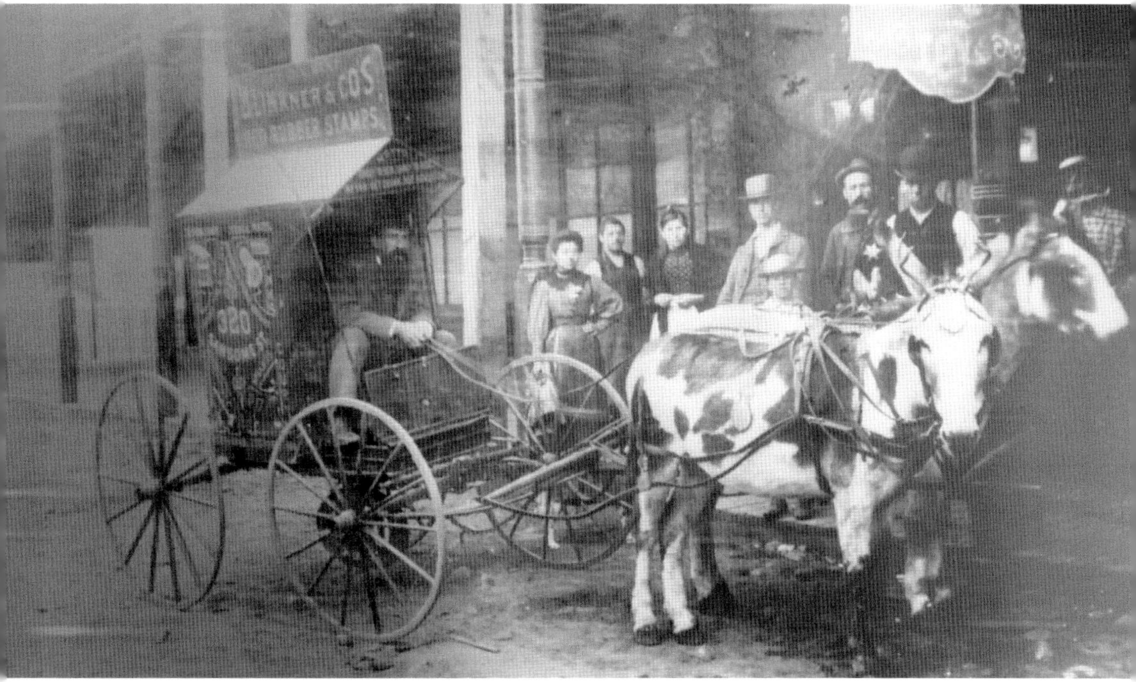

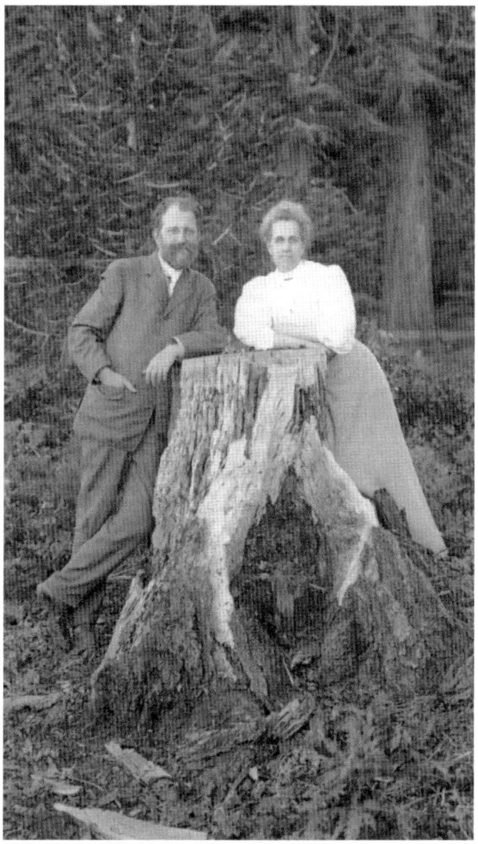

Stop Here, This is the Place
The Golden Gate district of Oakland was once the town of Klinknerville, named by realtor and promoter Charles Klinkner. Klinkner was a born salesman and showman who was known for such stunts as painting mules red, white, and blue and putting signs on dogs to advertise his ventures. In addition to houses, Klinkner developed Klinkner Hall, which housed the local post office and Klinkner Drugs, as well as a baseball field where the Oakland Oaks later played. (Courtesy Oakland History Room, Oakland Public Library.)

The Earthquake Governor
Dr. George Pardee (pictured with wife, Helen Pardee) followed in the footsteps of his father, Dr. Enoch Pardee. They were both medical doctors and served as mayors of Oakland. The younger Pardee also served one term as governor of California and was noted for his environmental conservation. He was the first governor born in California and was governor during the 1906 earthquake. The Pardee family home on Eleventh Street in Oakland is now a museum open to the public. (Courtesy Pardee Family Home Museum.)

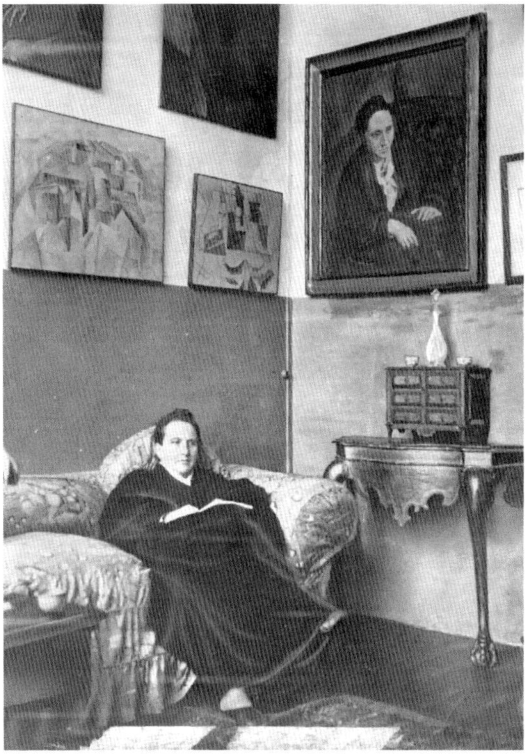

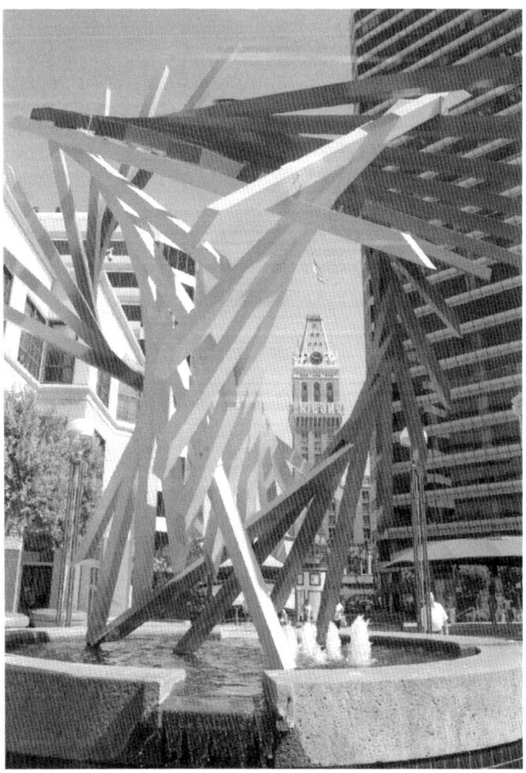

"There is No There There"
Writer, poet, and art collector Gertrude Stein was born in Pittsburgh, Pennsylvania, and her family only lived in Oakland for 11 years, but her five small words have had a large impact on Oakland over the years.

While some people think she was showing a lack of respect for Oakland, Stein was lamenting in *Everybody's Autobiography* (1937) that none of the things she remembered from her childhood were still there. The palatial Tubbs Hotel, where her family first lived in Oakland, had long since burned down, and the bucolic neighborhood east of Lake Merritt, where the family home had been, was now full of apartments, new houses, and nearby Highland Hospital. Oakland had grown from 35,000 people in 1880 when her family arrived to almost 300,000 people when she visited again in 1935.

Oaklanders have long bristled at any disrespect shown to their beloved town. So that no one else can claim "there is no there there," in 1988, sculptor Roselyn Mazzilli installed a work titled "There!" in the City Center Plaza. (Top, courtesy Library of Congress; bottom, author's collection.)

Animal Welfare Advocate

In addition to writing one of the first vegetarian cookbooks, published in 1898, Henrietta Latham and her husband, James, were animal welfare advocates. In her later years, Latham was also a noted watercolor painter. The Latham Fountain at Broadway and Telegraph Avenues was erected by the Lathams' children in memory of their parents. (Author's collection.)

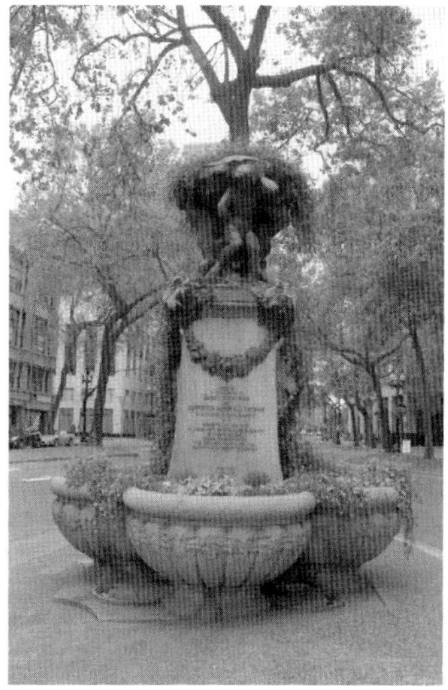

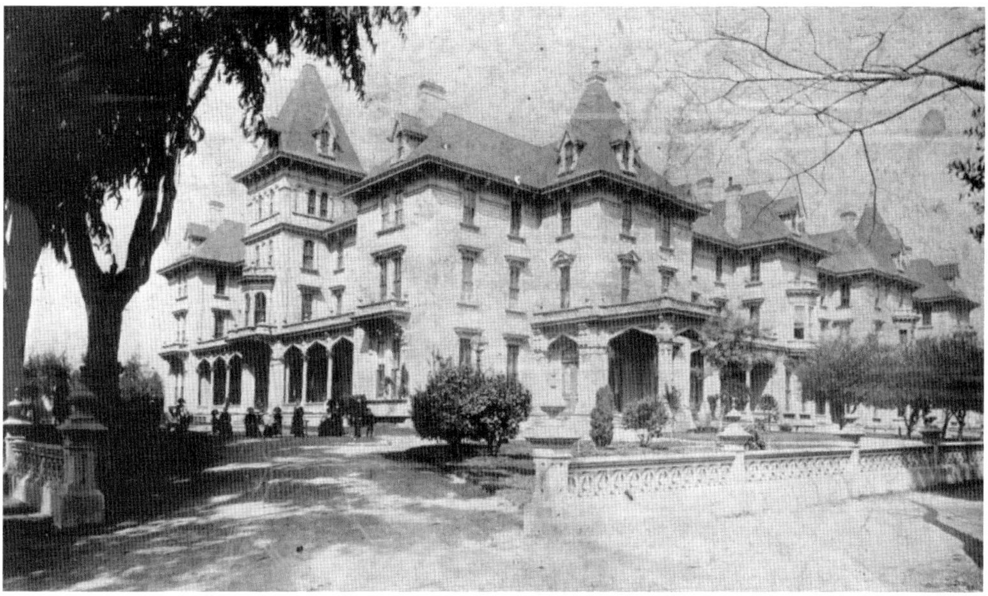

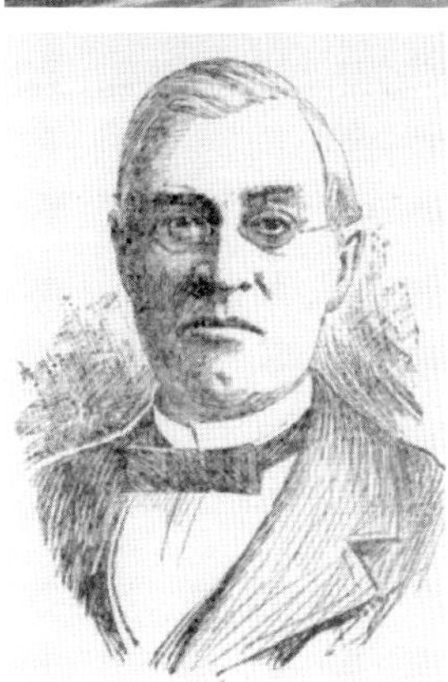

Businessman, Hotelier, Cemetery Founder

Not many people in Oakland know the name of Hiram Tubbs, but in addition to owning a successful business making ropes for ships and other uses, Tubbs was one of the founders of the Mountain View Cemetery and one of the first to construct a mausoleum there. Tubbs was best known for the palatial Tubbs Hotel, east of Lake Merritt, where a young Gertrude Stein lived when her family first moved to Oakland. (Above, courtesy Oakland History Room, Oakland Public Library; left, from *San Francisco Call*, retrieved from the California Digital Newspaper Collection.)

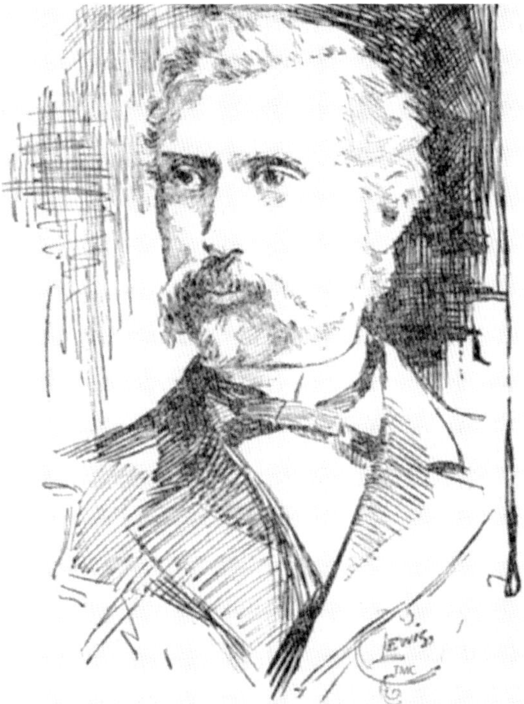

HUGH DIMOND.
San Francisco Call, January 15th, 1896

Namesake of the Dimond District
While Hugh Dimond made some money mining in the 1849 Gold Rush, he made more selling supplies to other would-be miners and made his fortune in the wholesale liquor business in the Bay Area. Dimond bought land that formerly belonged to Henderson Luelling and built an imposing house in what is now Dimond Park. His son Denis built the adobe cottage that was later known as the Boy Scout Hut. (From *San Francisco Call*, retrieved from the California Digital Newspaper Collection.)

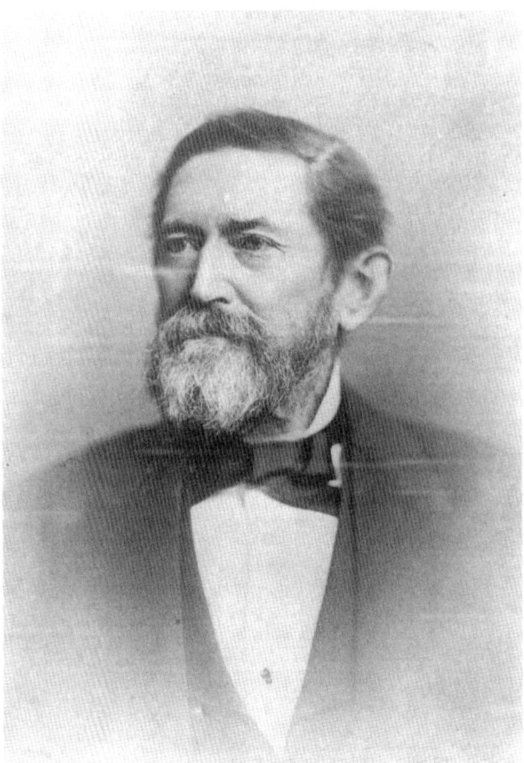

Texas Ranger, Oakland Founder
Jack Coffee Hays, pictured around 1875, was renowned for hunting down the Comanche people during his days as a Texas ranger. After a stint as sheriff in San Francisco, Hays settled in Oakland at the Fernwood Estate in what is now Montclair. Hays was also a founder of Oakland's Union Savings Bank and a large shareholder in the Oakland Gas Light Company. (Courtesy Oakland Museum of California, gift of Robley McMullin.)

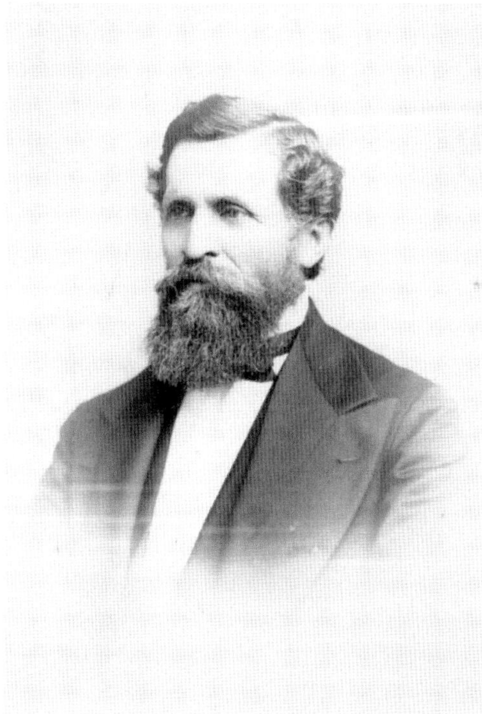

Organizer of Oakland High School
After serving as the principal of Irving Elementary School, Joseph Burwell McChesney organized Oakland High School and was the principal from its founding in 1869 until 1901. McChesney also served as president of the Oakland Library Association, predecessor of the Oakland Free Library. McChesney's daughter, Clara Taggart McChesney, became an artist, well-known in New York and Paris. (Courtesy Oakland History Room, Oakland Public Library.)

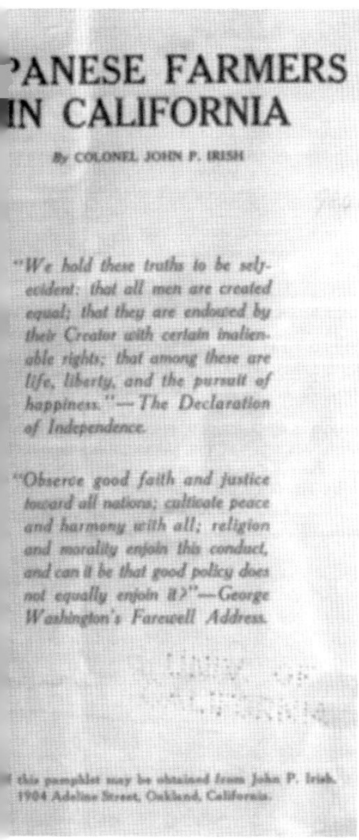

'ANESE FARMERS
IN CALIFORNIA

By COLONEL JOHN P. IRISH

"We hold these truths to be self-evident: that all men are created equal; that they are endowed by their Creator with certain inalienable rights; that among these are life, liberty, and the pursuit of happiness."—The Declaration of Independence.

"Observe good faith and justice toward all nations; cultivate peace and harmony with all; religion and morality enjoin this conduct, and can it be that good policy does not equally enjoin it?"—George Washington's Farewell Address.

this pamphlet may be obtained from John P. Irish, 1904 Adeline Street, Oakland, California.

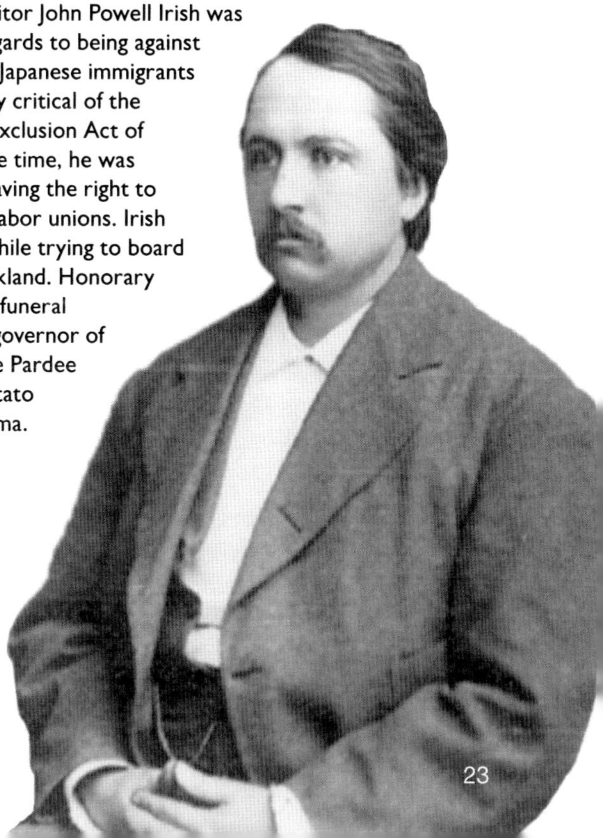

Outspoken Editor
Oakland Times editor John Powell Irish was progressive in regards to being against discrimination of Japanese immigrants and was especially critical of the hateful Chinese Exclusion Act of 1882. At the same time, he was against women having the right to vote and against labor unions. Irish died from a fall while trying to board a streetcar in Oakland. Honorary pallbearers at his funeral included former governor of California George Pardee and Japanese "potato king" George Shima. (Right, courtesy Rich Samuels; left, courtesy San Francisco Public Library.)

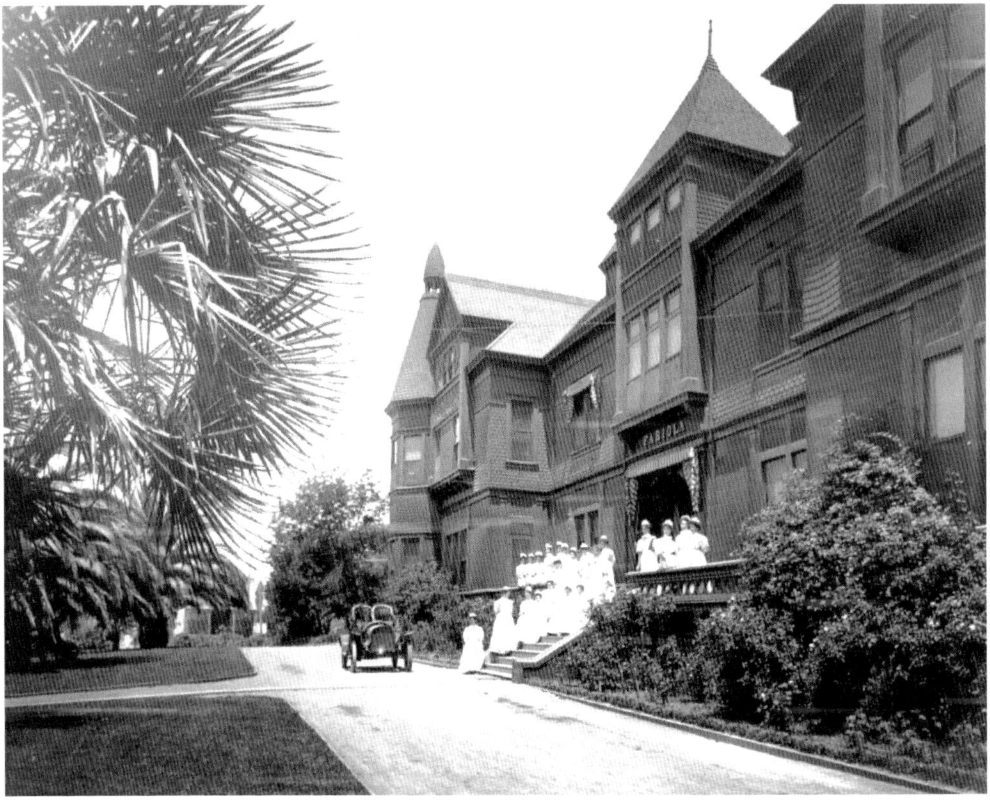

Fabiola Founder

After witnessing a terrible carriage accident in Oakland and learning that the victim had to be transported 10 miles to San Leandro, Kate Kirkham organized her friends and started the Fabiola Association to provide medical treatment for all, regardless of financial situation. Kirkham served as the first president of Fabiola Hospital (pictured), built in 1887 and named for Saint Fabiola, a matron who built a hospital in fourth-century Rome. (Courtesy Oakland History Room, Oakland Public Library.)

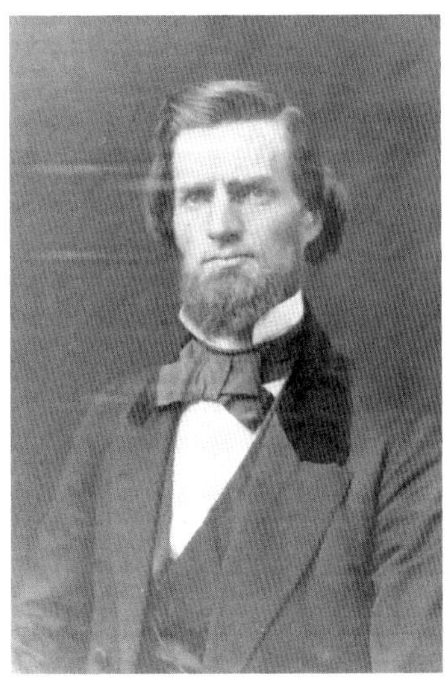

Controversial Theologian

Rev. Laurentine Hamilton was the pastor of the First Presbyterian Church of Oakland in 1864, but five years later, he was charged with heresy. He resigned, and most of the congregation joined him at the newly formed Independent Church of Oakland, which later became the First Unitarian Church of Oakland. The church building has survived two major earthquakes and urban renewal. Mount Hamilton, east of San Jose, is named for Reverend Hamilton. (Courtesy San Jose Public Library.)

Mother of Civil Rights in California
Mary Ellen Pleasant was the daughter of an African American mother and a merchant from Hawaii. After working off indentured servitude, Pleasant worked as a tailor, and then worked with her husband to free slaves. After her first husband died, she married John James Pleasant and continued freeing slaves. The Pleasants came to California around the time of the 1849 Gold Rush, and Pleasant worked in eating establishments that catered solely to men. With information she picked up, she invested money and made a fortune. Sadly, she lost her fortune and died penniless. (Courtesy African American Museum & Library at Oakland.)

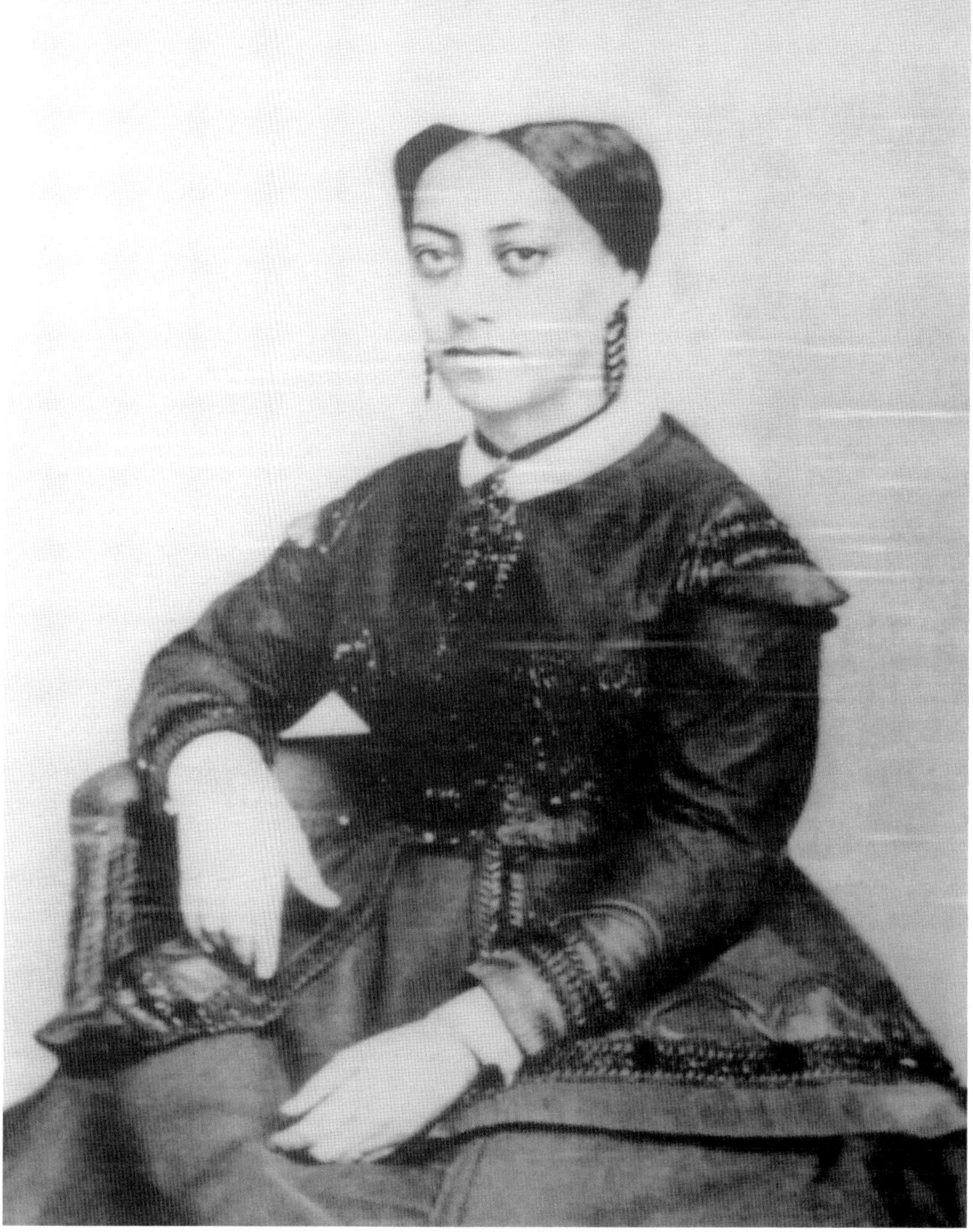

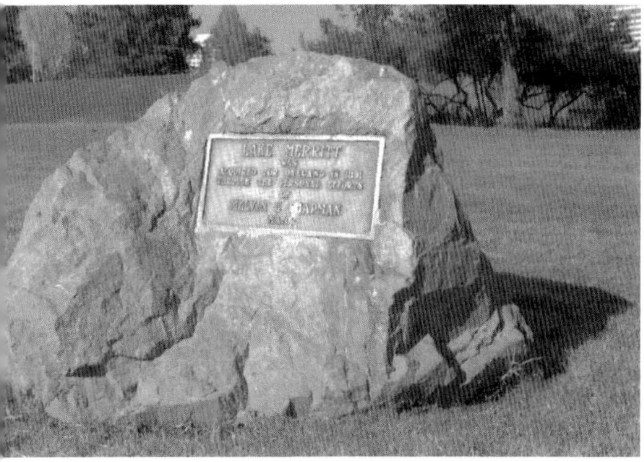

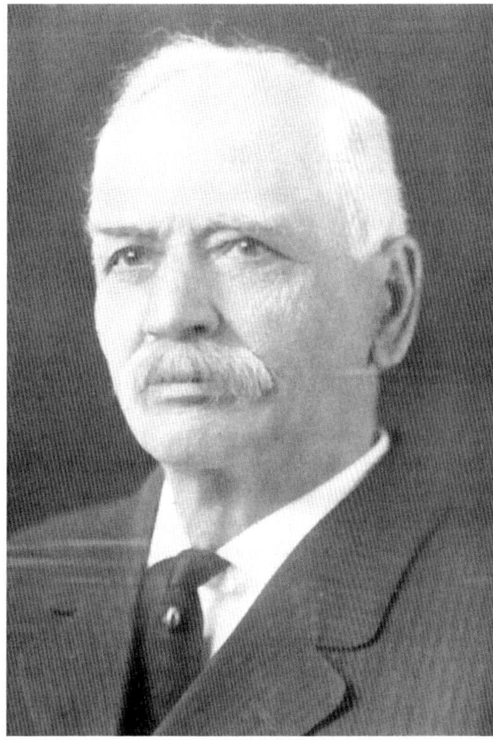

Lawyer, Legislator, Mayor

Melvin Canfield Chapman was a lawyer and served in the California state legislature. But he should be remembered in Oakland as the 28th mayor from 1891 to 1893, who was influential in acquiring the land around Lake Merritt and making it into Oakland Park. (Above, author's collection; right, from *Davis' Commercial Encyclopedia*, courtesy Oakland History Room, Oakland Public Library.)

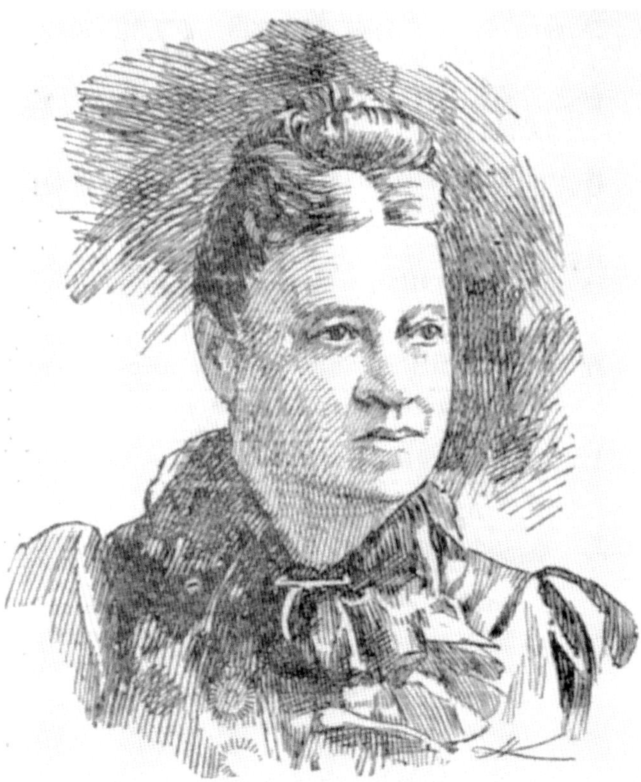

School for Girls

Millicent Kittredge Blake established the first school for girls west of the Mississippi River, the Oakland Seminary for Young Ladies. She was the sister of early settler Francis Kittredge Shattuck and married Shattuck's business partner, George Blake. The Oakland Convention Center now stands on what was the Blake property in downtown Oakland. (From *San Francisco Call*, retrieved from the California Digital Newspaper Collection.)

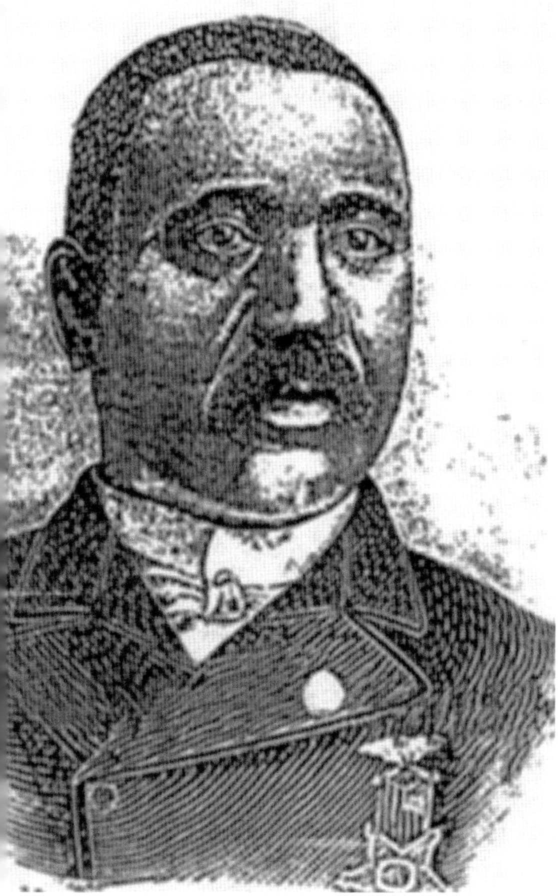

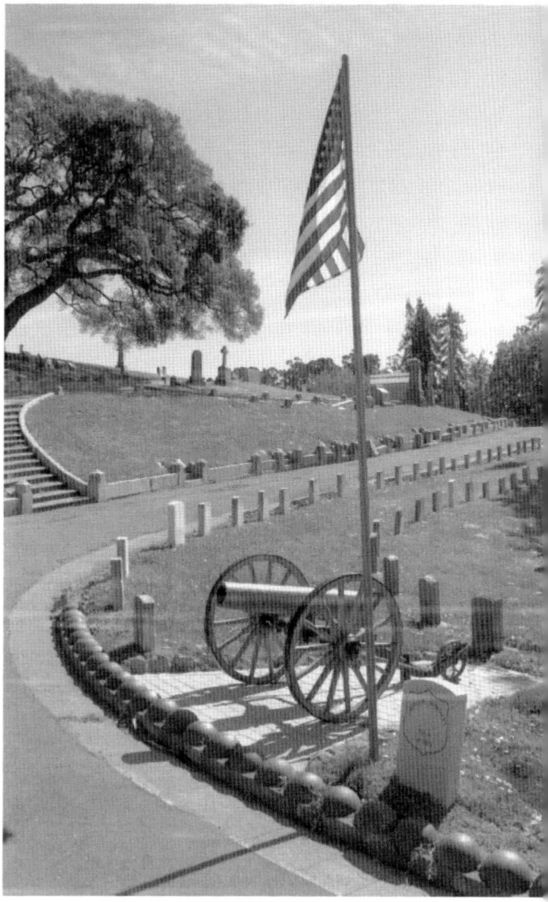

Slave, Civil War Veteran, Minister

Obediah Summers was born into slavery in Missouri, and his master paid for Summers to take his place in the Confederate army as a "servant." He was captured in 1862 and enlisted in the Union army. After the Civil War, Summers became a minister and eventually came to California, where he served as the first black chaplain of the California state legislature. Summers was not originally buried in the Grand Army of the Republic plot in Mountain View Cemetery, but his descendants petitioned to have his remains moved, and a new marker was installed. (Left, courtesy Myrna Adams; right, author's collection.)

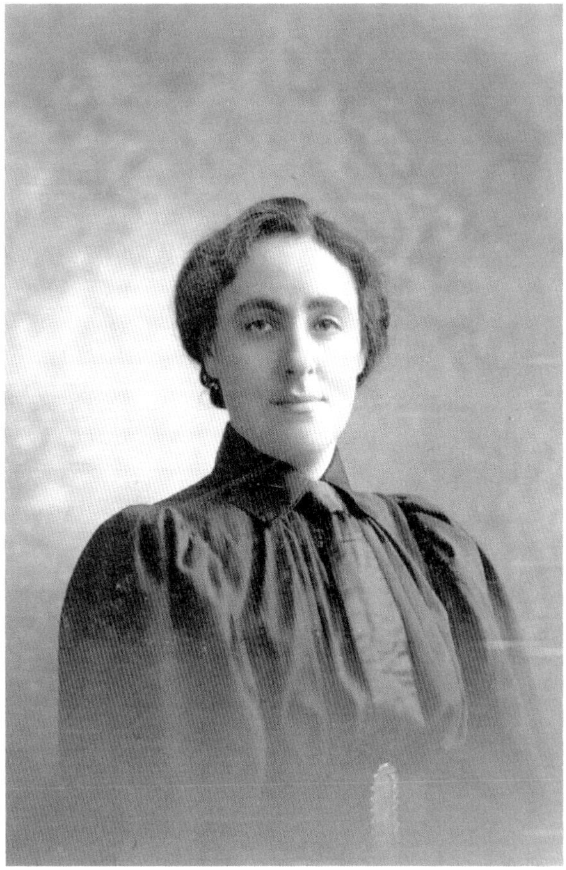

Girl Rabbi of the Golden West
While never officially ordained, Rachel "Ray" Frank was the first Jewish woman to formally preach from the pulpit in the United States. While teaching at the First Hebrew Congregation in Oakland, her students included Gertrude Stein and Judah Leon Magnes, who later became a prominent reform rabbi. (Courtesy Collection of American Jewish Historical Society.)

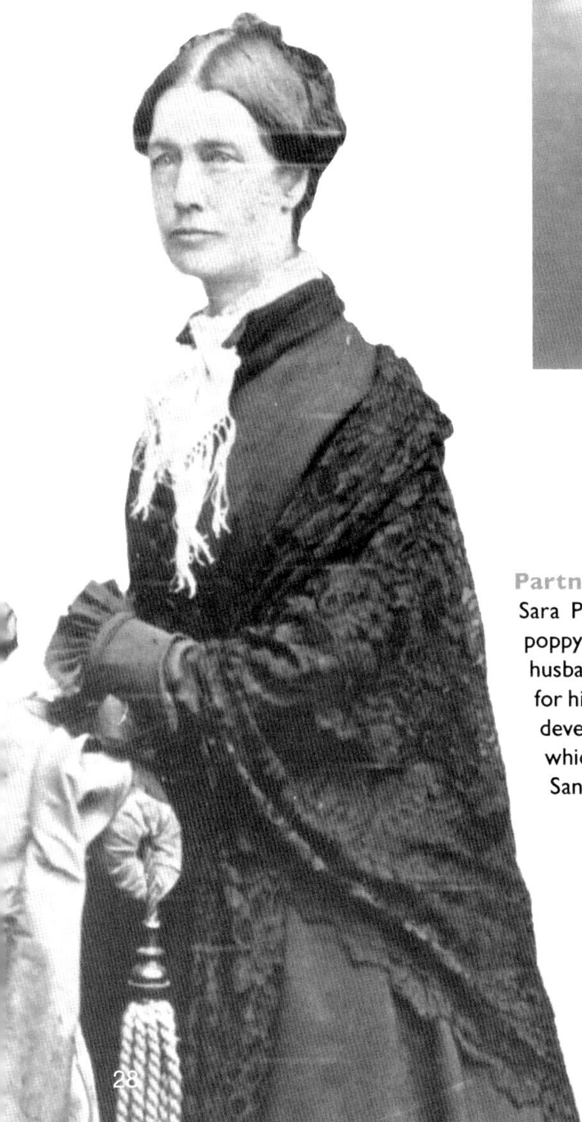

Partners in Botany
Sara Plummer Lemmon endeavored to get the California poppy named the state flower. She partnered with her husband, John Gill Lemmon, frequently drawing illustrations for his botanical writings as well as her own. Together, they developed the Lemmon Herbarium on Telegraph Avenue, which was eventually donated to UC Berkeley. (Courtesy Santa Barbara Historical Museum.)

Namesake of Lake Merritt

Dr. Samuel Merritt (farthest back) was the 13th mayor of Oakland, but his impact on Oakland went far beyond his 16 months in office. Originally a physician, Merritt largely switched to real estate after a day trip to Oakland.

Merritt purchased land near the body of water that was then known as Laguna Peralta, subdivided the land, and built a number of residences, including the Italianate Victorian style now known as the Camron-Stanford House. In his time as mayor, Merritt is credited with helping ensure that Oakland became the terminus of the first transcontinental railroad. He was also responsible for creating the dam at Twelfth Street to deepen the lake, lobbying to have the lake declared the first wildlife refuge in the country in 1870. In addition, he was the first president of the Oakland Library Association.

Merritt was one of the founders of Mountain View Cemetery, where his mausoleum graces Millionaire's Row. After Merritt's death, his sister Catherine Merritt Garcelon carried out his wishes and founded Samuel Merritt Hospital, which included a nursing school. Today, Samuel Merritt University provides advanced degrees in a number of health disciplines.

Also pictured are Robert Louis Stevenson, author of *Treasure Island* (standing at right); his wife, Fanny van de Grift Osbourne (seated at right); her son from a previous marriage, Lloyd Osbourne (standing at left); and Thomas T. Dargie (standing at center). Stevenson chartered Merritt's yacht *Casco* for one of his voyages across the South Pacific in 1888. The other two women are unidentified. (Courtesy Oakland History Room, Oakland Public Library.)

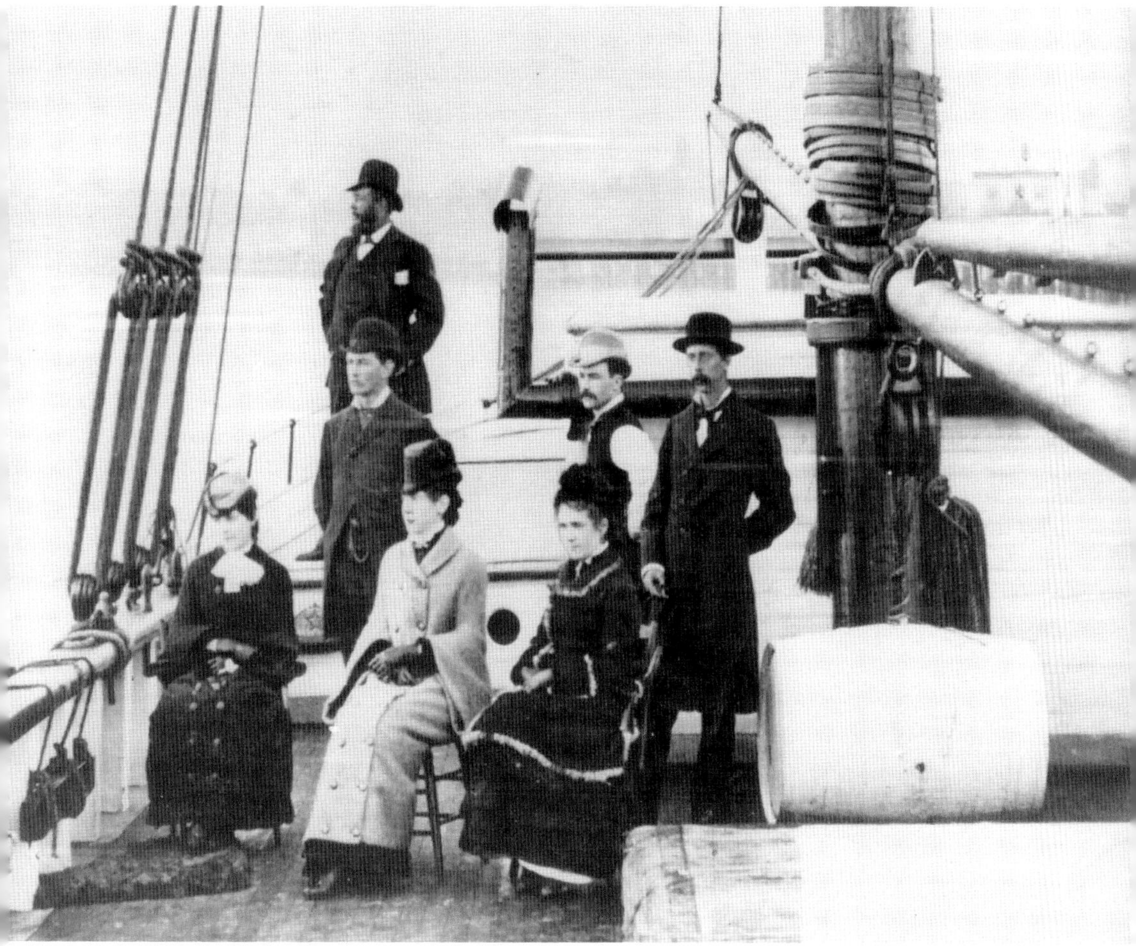

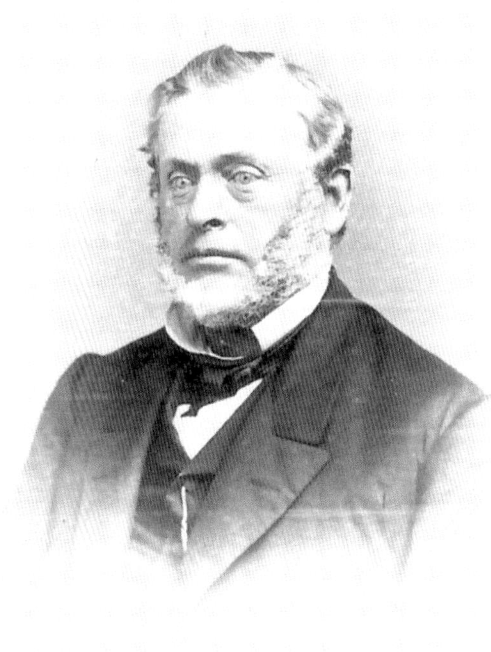

Early Settler of Temescal

Solomon Ellsworth Alden once owned much of what is now the Temescal neighborhood. In addition to his farm, Alden was also one of the founding trustees of Mountain View Cemetery and a director of the Oakland Savings Bank. The local post office was known as the Alden Post Office, and the Oakland branch library, built in 1918, was originally known as the Alden branch. (Courtesy McElrath family private collection.)

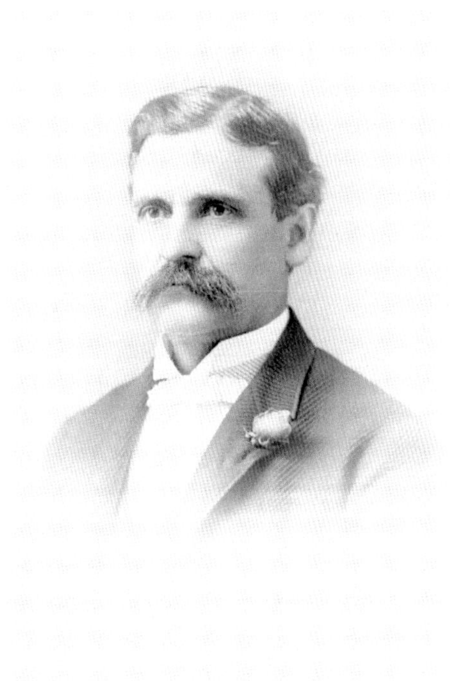

Mills Trustee, Sierra Club Founder, Mayor

Warren Olney served as a trustee of Mills College for 34 years and as mayor of Oakland during the "water wars" between Dingee and Chabot, but he was also friends with John Muir and was one of the founding members of the Sierra Club. The club initially met in Olney's office, and he wrote the club's first charter. (Courtesy Special Collections, F.W. Olin Library, Mills College.)

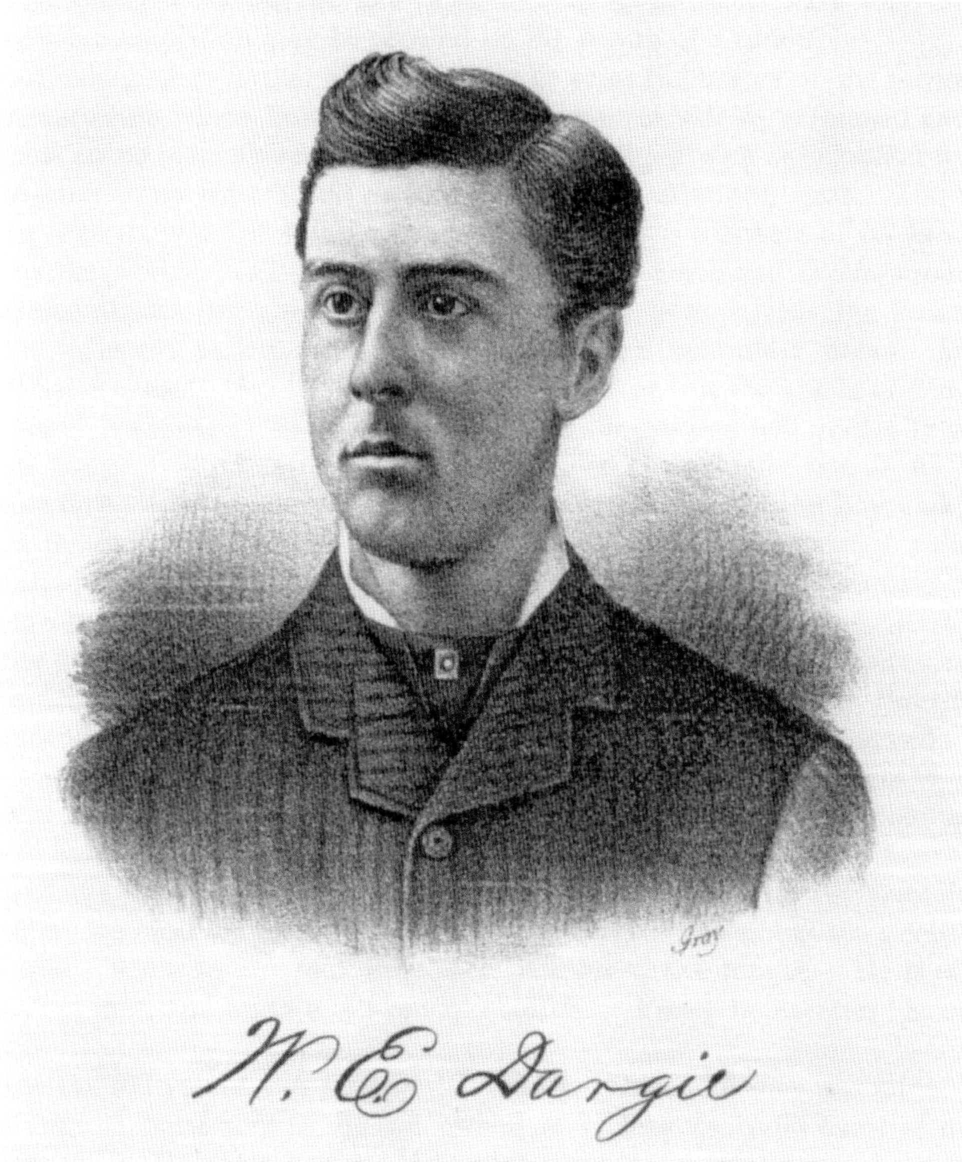

Oakland Tribune Owner and Publisher
William Edward Dargie was a longtime owner and publisher of the *Oakland Tribune*, starting at the age of 22, when he used a loan from A.K.P. Harmon to buy a controlling interest in the newspaper. While he did much to modernize the paper, he was not universally loved. The *San Francisco Call* wrote, "The worst thing that ever happened to Oakland and Alameda county was William E. Dargie." (From *History of Alameda County* by M.W. Wood, author's collection.)

The Black Ahab

William Shorey was a whaling ship captain known to his crews as the "Black Ahab" and was the only black captain on the West Coast at the time. Despite long, dangerous voyages, his wife, Julia Ann, and their children sometimes accompanied Shorey. Shorey was active in politics and hosted a dinner for Booker T. Washington, who was raising funds for Tuskegee University. (Courtesy San Francisco Maritime National Historical Park Research Center, P00.21578x.)

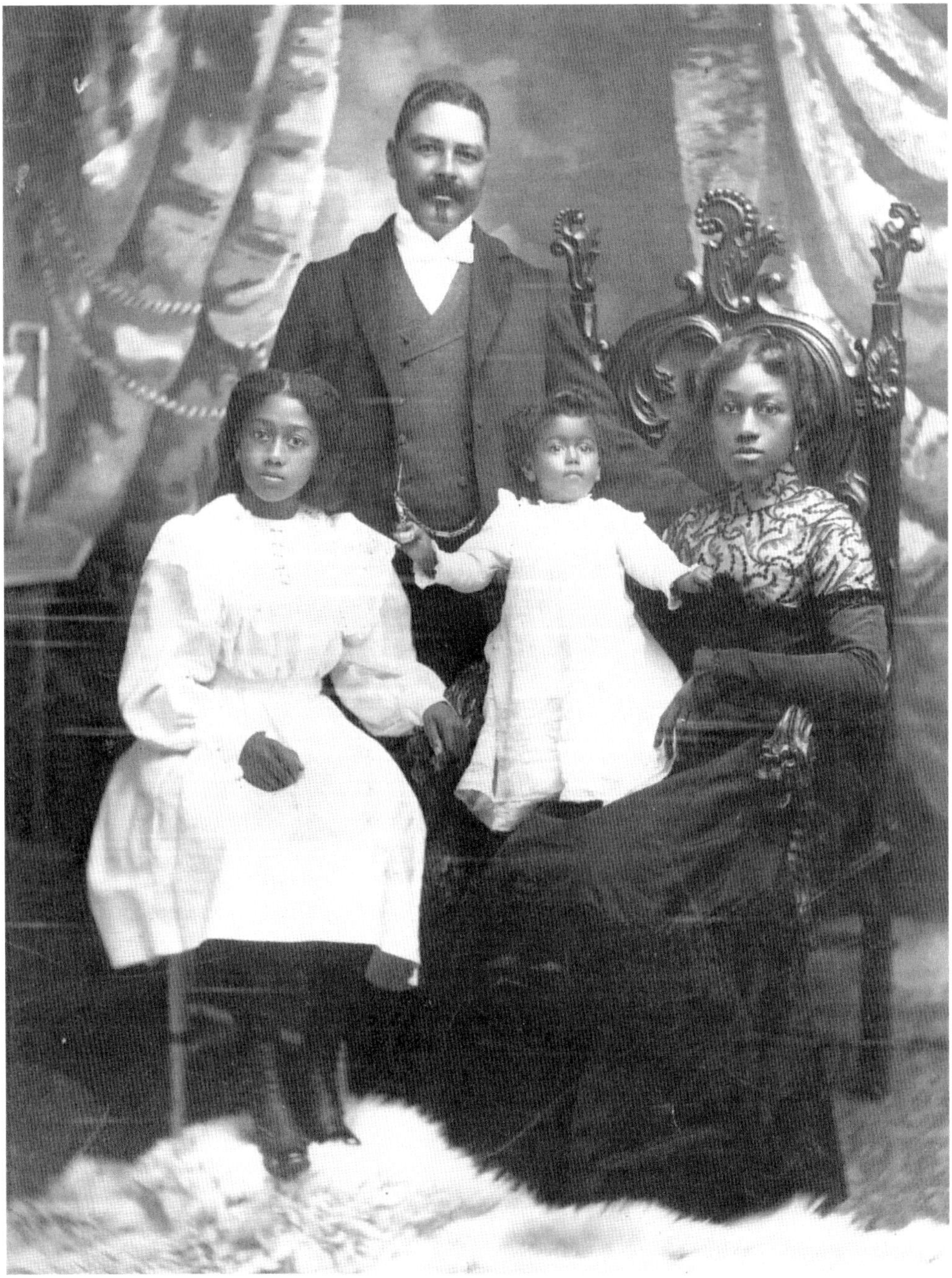

The Borax King

Francis Marion "Borax" Smith made his fortune in borax mining and made "20 Mule Team Borax" a household phrase. In Oakland, he invested in real estate and created the Key System for streetcars and ferries.

After making his fortune with the discovery of a large borax deposit in Nevada, Smith began investing in Oakland real estate and buying streetcar lines. He formed the Realty Syndicate with Frank C. Havens in 1895 to manage their real estate holdings, and in 1902, consolidated various streetcar lines into the Key System, with the goal of getting people out to see and buy property. The Claremont Hotel was built as a destination resort and opened in 1915.

He and his wife, Mary R. Smith, regularly entertained and hosted fundraising events at their estate. Their mansion, Oak Hall, had 42 rooms, including 15 bedrooms, a ballroom, a bowling alley, an attached conservatory, and a large pipe organ. The 35-acre grounds of Arbor Villa included grape and rose arbors, groves of birch and pine trees, numerous gardens, tennis and croquet courts, an archery range, stables, several guesthouses, and other structures.

Mary R. Smith was inspired by Benjamin Farjeon's *Blade O' Grass*, about orphans in London, and the Smiths took in and adopted a number of homeless girls. In 1901, the Smiths started an orphanage, the Home for Friendless Girls. They constructed multiple cottages for the girls to live in, each managed by a house mother. These beautiful houses were designed by local architects, including Julia Morgan, Walter J. Mathews (who also designed Oak Hall for the Smiths), and Bernard Maybeck. (Both, courtesy Oakland History Room, Oakland Public Library.)

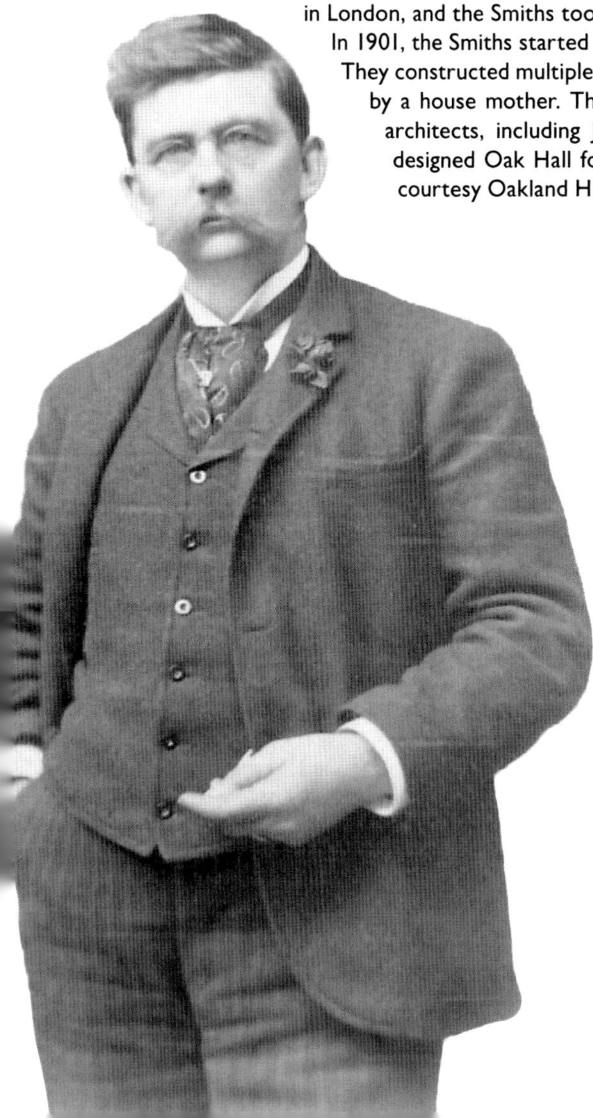

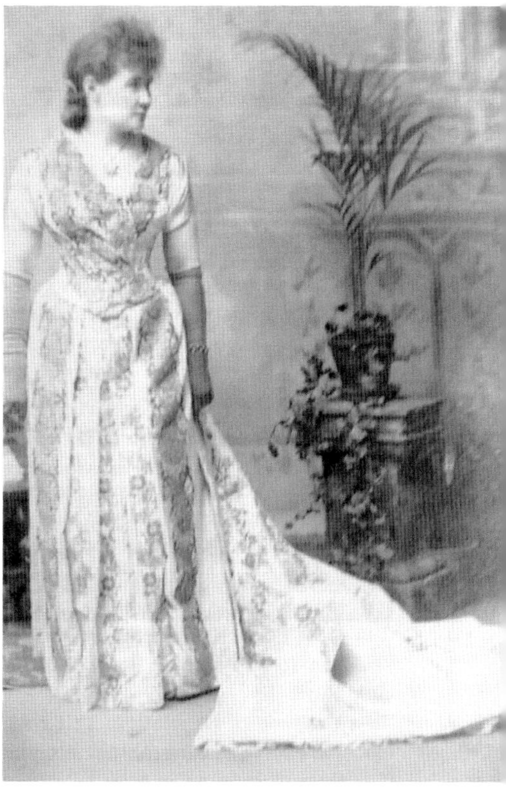

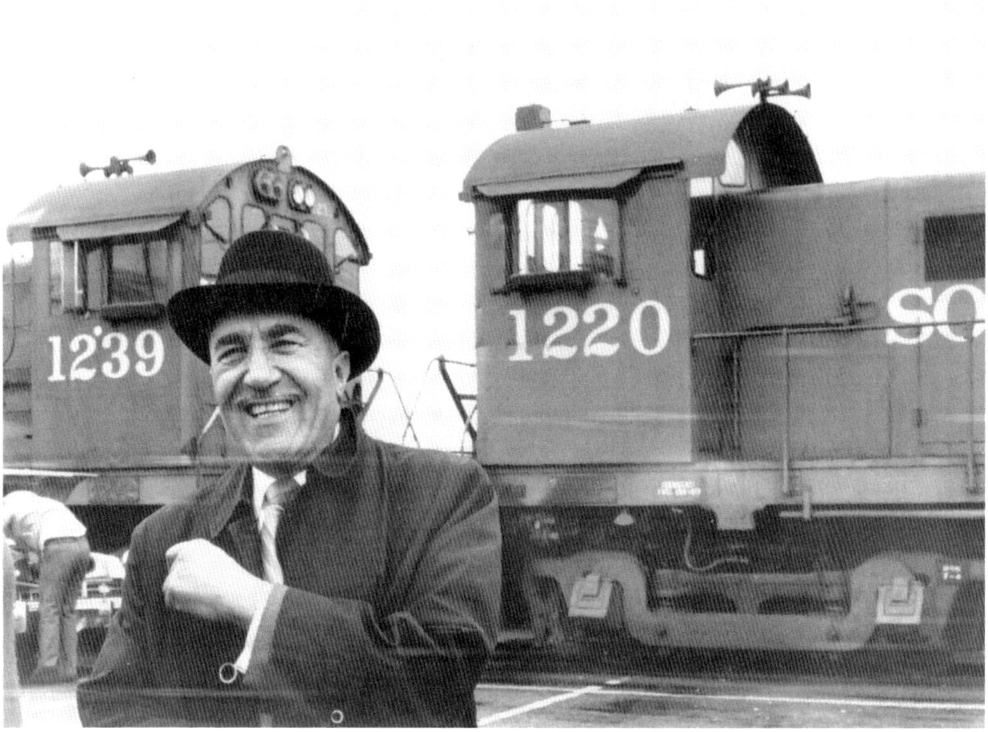

Civil Rights and Labor Leader

Cottrell Laurence Dellums, better known as C.L. Dellums, had dreams of going to UC Berkeley and becoming a lawyer. Denied the opportunity because of his race, he went to work as a Pullman porter. He eventually became the international president of the Brotherhood of Sleeping Car Porters and is remembered with a statue at the Jack London Square train station. Dellums was also the uncle of US representative and later Oakland mayor, Ron Dellums. (Courtesy Oakland History Room, Oakland Public Library.)

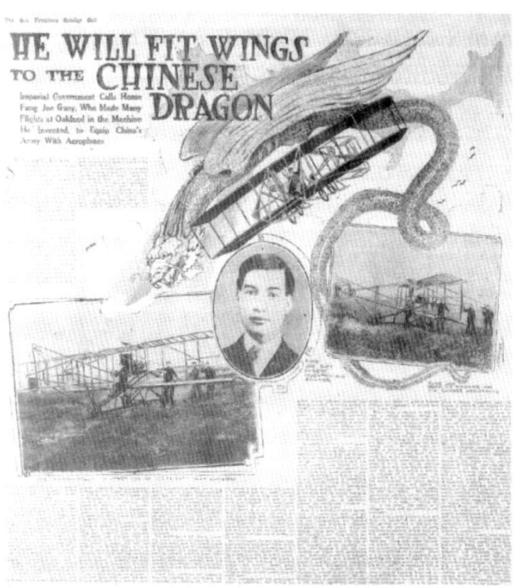

Father of Chinese Aviation

In the early days of powered flight, Feng Ru was a little-known pioneer. On September 21, 1909, Ru was the first person to pilot an airplane on the West Coast, flying over Oakland and Piedmont. His Oakland workshop was near where Laney College now stands. (From *San Francisco Call*, retrieved from the California Digital Newspaper Collection.)

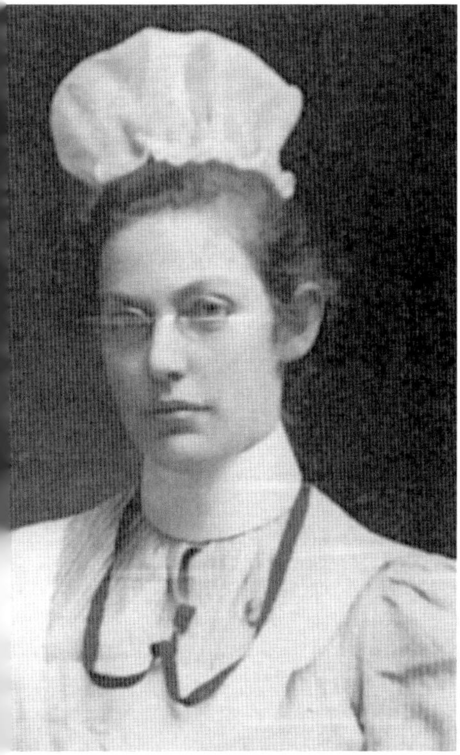

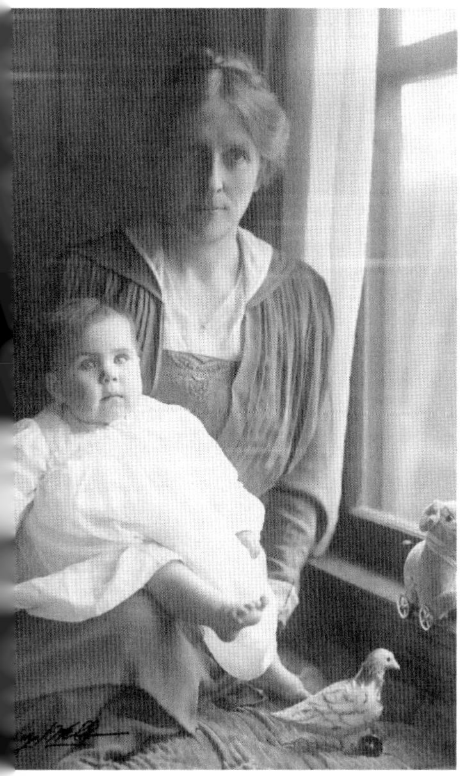

Founders of Children's Hospital Oakland
Bertha Wright (top) and Mabel Weed (bottom) came from different backgrounds, but both recognized the need for affordable hospital care and specialized health care for children.

Bertha Wright graduated from the California Women's Hospital School of Nursing in 1901. Following the 1906 San Francisco earthquake, she treated patients in a tent in Golden Gate Park. In 1909, she became the first school nurse and first public health nurse in Alameda County. Wright was a highly successful fundraiser and formidable activist for health and feminism, who could stop people in their tracks with her stare. Mabel Weed (she was adamant about being called "Miss Mabel Weed") was a social worker, involved in numerous social welfare organizations and charities in Alameda County. She and Wright met while working at the Berkeley Charities Organization.

In 1912, they started working with other women to create the Baby Hospital, the first West Coast hospital specifically for babies and children. A benefit event was held at the Hotel Oakland in 1913, and local luminaries included Gertrude Mott, Josephine Capwell, and Virginie de Fremery. The hospital was opened in 1914 with 38 beds. Rates were $2.50 per day for a private room or $1 for a bed in the wards, but families who were not able to pay were not charged. One hundred years later, the University of California, San Francisco Benioff Children's Hospital Oakland is a nationally recognized teaching hospital, with a research institute, pediatric AIDS unit, and more. (Top, courtesy Children's Hospital; bottom, courtesy K. Bodding.)

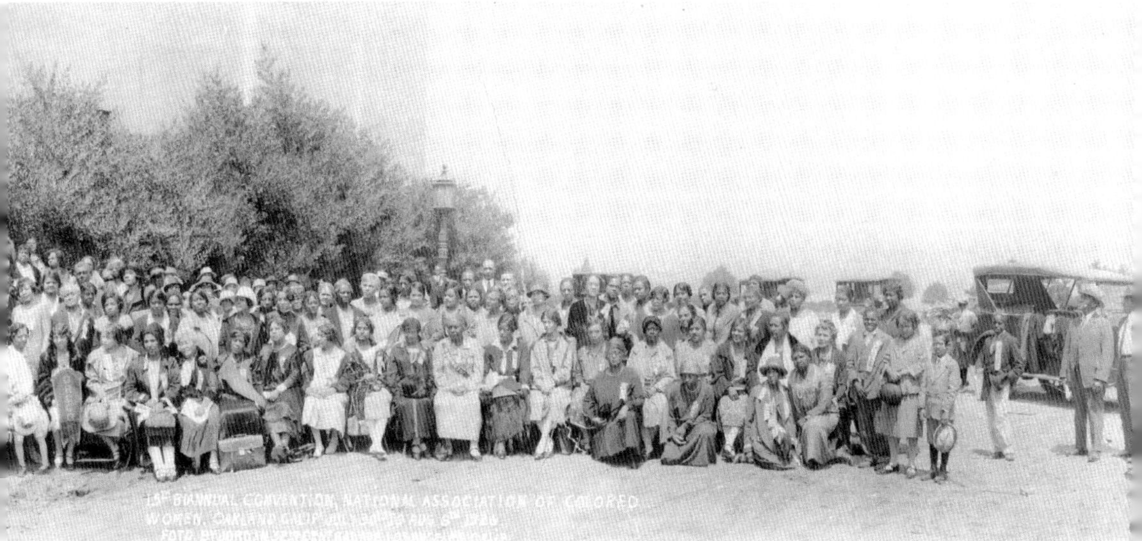

Groundbreaking Journalist and Historian

Delilah Beasley (third row, third woman from right) wrote a weekly column for the *Oakland Tribune* from 1923 to 1934 and was the first African American woman to be regularly published in a major metropolitan newspaper. In addition to writing about national politics and goings-on in black society, she confronted misconceptions and campaigned against press use of explicitly derogatory words when writing about blacks.

Beasley did not limit her words to paper. At a protest of more than 800 people about the integration of the proposed International House at UC Berkeley, she "passionately defended the concept to a disgruntled and stunned audience. And it was Beasley who stood up to the protests of property owners who feared that I-House would cause Berkeley to be overrun with Blacks and Asians," according to *International House: An Informal History* by Joseph Lurie.

Beasley also wrote *The Negro Trail Blazers of California* in 1919, which documented for the first time the contributions of black men and women in early California, including in the 1849 Gold Rush.

This photograph was taken at the 15th Biannual Convention of the National Association of Colored Women, held in Oakland July 30–August 6, 1926. (Courtesy General Photograph Collection, MS 180, African American Museum & Library at Oakland.)

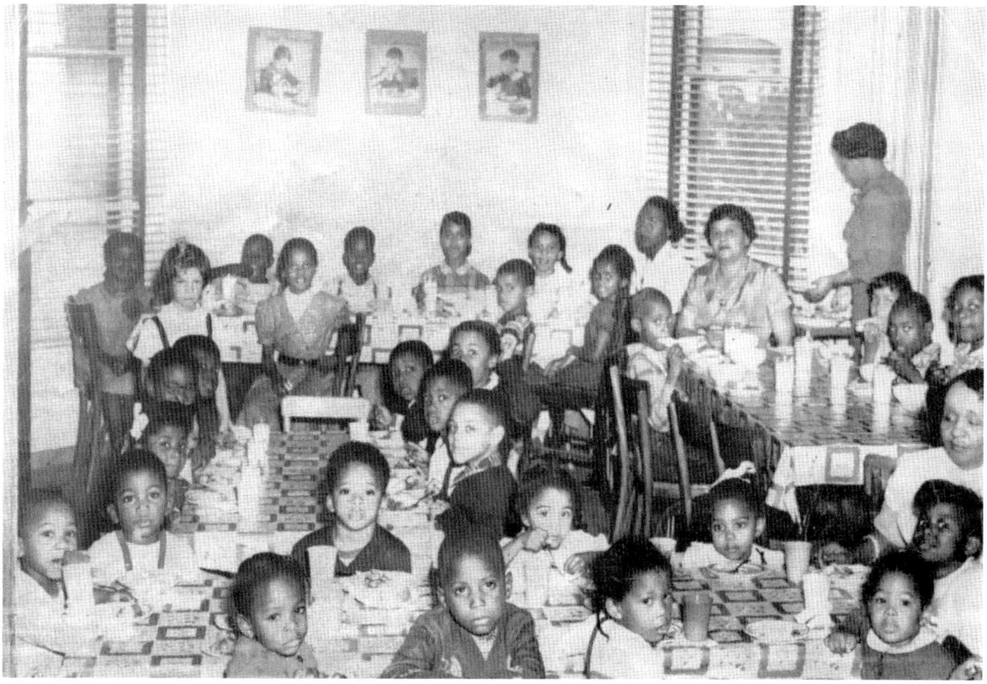

A Haven for Children

Fannie Franklin Wall was active in society, and was not afraid to ask people to get things done. In addition to being active at the First African Methodist Church, Wall was active in the King's Daughters Circle, the NAACP, and numerous other organizations. On many occasions, Wall staked out mayor Davies's office, refusing to leave until he addressed her concerns about a particular community issue. Wall was also the grandmother of pilot and athlete Archie Franklin Williams. The Fannie Wall Home for Children (shown here in 1953) was started in 1914 and named in her honor. (Courtesy African American Museum & Library at Oakland.)

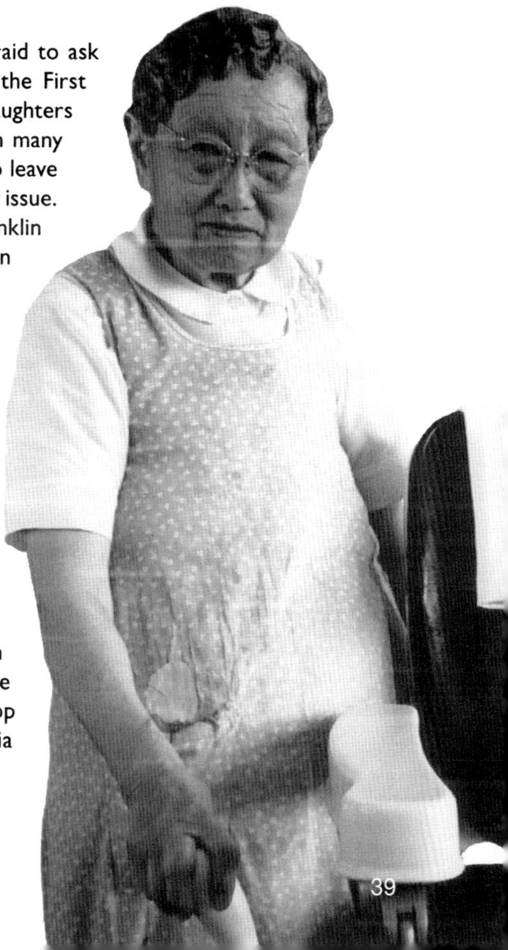

First Chinese Woman Barber

Born in 1894 in a Chinese gold mining camp, Lon Yoke Wong Fong, better known as Fong Get Moo, was the first woman barber in Oakland's Chinatown. Fong was well known and gave candy to her customers after cutting their hair in her shop at Harrison and Eighth Streets. (Courtesy Clifton Fong via William Gee Wong.)

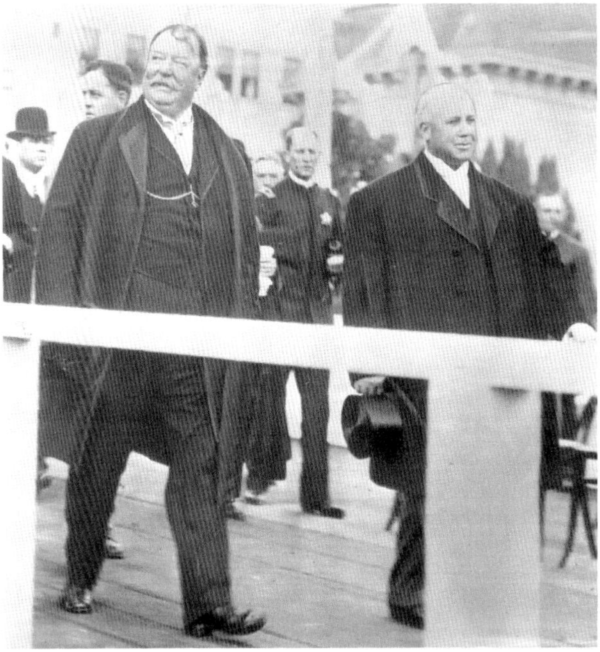

The Mayor who Built Oakland

While George Pardee may have been the "earthquake governor," Frank K. Mott (on right next to Pres. William Howard Taft) was the "earthquake mayor," heading Oakland during the 1906 San Francisco Earthquake and helping absorb the thousands of refugees into Oakland. There were numerous civic improvements during his time in office, including the construction of the new city hall in 1914, which some called "Mott's wedding cake" because of its layered design. (Courtesy Oakland Tribune Collection at the Oakland Museum of California, gift of ANG Newspapers.)

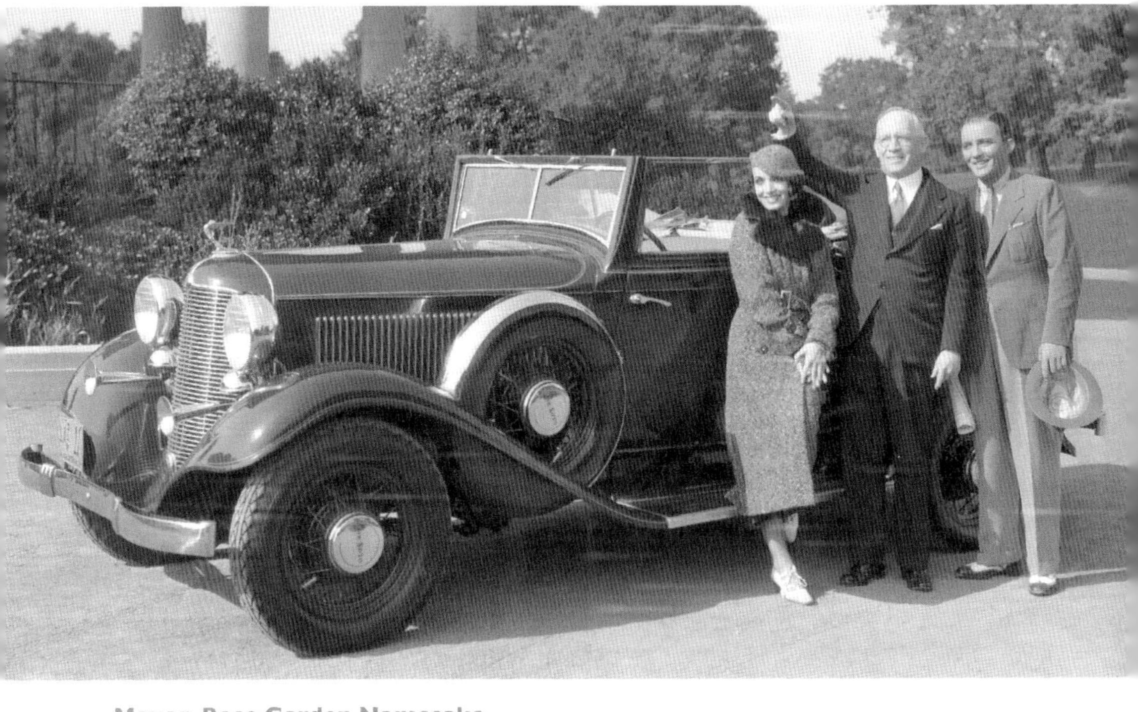

Mayor, Rose Garden Namesake

Fred Morcom, pictured here at center near the Lake Merritt Bandstand with singer Bing Crosby at right, was the 37th mayor of Oakland and later served as the council member at large. His name is most associated with the Morcom Rose Garden. Morcom ceremonially planted the first rosebush in the garden in 1933, and the garden was renamed in his honor 20 years later in 1953. (Photography by M.L. Cohen Company, courtesy Oakland Museum of California, gift of Fred M. and Shannon J. Squires.)

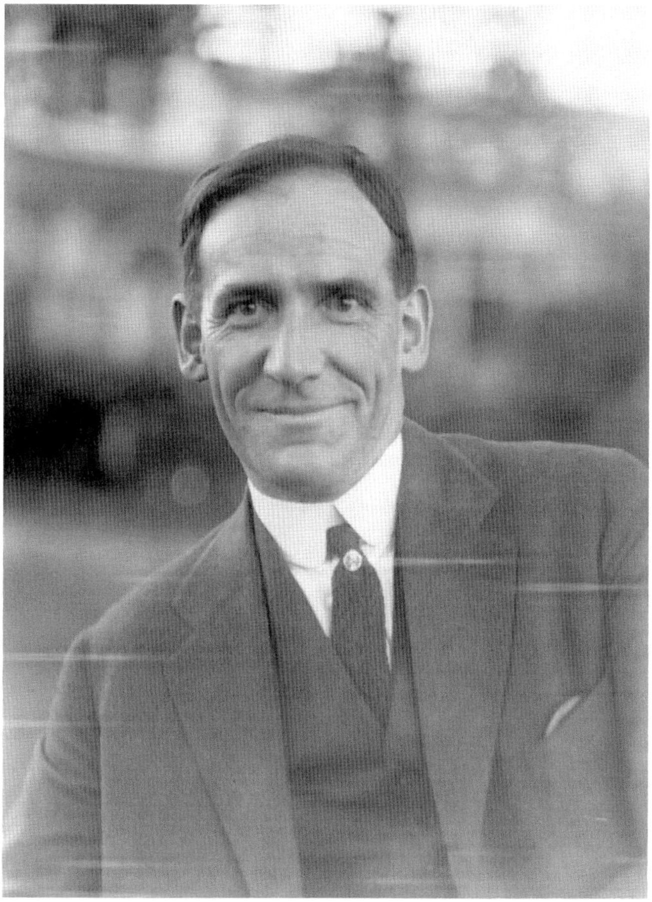

Chemist, Inventor, Philanthropist
Neither Frederick Cottrell nor the electrostatic precipitator he patented in 1908 are household names, but we all have him to thank for cleaner air. After graduating from Oakland High School at 16, then from University of California, Berkeley in three years, Cottrell taught chemistry and saved his money for higher education. In 1912, he and Charles Wolcott created the Research Corporation, which helped fund numerous research projects, including Robert Goddard's work in rockets and Ernest Lawrence's invention of the cyclotron. (Courtesy Research Corporation for Science Advancement.)

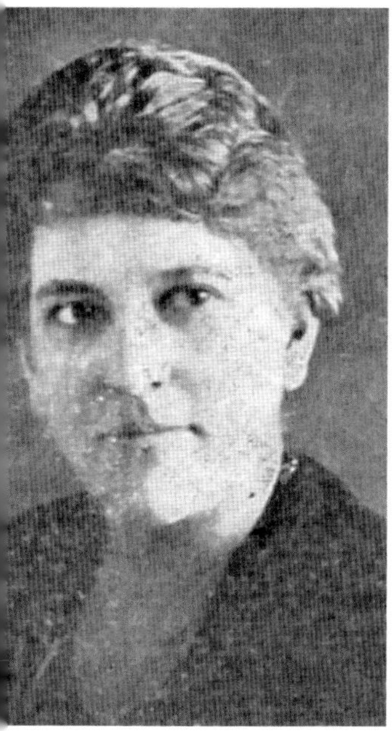

Local Booster and Businesswoman
Gladys Barndollar was a pioneer in direct mail marketing. As head of the women's bureau of the Oakland Chamber of Commerce, Barndollar created an "Oakland Label" program, not unlike today's Oakland Grown program, to encourage people to buy from small, local businesses. (Both, from *Business Women's Herald*, retreived from the Internet Archive)

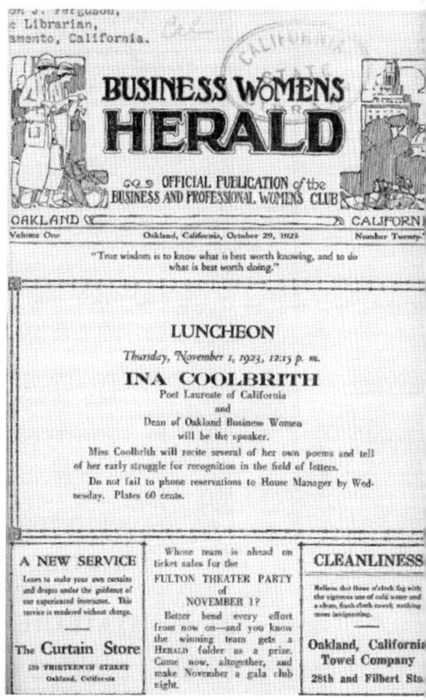

e Librarian,
amento, California.

BUSINESS WOMENS HERALD

OFFICIAL PUBLICATION of the BUSINESS AND PROFESSIONAL WOMENS CLUB

OAKLAND — CALIFORN

Volume One | Oakland, California, October 29, 1923 | Number Twenty-

"True wisdom is to know what is best worth knowing, and to do what is best worth doing."

LUNCHEON

Thursday, November 1, 1923, 12:15 p. m.

INA COOLBRITH
Poet Laureate of California
and
Dean of Oakland Business Women
will be the speaker.

Miss Coolbrith will recite several of her own poems and tell of her early struggle for recognition in the field of letters.

Do not fail to phone reservations to House Manager by Wednesday. Plates 60 cents.

A NEW SERVICE

Learn to make your own curtains and drapes under the guidance of our experienced instructor. This service is rendered without charge.

The Curtain Store
530 THIRTEENTH STREET
Oakland, California

Whose team is ahead on ticket sales for the
FULTON THEATER PARTY
of
NOVEMBER 1?
Better bend every effort from now on—and you know the winning team gets a HERALD folder as a prize. Come now, altogether, and make November a gala club night.

CLEANLINESS

Relieve that three o'clock fag with the vigorous use of cold water and a clean, fresh cloth towel; nothing more invigorating.

Oakland, California Towel Company
28th and Filbert Sts.

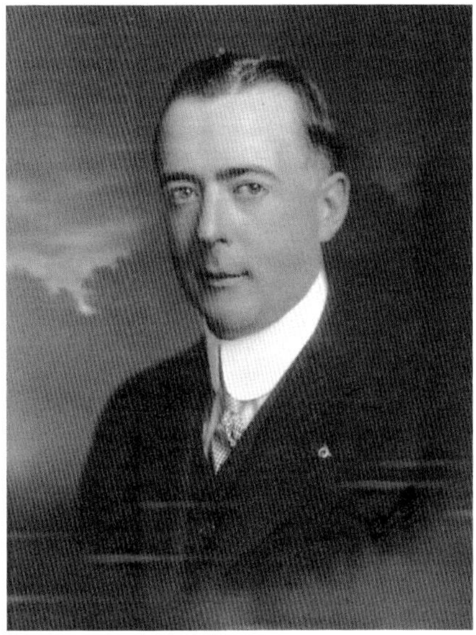

First Public Works Commissioner

In addition to running a carpet business with his father, Oakland native Harry Anderson was elected the first public works commissioner of Oakland in 1911. While on council, Anderson oversaw the construction of the new city hall (completed in 1914), the Oakland Municipal Auditorium (completed in 1915), and new schools. (Courtesy Harry Severin.)

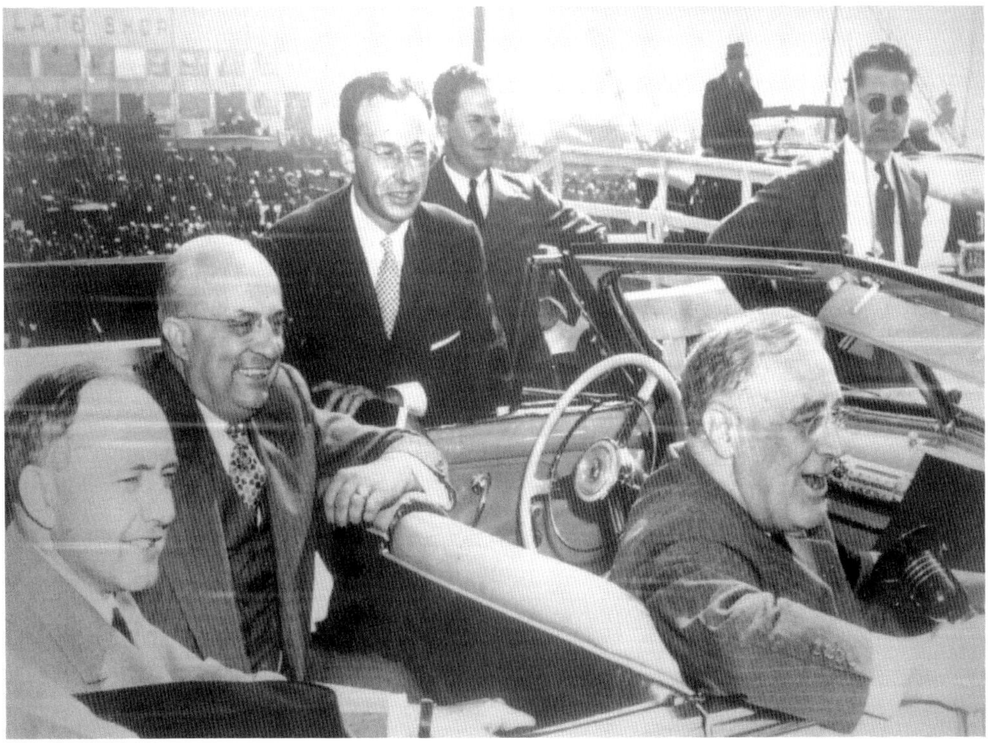

American Industrialist

Industrialist Henry J. Kaiser (second from left, behind Pres. Franklin D. Roosevelt, at front right) was a bold businessman. Kaiser started in the construction business, building Hoover Dam near Las Vegas as his first big contract. He later diversified into shipbuilding, steel, aluminum, healthcare, and even automobiles. Kaiser Center on Lake Merritt was once his world headquarters, and today, Kaiser Permanente health care is one of the largest employers in Oakland. (Courtesy Oakland History Room, Oakland Public Library.)

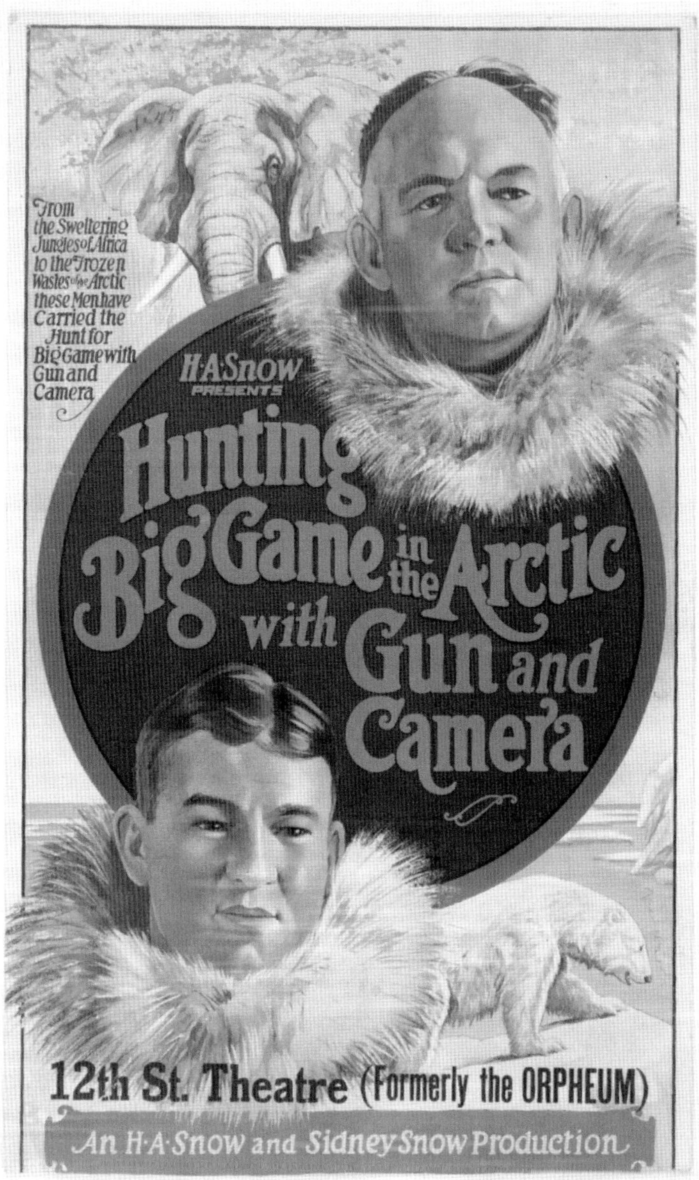

"Build Me a Museum, and I'll Fill 'Er Up"

Henry Snow was an adventurer and big game hunter who donated his extensive collection to Oakland to start the Snow Museum of Natural History in 1922. The collection was housed in the former Cutting Mansion, where Snow Park now sits, and included tens of thousands of specimens, mostly collected in Africa. The collections from the Snow Museum of Natural History were later merged with others to form the Oakland Museum of California.

Snow also started the first Oakland Zoo, which was then moved to what is now Joaquin Miller Park. The land for the zoo's current home in Knowland Park was not purchased until the 1940s.

Snow died of blackwater fever, a disease he picked up while hunting in Africa. The Snow family grave in Mountain View Cemetery is marked with a lion. (Courtesy Oakland Museum of California, gift of Mr. and Mrs. George Neubert.)

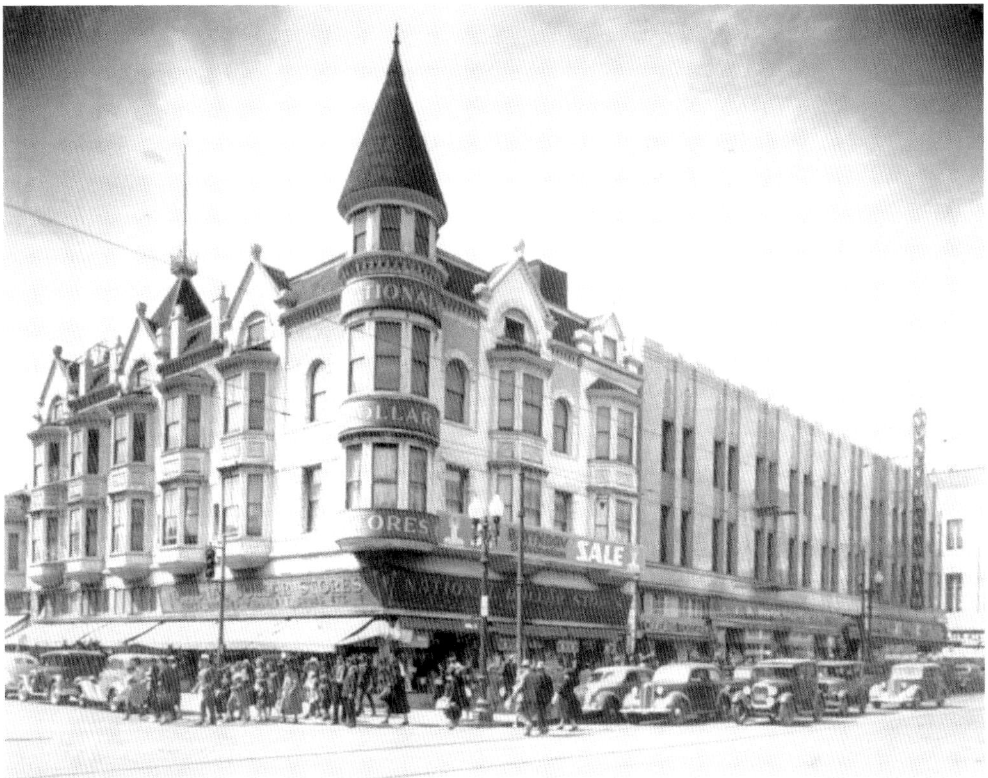

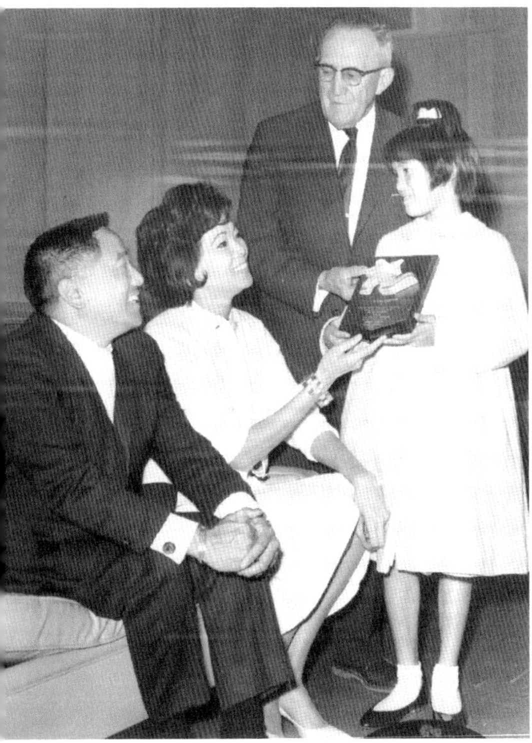

Businessman and Philanthropist

Starting with a small store in Vallejo in 1901, Joe Shoong quickly bought out his three partners and moved the shop to San Francisco. He added more stores, and in 1928, the chain was renamed National Dollar Stores. Shoong made a point of having a Chinese manager in almost every store in the chain.

Shoong was active in the Oakland Chinese American community, with the family entertaining many prominent people in their Julia Morgan–designed home in Adams Point. Joe and his wife, Rose, even hosted the leader of the Republic of China, Chiang Kai-Shek, who was guarded by the FBI during his visit.

Shoong generously donated much of his fortune to various causes, including a scholarship endowment for Chinese American students at the University of California, Berkeley, the construction of a Chinatown community center, and the creation of a Chinese language school (the Shoong Family Chinese Cultural Center). Shoong and his son Milton (at left with his family) also donated money toward the renovation of the Paramount Theatre and supported the Children's Fairyland Treetop Teahouse and Dragon Slide. (Both, courtesy Oakland History Room, Oakland Public Library.)

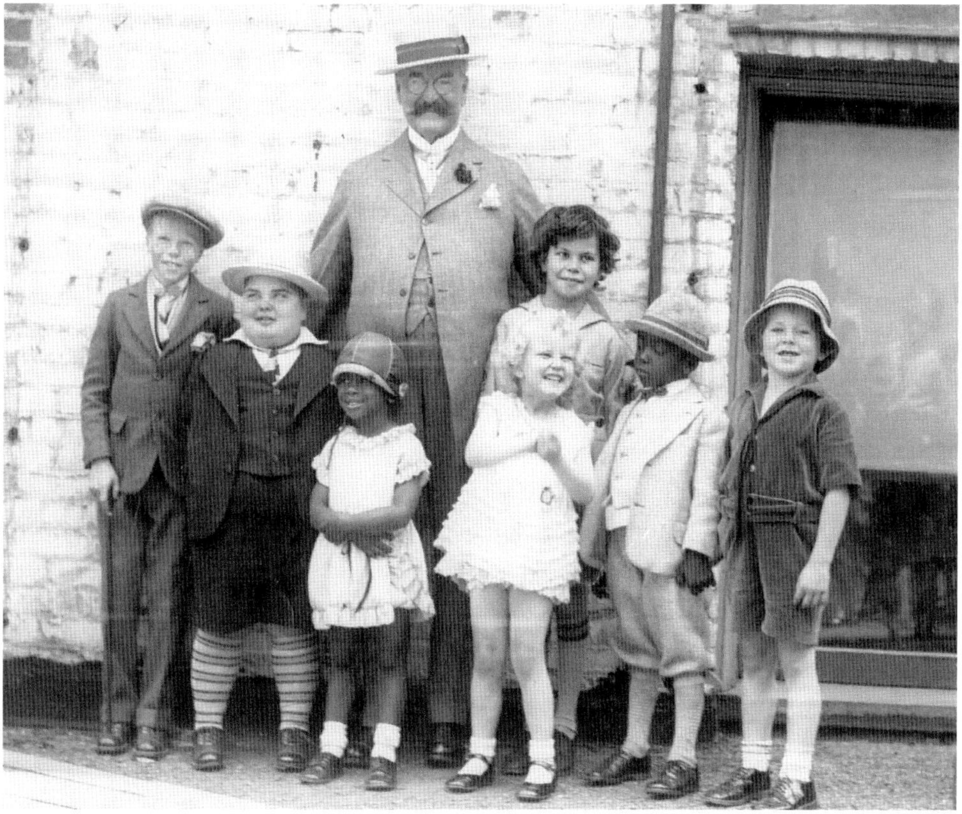

His Honor, The Buckaroo

John L. Davie (shown with the cast of the *Our Gang* films) was Oakland's longest-serving and most popular mayor and a larger-than-life character. Davie was elected five times, serving from 1895 to 1897 and 1915 to 1931. He is also the only Oakland mayor to date to have written an autobiography, fittingly titled *His Honor, the Buckaroo.*

Davie was born in upstate New York in 1850, and his varied life included working as a mule driver on the Erie Canal, studying law in Chicago during the Great Chicago Fire, working as a ranch hand in Nevada, and working as an actor, opera singer, butcher, feed store owner, and bookstore owner in the Bay Area. His bookstore put him in contact with Oakland's literati, including Ina Coolbrith, Joaquin Miller, a young Jack London, and Rev. John Knox McLean.

Much of Davie's popularity came from a "David and Goliath" struggle with the railroads over a stranglehold on Oakland's waterfront. He constructed a wharf to serve his feed and coal business, did battle with railroad thugs, and introduced a ferry service as the only competition to the railroad's ferries. He eventually earned his law degree and argued his case all the way to the Supreme Court, where he won a partial victory.

Among Davie's civic accomplishments during his years in office were the creation of the Port of Oakland and East Bay Municipal Utility District, the 1927 construction of the Oakland International Airport, the construction of the Posey Tube to Alameda, the construction of Skyline Boulevard (with city prisoners providing the labor), and the opening of fine art and natural history museums, including the Snow Museum.

Despite these many accomplishments, the only site in Oakland to bear the Davie family name is the Davie Tennis Stadium. Davie retired to the Hotel Oakland, where he would "hold court" in the lobby, dapperly dressed and with his signature red carnation in his lapel. (Courtesy Oakland History Room, Oakland Public Library.)

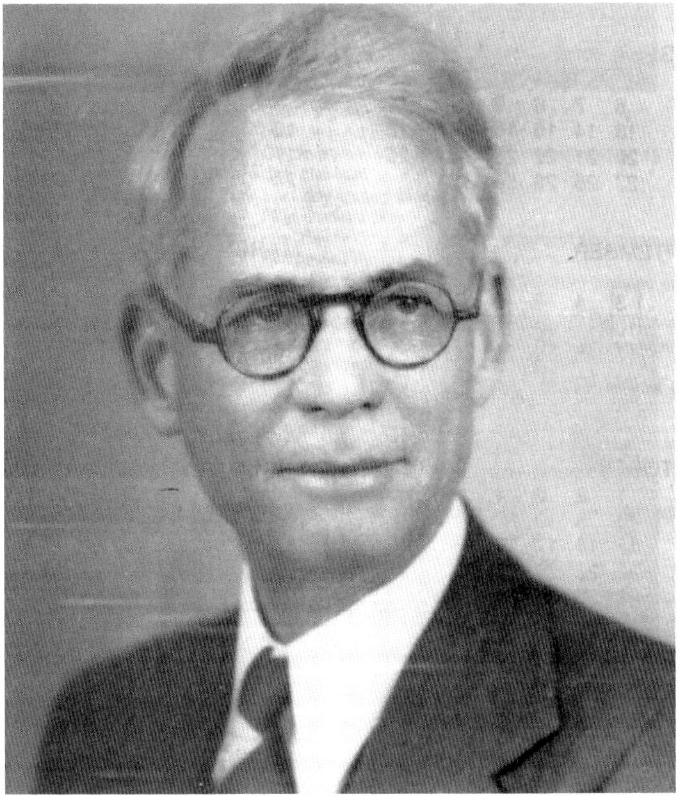

Journalist and Educator

Joseph Laney was a successful journalist and publisher but also a strong believer in the value of a vocational education. Against strong resistance from both labor unions and management, Laney brought the sides together and showed the benefits of a free vocational trade school. He founded the Oakland Central Trade School, which was later renamed Laney College in his memory. Laney College is now one of four campuses of the Peralta Community College District. (Courtesy Laney College.)

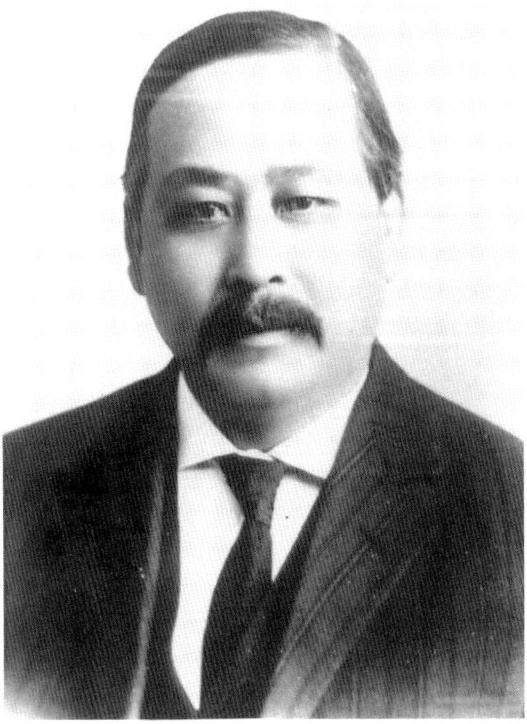

Canning Pioneer

In addition to owning four canneries around the Bay Area, Lew Hing was president of the Bank of Canton. Lew's Pacific Coast Canning Company in West Oakland used state of the art technology, but he still made a point of opening and tasting samples from the previous day's production. He provided food and shelter to refugees from the 1906 earthquake, and his canned goods helped provide relief for war-torn Europe following World War I. (Courtesy Jean Moon Liu via William Gee Wong.)

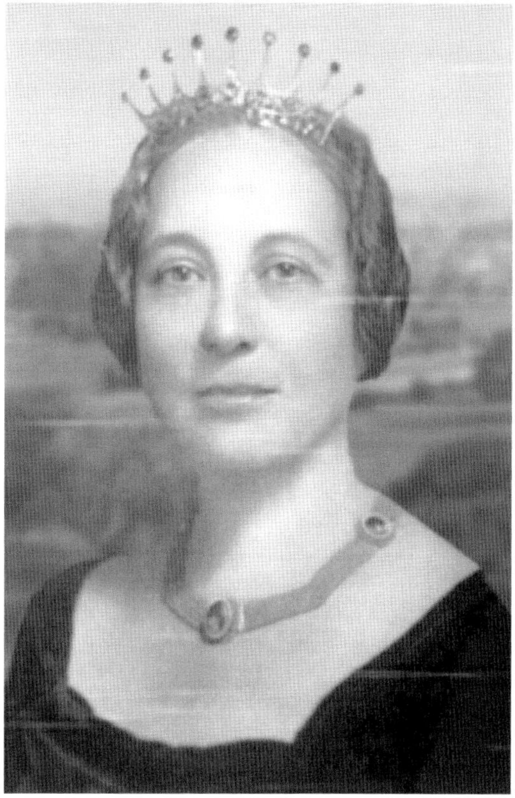

Brick Company Heiress

More famously known as the Countess Dandini, Lillian Remillard was the heiress of the Remillard Brick Company fortune. Remillard bricks were used to construct numerous buildings around the Bay Area, including the First Unitarian Church and the second iteration of Oakland High School. In 1932, Remillard married a poor nobleman, Count Dandini of Cesena, Italy. Their marriage did not last, but she kept the title. Remillard is also thought to have tutored a young Jack London in the Remillard family home, which still stands in Preservation Park. (Courtesy Carolands Foundation.)

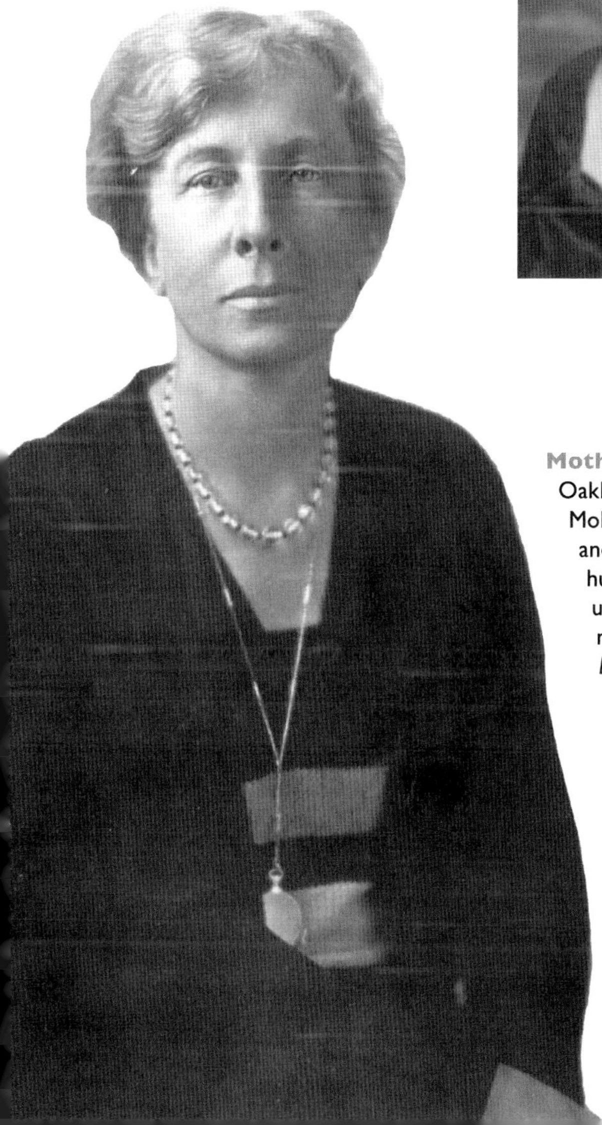

Mother of Modern Management

Oakland High School graduate Dr. Lillian Evelyn Moller Gilbreth was a pioneering psychologist and industrial engineer. Gilbreth and her husband were efficiency experts. Their unusual life as parents of 12 children was made famous by the book and movie *Cheaper by the Dozen*. Gilbreth was the granddaughter of early Oakland businessman Frederick Delger. (Courtesy Smithsonian Institution, SIA2008-1924.)

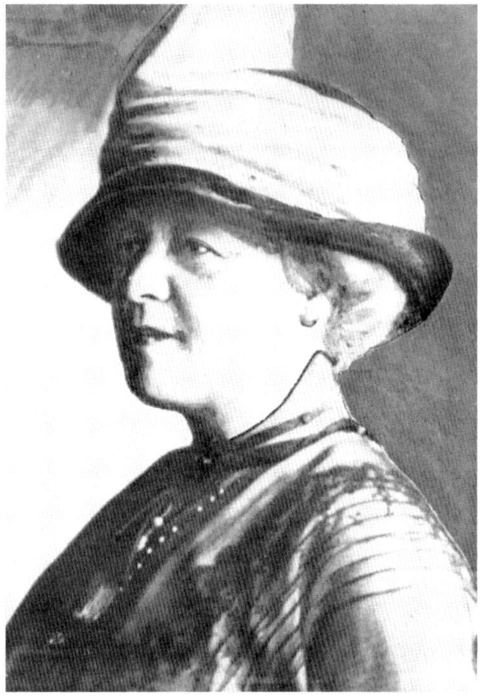

Newspaper Editor and Suffragist
In the early 1900s, when most women in society did not work outside the home, Mollie Conners was editor and publisher of the weekly *Oakland Saturday Night* newspaper and an outspoken suffragist. Later, she was the society editor of the *Oakland Tribune* and was active in the Ebell Society. (From *San Francisco Call*, retrieved from the California Digital Newspaper Collection.)

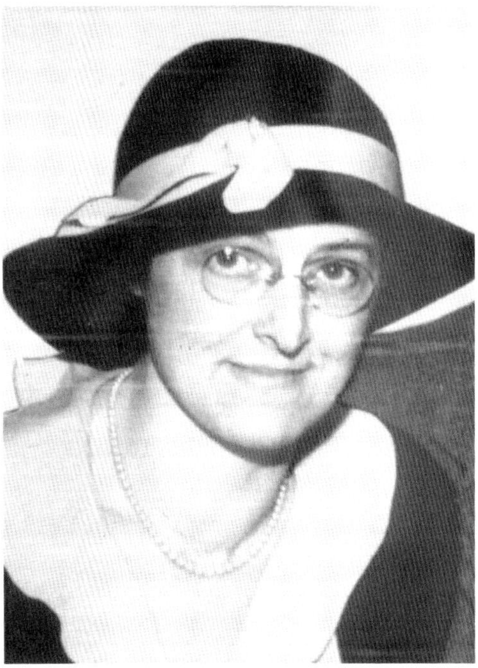

First Woman on City Council
In 1931, Wilhelmine Yoakum was the first woman elected to the city council of Oakland. When she ran again in 1933 as an incumbent, she was the only woman among 45 candidates but was only narrowly defeated. It was more than 15 years until Florence Fletcher was elected in 1949 and 25 years after that until Mary Moore (see page 114) was elected in 1977. (Courtesy City of Oakland.)

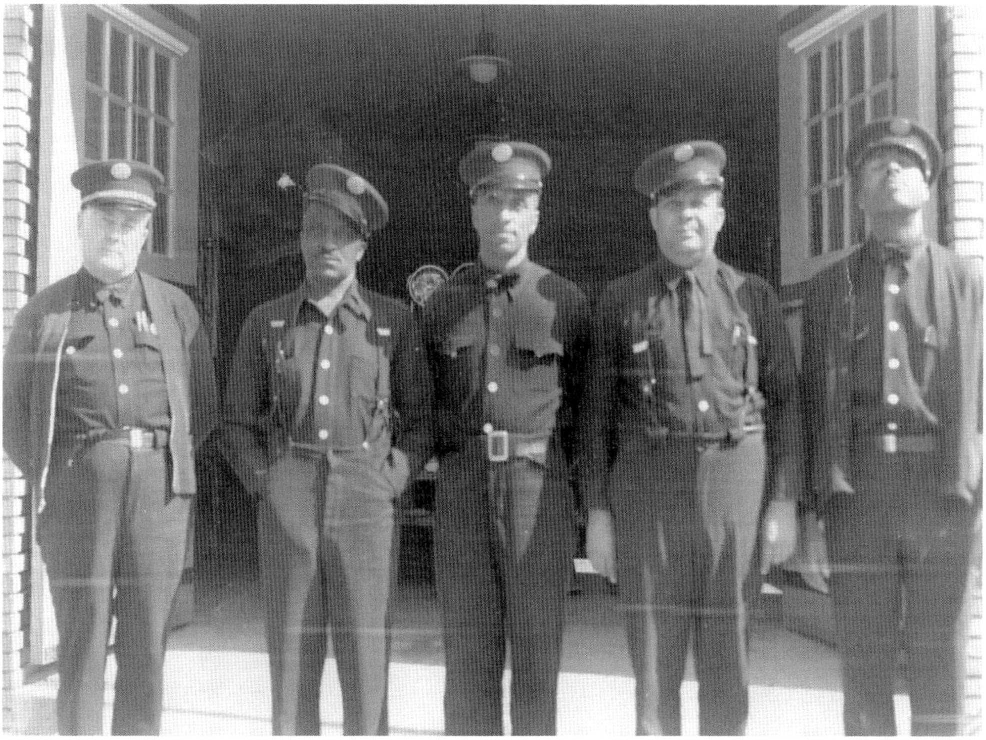

Pioneering Firefighter

While Royal Towns (second from right, with segregated Engine Company No. 22) was not the first black firefighter in Oakland, he was instrumental in desegregating the department. Despite easily passing the entrance exam, Towns's application was destined for the wastebasket until a former employer intervened. After collecting data showing African Americans in fire departments in other cities like New York were being promoted, Towns became the first to be promoted in the Oakland Fire Department. (Courtesy Oakland Fire Department archives.)

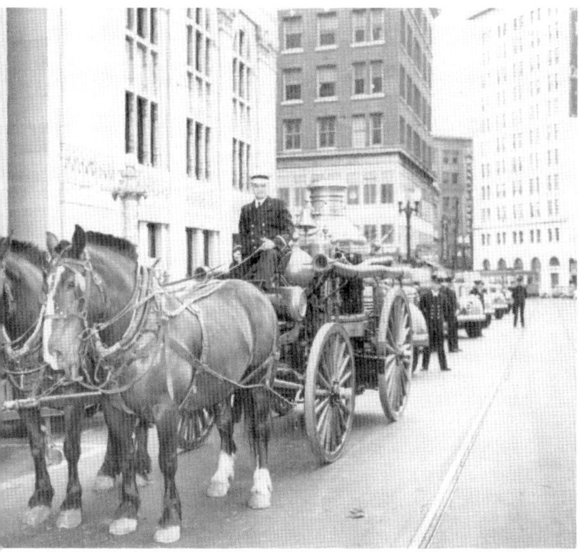

From Horses to Fire Engines

William Lutkey had a lengthy career at the Oakland Fire Department and saw firefighting equipment evolve from horse-drawn wagons to modern fire engines. He joined the department in 1901, became a captain in 1910, and was chief of the department in 1927, a position he held until his retirement in 1947. His tenure included the Great Depression in the 1930s, when the department had to make due with no pay increases or additional personnel. (Courtesy Oakland Fire Department archives.)

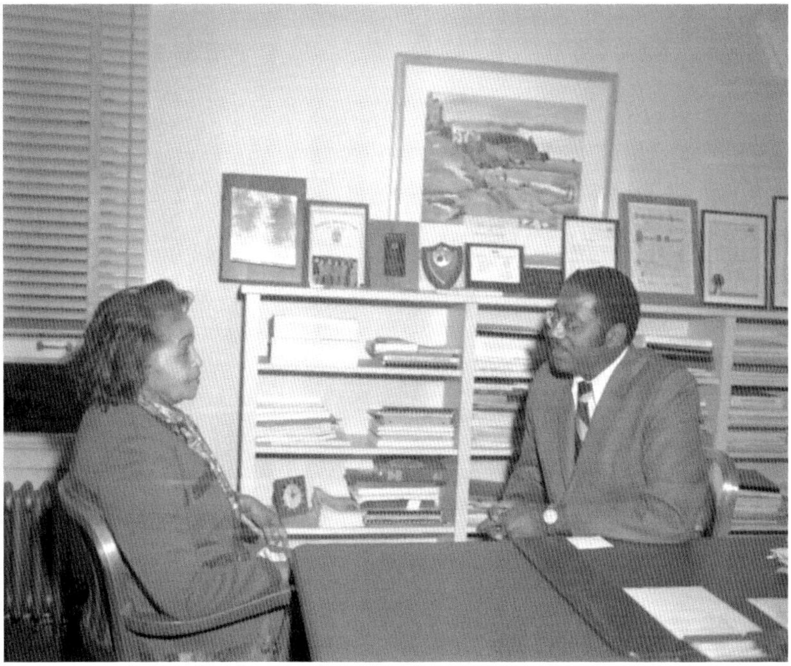

First Black Teacher, OUSD Superintendent

In 1926, Dr. Ida Louise Jackson (left) became the first black teacher in Oakland public schools. Her appointment to Prescott Elementary School was met with protests and attempts to have her reassigned, but her students—including white children—helped her through.

More than four decades later, Dr. Marcus Foster (above right and below) became the first black superintendent of the Oakland Unified School District and the first to head a major US school district. Foster was assassinated by the Symbionese Liberation Army, who used bullets with cyanide, because they mistakenly believed he supported student IDs and police in schools. (Both, courtesy Oakland History Room, Oakland Public Library.)

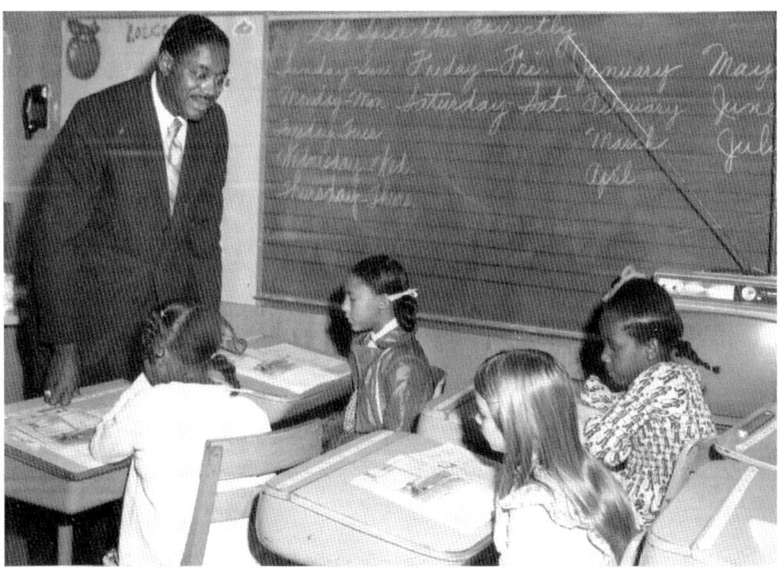

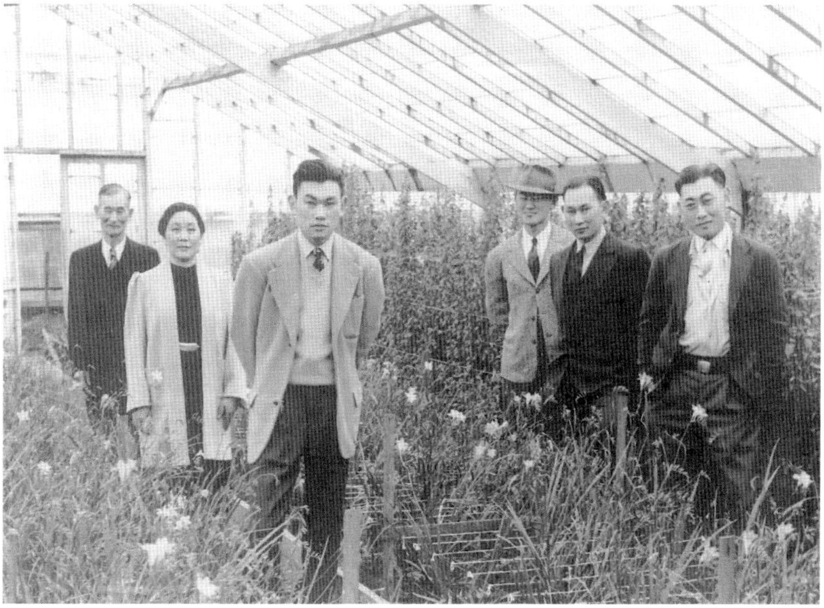

Refused World War II Internment

To support the war effort, Castlemont High School graduate Fred Korematsu went to work in the shipyards but was fired because of his Japanese ancestry. Korematsu underwent plastic surgery and tried to pass as Filipino and Hawaiian. Rather than report for internment in 1942, he went into hiding, but he was caught and his family sent to the internment camp at Topaz, Utah. Pictured from left to right are Kakusaburo, Kotsui Aoki, and brothers Fred (Toyosaburo), Joe (Junichi), Harry (Takashi), and Hi (Hiroshi).

Korematsu's case went all the way to the US Supreme Court, but he lost in a 6-3 decision. Finally, in 1983, his case was formally vacated, and in 1998, Pres. Bill Clinton awarded Korematsu the Presidential Medal of Freedom. A replica of the medal adorns his grave marker in Mountain View Cemetery. (Above, courtesy Karen Korematsu and the Korematsu Institute; below, author's collection.)

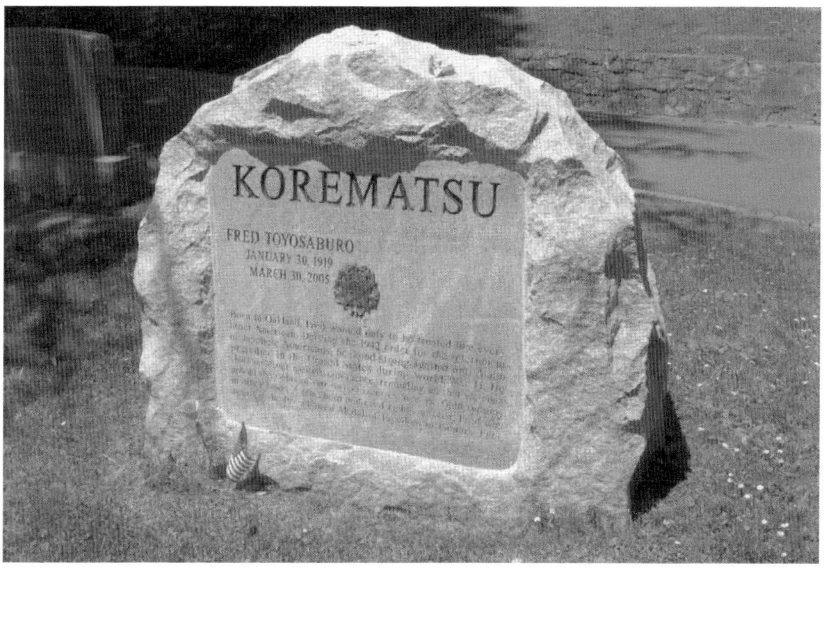

Education Leader, Pioneering Doctor

Joseph Lee was a leader in education in Oakland public schools, working his way up through the ranks beginning in 1938. Lee eventually served as principal of several schools before he retired more than four decades later. In the 1930s, Lee was also a member of the Wa Sung Athletic Club baseball team (see page 82) and served as the first president of the Wa Sung Community Service Club in 1953. Dr. Janet Chan Lee was the first Chinese American woman from Oakland to receive a medical degree from the University of California, San Francisco and graduated at the top of her class. She started her obstetrician-gynecology practice in 1943 and practiced medicine until her retirement in 1985. (Courtesy Dr. Janet Lee via William Gee Wong.)

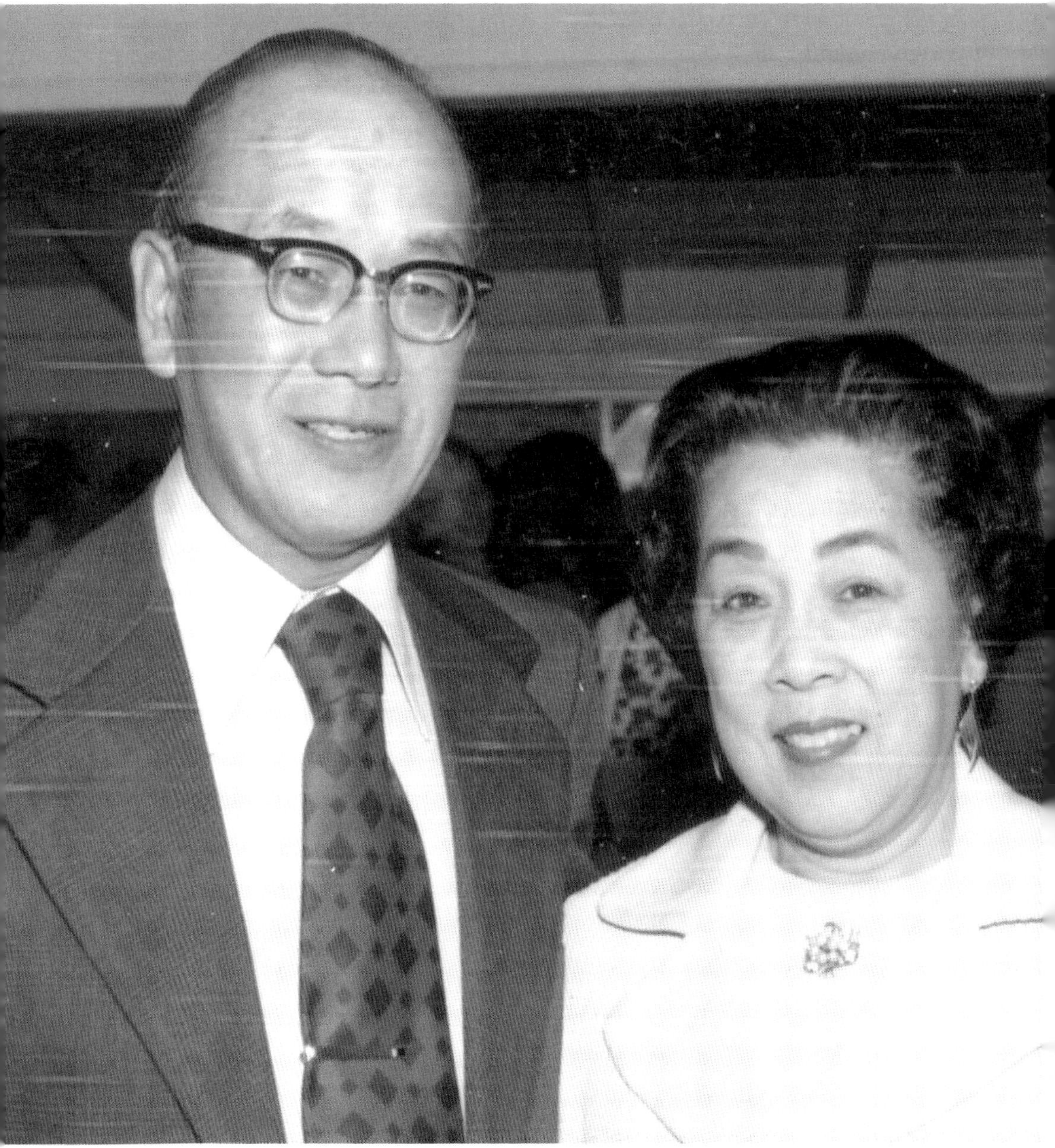

CHAPTER FOUR

New Era, New Politics

I believe that there is a willingness now to work with a mayor who happens to be black.

—Lionel J. Wilson

Oakland has long been a diverse city, but not necessarily an egalitarian one. The first known residents were the Ohlone people; the first settlers included Afro-Latinos from New Spain. The Gold Rush, and later the railroads, brought a variety of people from all over to settle in the Bay Area. With a few exceptions, the people with wealth and power were white men, but that started to change around World War II.

The end of World War II saw the rise of the automobile. This led to a more mobile population, the decline of transit, and a boom in freeways and suburbs. Unfortunately, this also enabled and encouraged "white flight" from Oakland and other cities.

Oakland's Latino community started organizing in the 1950s and 1960s in response to continued discrimination and the destruction of neighborhoods by freeways and urban renewal.

The 1960s saw the rise of the Black Panther Party. While people tend to focus on individual acts of violence by or against party members, the Black Panthers should also be remembered for creating a free breakfast program for schoolchildren and free medical clinics and holding teach-ins to educate people about their history and rights. Some people in the Latino community started a local branch of the Brown Berets with similar goals.

All these changes led to the election of the first black mayor of Oakland, former judge Lionel Wilson, who "the establishment" viewed as a "safe" black candidate compared to the opposing candidate, Black Panther Bobby Seale, who was defeated in a runoff in the previous election. However, Wilson was passionate about equality and went on to serve multiple terms.

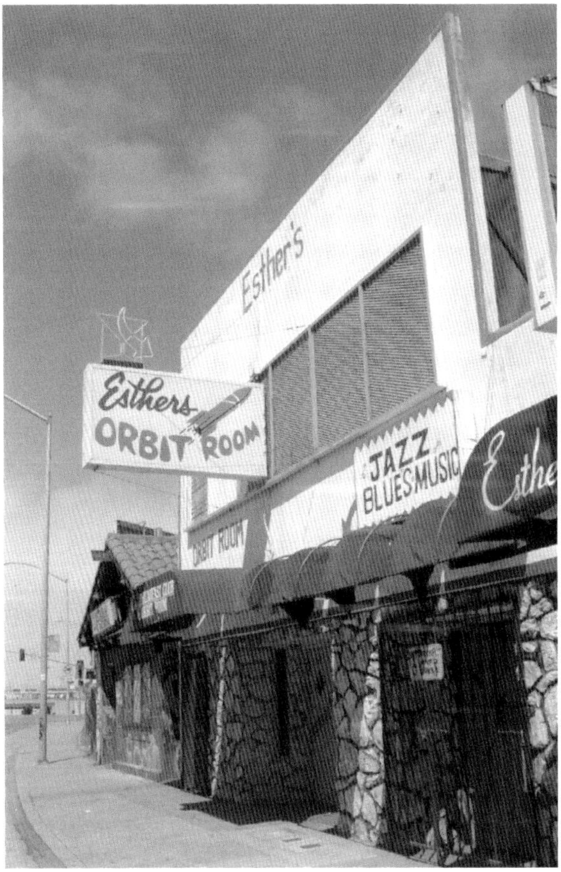

Esther's Orbit Room

After coming to Oakland in the 1940s, Esther Mabry worked at Slim Jenkins Supper Club (see page 90), saved her tips, and opened her own restaurant, Esther's Breakfast Room. The Mabrys expanded the business to offer cocktails and live music, and the Orbit Room opened in 1963. It was among dozens of jazz and blues clubs along Seventh Street that once made Oakland the "Harlem of the West." Noted performers included B.B. King, Lou Rawls, Etta James, and Al Green. (Author's collection.)

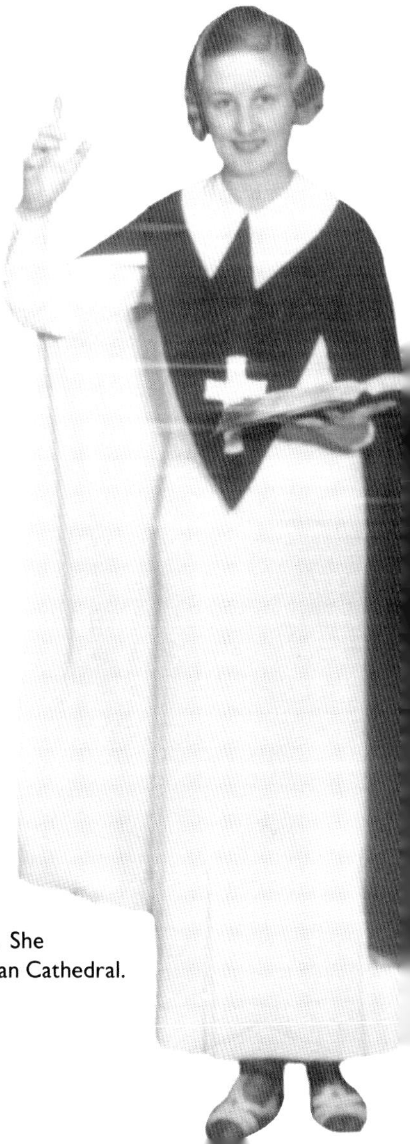

The "Girl Evangelist"

Dr. Bebe Patten was an early supporter of racial equality; in the 1930s and 1940s, several of her revivals were attacked after she preached against racism and social injustice in the South. After leading a series of revivals at the Oakland Auditorium in 1944 with as many as 5,000 people a night, Patten founded the Oakland Bible Institute, now known as Patten University. She also founded Patten Academy of Christian Education and Christian Cathedral. (Courtesy Bebe Patten Heritage Center.)

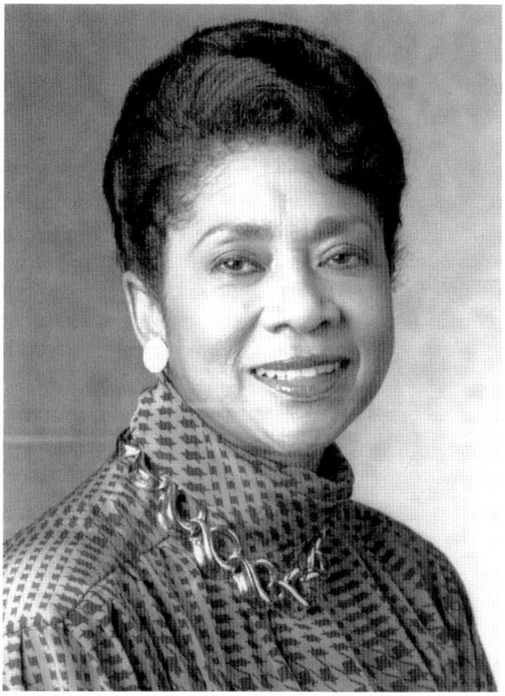

Grand Dame of Bay Area Journalism
Belva Davis (left; below center, receiving an award from the Ebony Museum of Arts in West Oakland) lived in a crowded West Oakland apartment and could not afford to go to college but said, "I always thought if I applied myself, I could be whatever I wanted to be." Beginning with freelance writing in 1957, Davis went on to have a lengthy radio and television career, and in 1966, became the first black woman television journalist on the West Coast. After decades on the air, Davis retired in 2012. (Both, courtesy Oakland Post Photograph Collection, MS 169, African American Museum & Library at Oakland.)

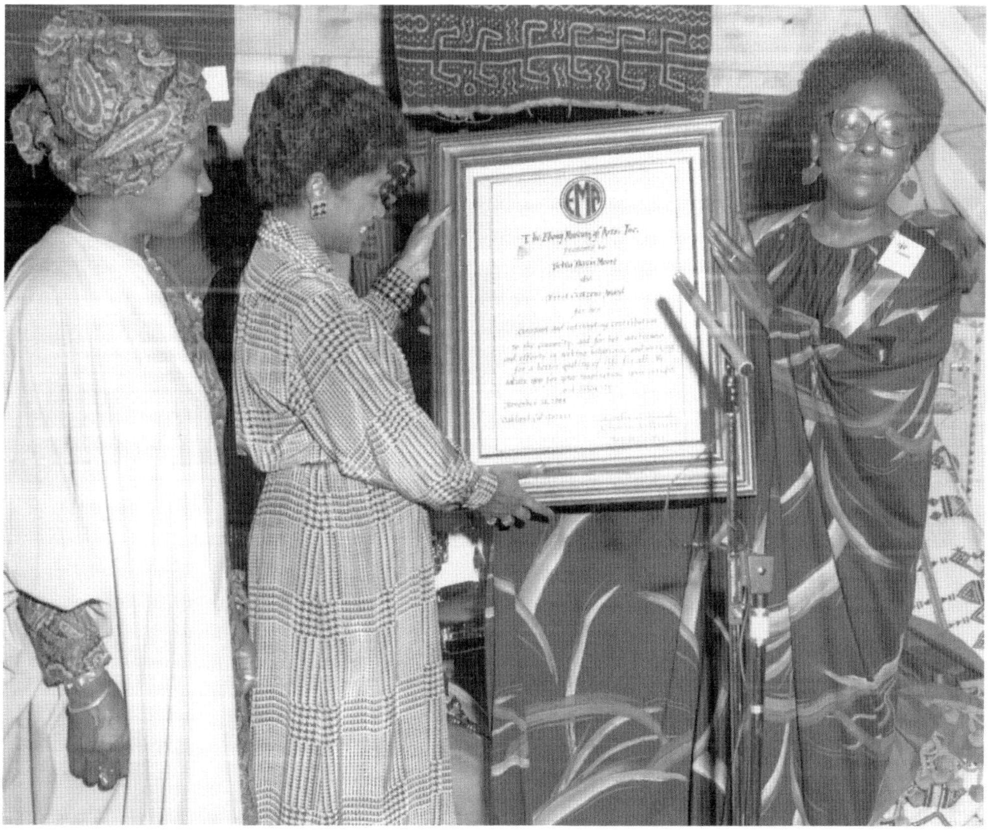

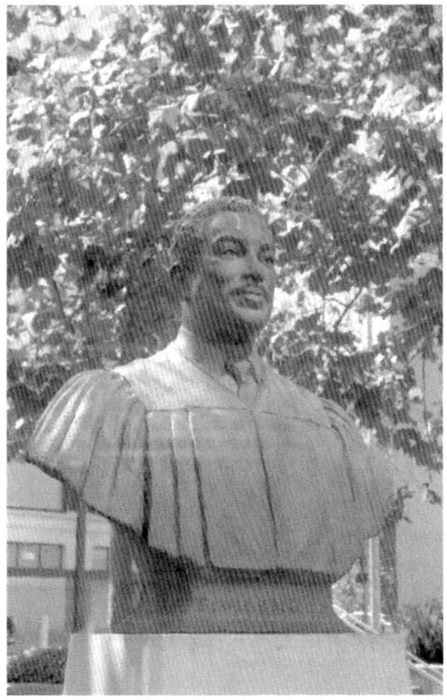

Judge and Social Justice Advocate

After serving as a highly decorated officer in the Navy during the Korean War, Donald McCullum went to work as a civil rights attorney in the 1950s. In addition to serving as city attorney of Berkeley and deputy district attorney of Alameda County, McCullum is best remembered as a judge in the Alameda County Superior Court until his death in 1988. The Donald P. McCullum Youth Court was named for him. (Author's collection.)

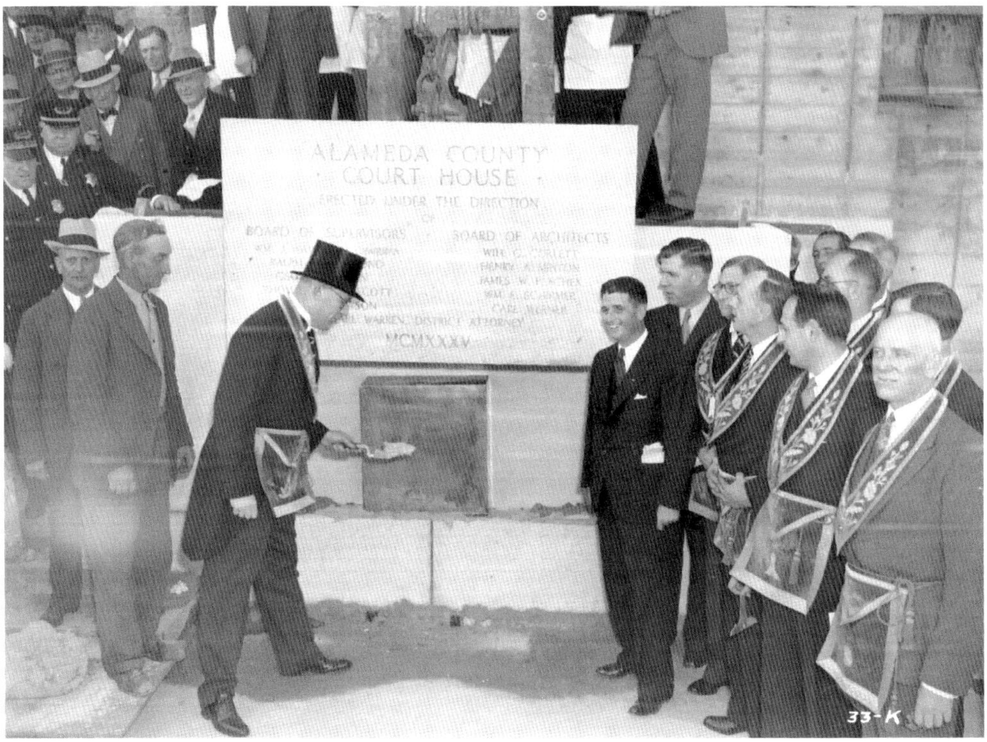

US Supreme Court Chief Justice

Earl Warren (with top hat, at the laying of the cornerstone for the new Alameda County Courthouse in 1935) had a lengthy career as a lawyer and judge, serving as deputy district attorney, district attorney, and attorney general of California and even as governor of California from 1943 to 1953. But Warren is best known as chief justice of the US Supreme Court, presiding over the landmark ruling *Brown v. Board of Education* in 1954, which outlawed segregation in schools. (Courtesy Oakland Museum of California, gift of Norma Stanberry.)

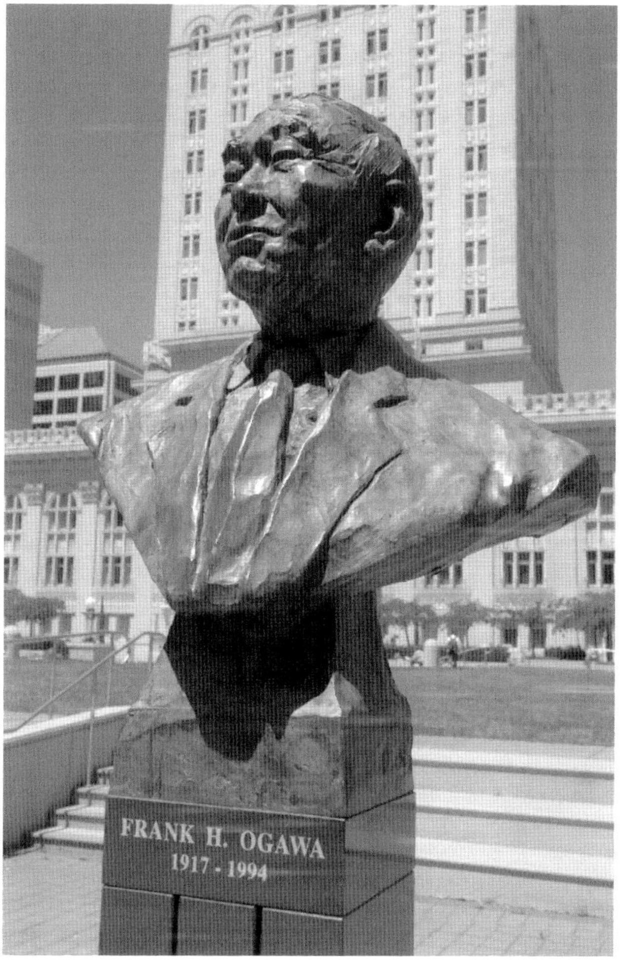

Civil Rights and Gardening

Frank Hirao Ogawa was the first Japanese American on the Oakland City Council and served 28 years, the longest tenure of any Oakland council member. But Ogawa's path to serving on council was not easy.

Ogawa was a Nisei (second generation Japanese) born in Lodi, California, but like many Japanese Americans during World War II, he and his wife, Grace Sumiye Ogawa, were forced to sell their possessions and were imprisoned in an internment camp. They slept on straw mattresses in a horse stall for six months before being shipped to the Topaz War Relocation Center in Utah, where they spent another three and a half years. Their daughter Nancy Lynne Ogawa was born in the camp and died at the age of two.

But the mistreatment did not turn Ogawa against the United States; instead, he strived to prove his loyalty. When he returned to Oakland, he became involved in civil rights and found work as a gardener. Saving his money, he eventually opened his own nursery.

Besides serving on the Oakland City Council, Ogawa also served on the Oakland Parks Commission, San Francisco Bay Conservation and Development Commission, and Bay Area Air Quality Management District.

After he died, the plaza in front of city hall was renamed Frank Ogawa Plaza in his honor by a unanimous vote of the city council. Also named in his honor are the Frank Ogawa Firescape Garden and the Torii Gate in Lakeside Park, which was dedicated in his memory. (Author's collection.)

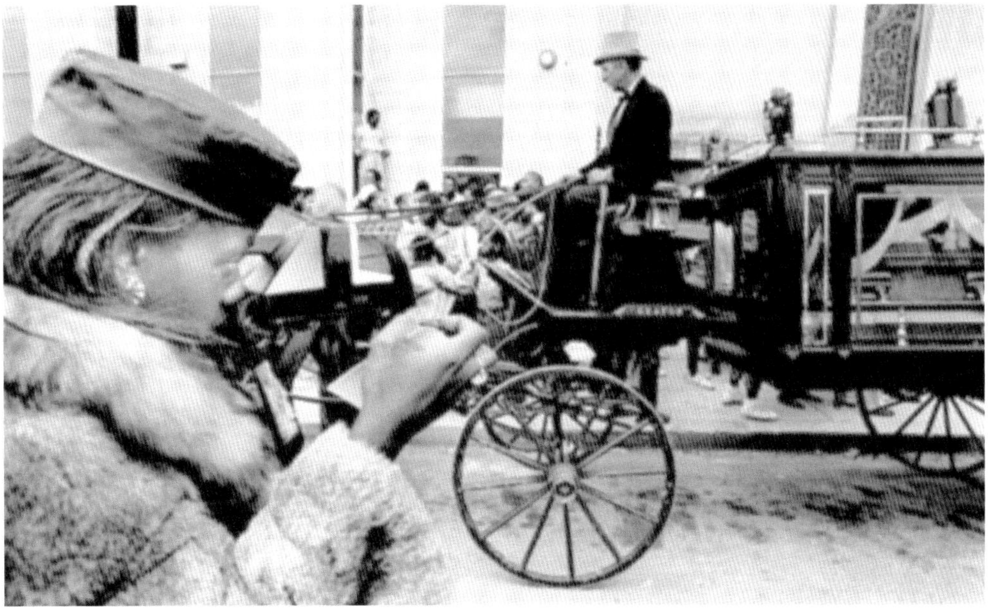

Notorious Drug Lord

After creating a large-scale drug operation, Felix "The Cat" Mitchell lived the high life, using his money for expensive cars, clothes, and parties. Mitchell also went to church and gave to charities, passing out toys and candy to children in the neighborhoods to cultivate his reputation. After Mitchell died in prison in 1986, people lined the streets to view his funeral procession, which included several Rolls-Royces and a horse-drawn, glass-walled carriage carrying Mitchell's body in a $6,000 bronze coffin. (Above, photograph by Mark Sarfati, courtesy East Bay Express; below, courtesy FBI/OPD files.)

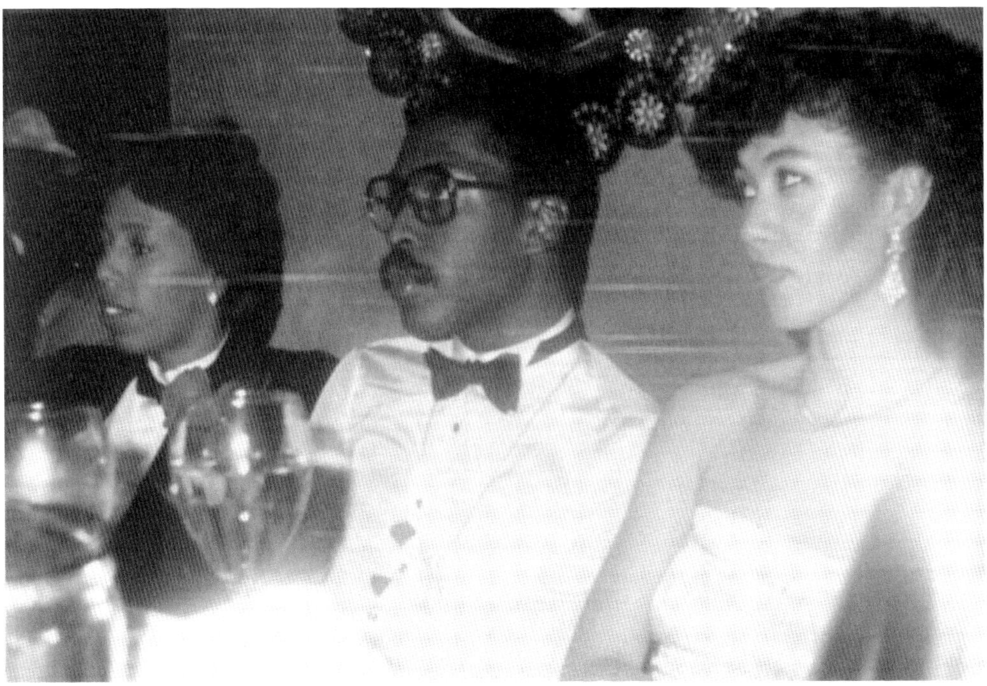

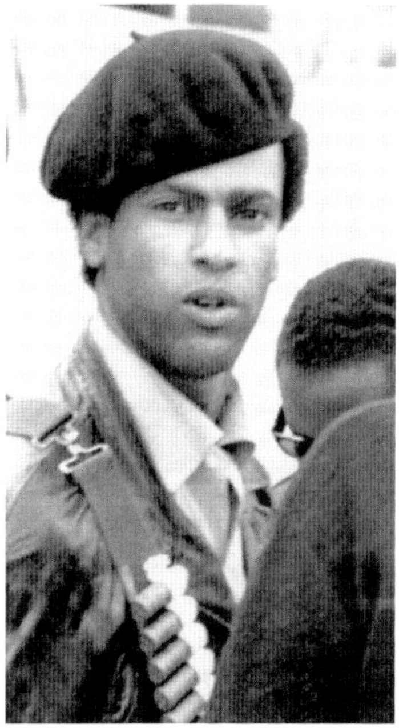

Black Panther Cofounder

Huey Newton graduated from Oakland Tech in 1959 without being able to read. After teaching himself to read, he eventually went on to earn a PhD. During his time at Merritt College, Newton met Bobby Seale, and the duo founded the Black Panther Party.

Violence seemed to linger around Newton. He was tried three times but never convicted in the shooting of Oakland police officer John Frey in 1967. In 1974, he fled to Cuba to avoid prosecution for the murder of Kathleen Smith. Then in 1989, Newton was shot and killed by a member of the Black Guerrilla Family, which included former Black Panthers who had become disenchanted with Newton. (Courtesy Oakland Post Photograph Collection, MS 169, African American Museum & Library at Oakland.)

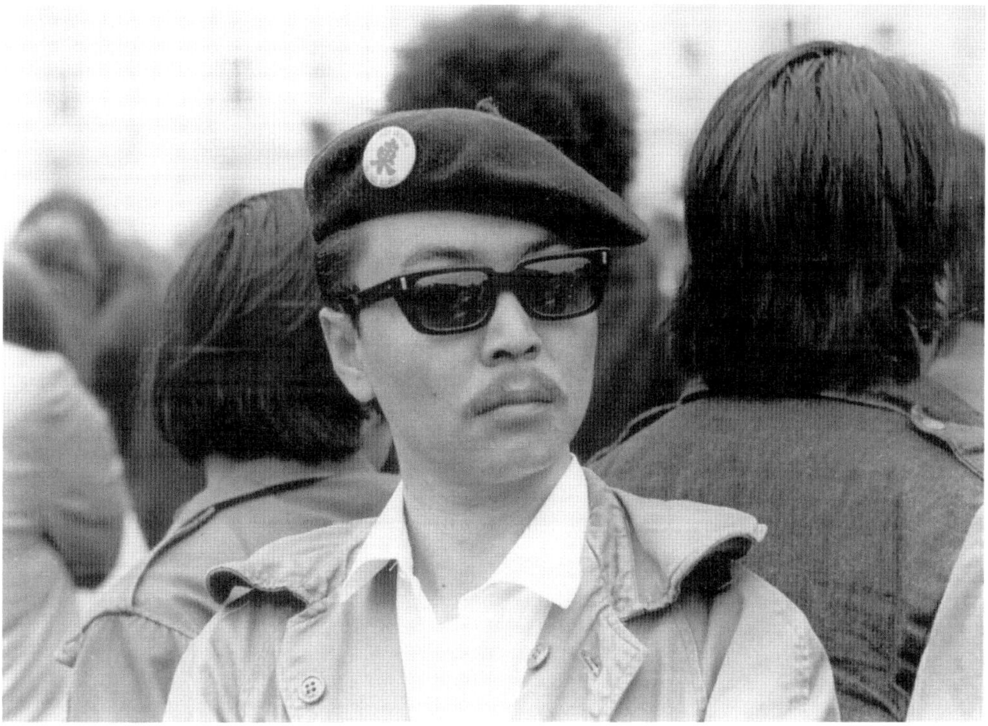

Samurai Among Panthers

After spending World War II in an internment camp with his family, Richard Aoki attended Merritt College in Oakland, where he met and became friends with Black Panther founders Huey Newton and Bobby Seale. In 2012, the FBI released papers showing Aoki had been an informant, but at the same time, he was supplying weapons and training to the Panthers. (Nikki Arai, Courtesy Nancy Park.)

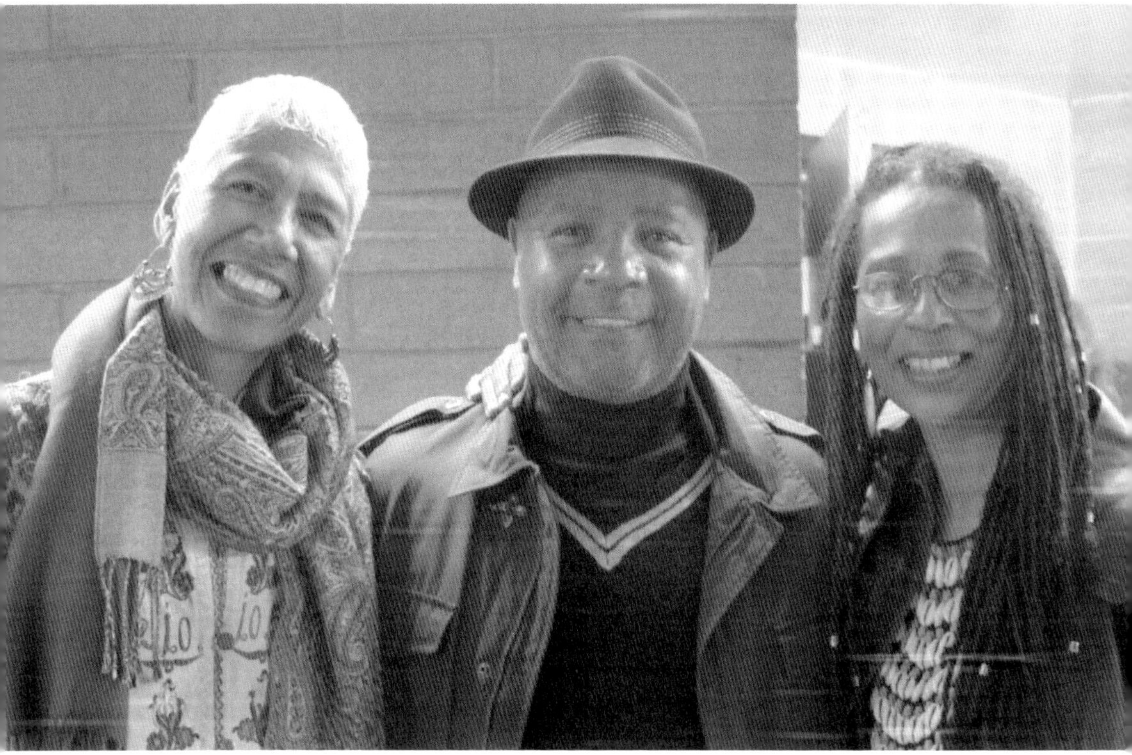

Black Panthers

Ericka Huggins (left) was the director of the Black Panther–run Oakland Community School, originally known as the Children's House. The school operated on liberation and empowerment principles with a curriculum that included education in both practical skills and community consciousness.

The distinctive art of Emory Douglas (center) helped give the message of the Black Panther Party a consistent look and portrayed the poor not as victims but with empathy. Douglas was the Panther's minister of culture from 1967 until the party disbanded in 1980, and his work was widely seen in *The Black Panther* magazine.

Joan Tarika Lewis (right) was the first woman to join the Black Panther Party in 1967. In addition to being an activist, Lewis is a talented jazz violinist, writer, illustrator, and teacher. (Courtesy Rasheed Shabazz.)

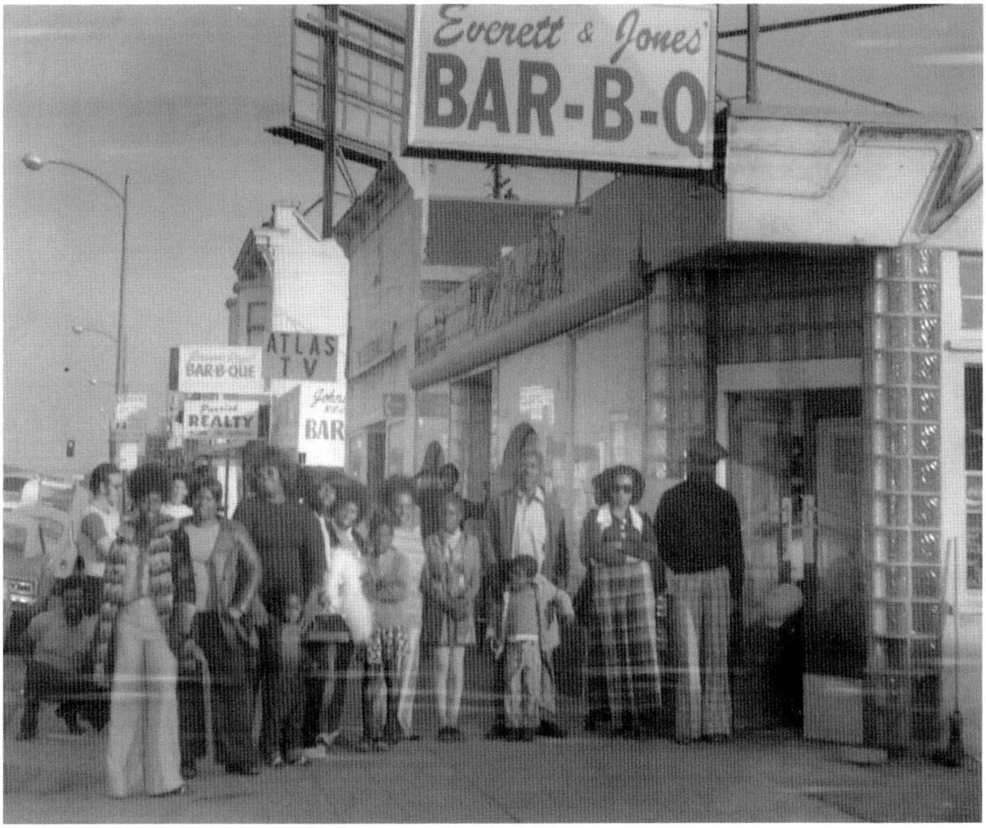

Everett and Jones Barbeque
With three small children and another on the way, Dorothy Turner Everett and her husband decided to leave rural Alabama and seek new opportunity in California. To support her children, Everett worked as a domestic, and also worked part-time tending a smoke pit for what was to become Flint's Bar-B-Q. She later became the restaurant's first manager.

Deciding to strike out on her own, Dorothy borrowed $700 from her good friend Cora "The Angel" McKinnon. With a week's line of credit, she opened Everett & Jones Barbeque. With her eight daughters, one son, and son-in-law (Jones) pitching in to fix up an old building on the corner of Ninety-Second Avenue and International Boulevard, Everett opened the restaurant in 1973.

Everett died in 2007, but Everett & Jones continues to be a family-run business, with restaurants in Berkeley, Hayward, and Oakland. It is considered one of the top barbecue restaurants in the country and continues the long history of barbecue in Oakland, which stretches from the 1800s to today. (Both, copyright Shirley Everett Dicko, used with permission.)

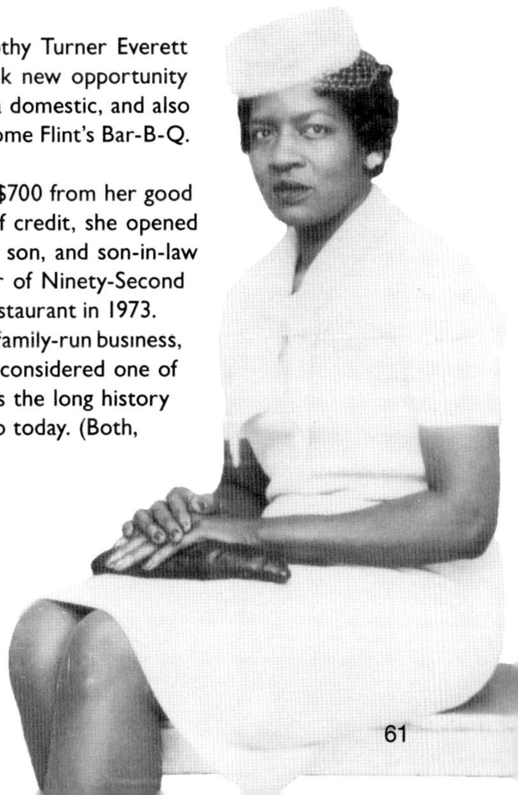

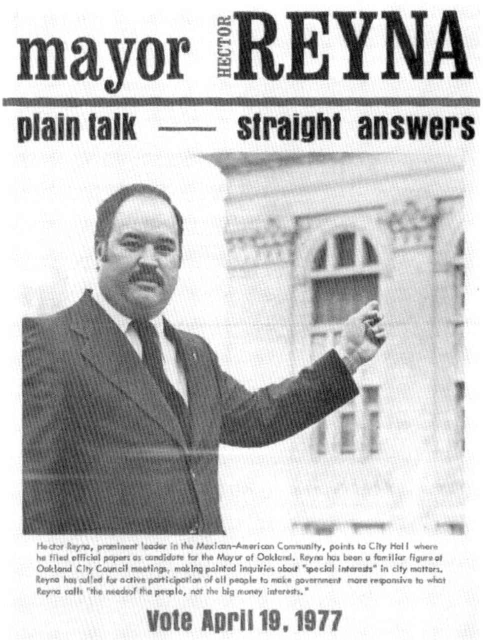
mayor HECTOR REYNA
plain talk — straight answers

Hector Reyna, prominent leader in the Mexican-American Community, points to City Hall where he filed official papers as candidate for the Mayor of Oakland. Reyna has been a familiar figure at Oakland City Council meetings, making pointed inquiries about "special interests" in city matters. Reyna has called for active participation of all people to make government more responsive to what Reyna calls "the needsof the people, not the big money interests."

Vote April 19, 1977

Businessman, Political Icon
After a disagreement about an ordinance that affected one of his businesses, Hector Reyna ran for city council and lost. Over the years, he ran for the boards of BART, AC Transit, and the East Bay Regional Parks District, as well as the state senate and US Congress. He ran against every Oakland mayor for 25 years but never won a single election. (Courtesy Oakland History Room, Oakland Public Library.)

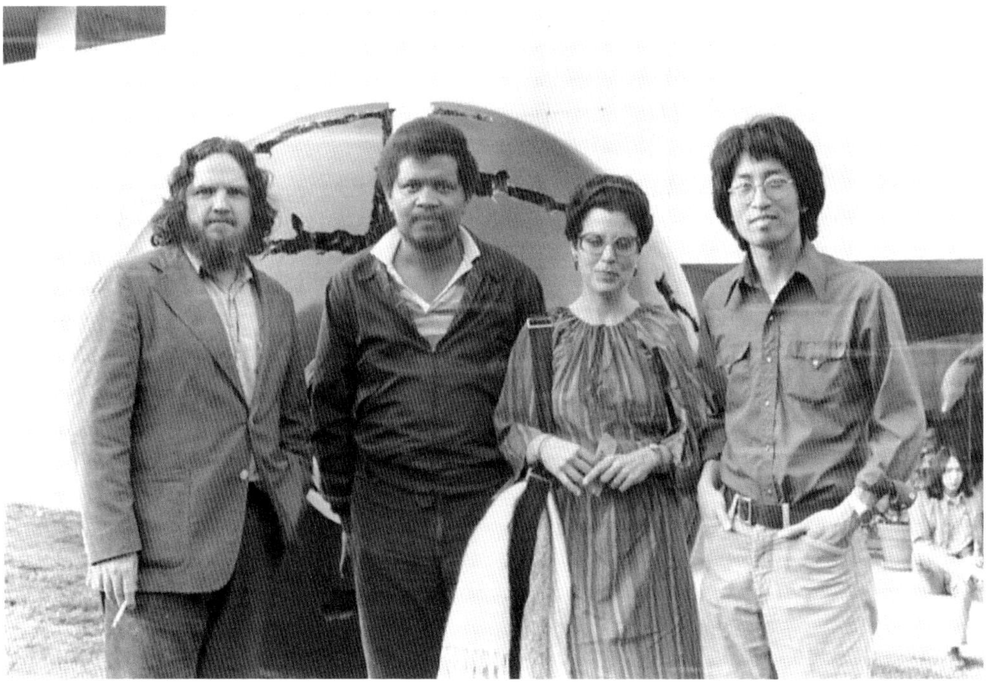

Historian, Poet, Lyricist, Author
Ishmael Reed (second from left, along with Bob Callahan, Carla Blank, and Shawn Wong) was part of the Black Arts Movement, which inspired numerous people—black, Latino, and Asian—to write about their backgrounds, histories, and experiences instead of assimilating into the dominant culture. Since retiring as a UC Berkeley professor, Reed has written a number of books, including *Blues City: A Walk in Oakland* (2003). (Courtesy Nancy Wong.)

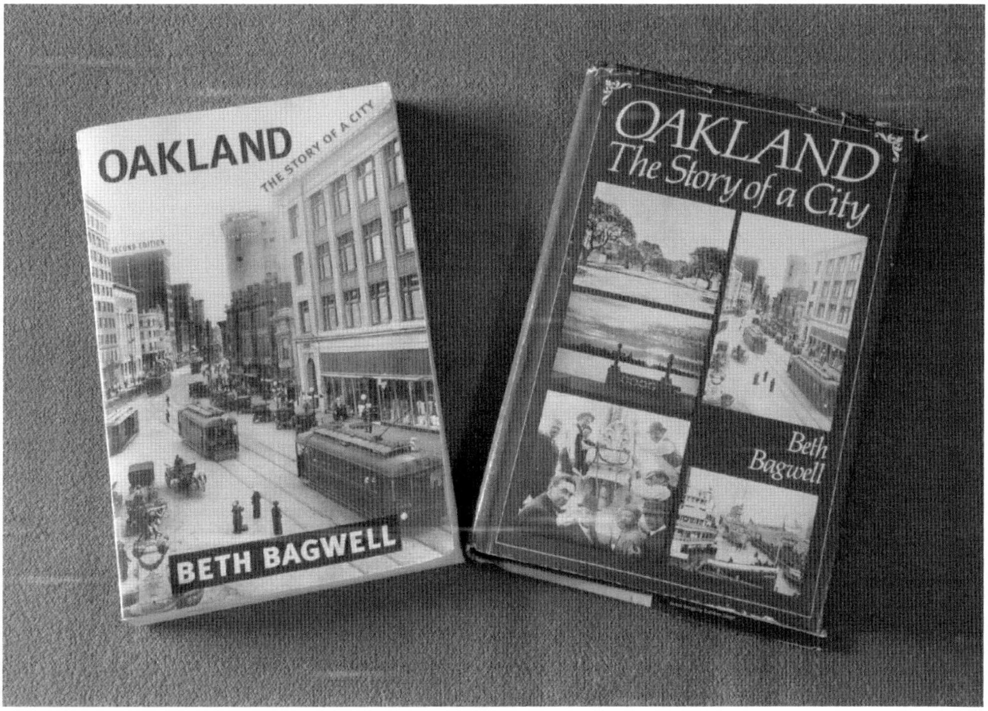

The Story of a City

Historian, preservationist, and author Beth Bagwell wrote *Oakland: The Story of a City* (1981), which is the definitive history book about Oakland. Bagwell was also one of the founders of the Oakland Heritage Alliance and served as the first chair of its board of directors. (Author's collection.)

Pioneering and Unconventional Broadcaster

Chuck Johnson founded Soul Beat Television in 1978, and while it was never known for high quality programming, it was much loved. It was one of the first stations to show music videos and broke Oakland artists like MC Hammer and Too $hort before they became mainstream. When the IRS briefly shut down Soul Beat because Johnson owed $37,000 in taxes, viewers responded by donating $40,000 in a week. Johnson even ran for mayor of Oakland in 1985. (Courtesy Oakland Post Photograph Collection, MS 169, African American Museum & Library at Oakland.)

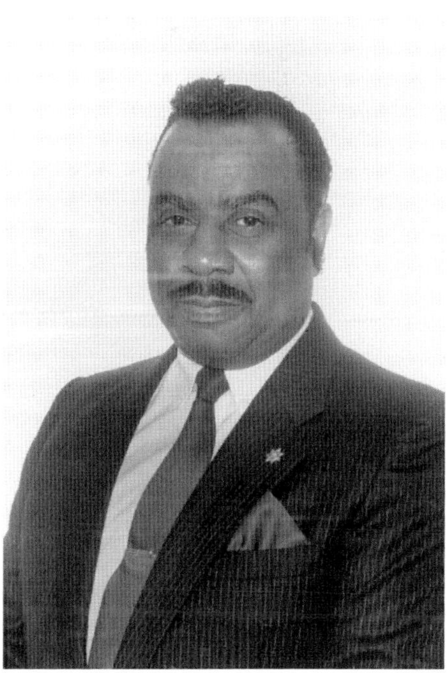

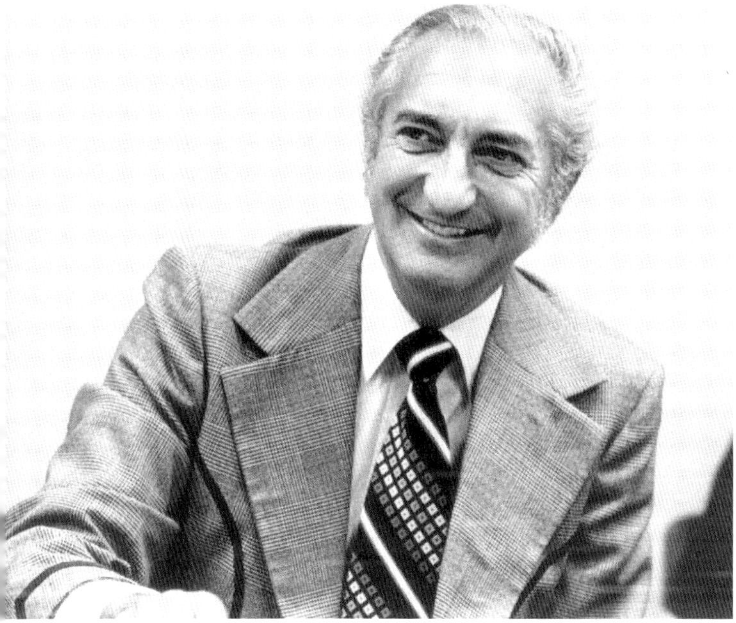

State Legislator for 37 Years
Nick Petris represented Oakland in the state senate and assembly for 37 years, advocating for affordable housing, farm workers, environmental concerns, and more. The Petris home was one of 2,700 that were destroyed in the Oakland Hills Firestorm in 1991, along with Petris's personal library of Greek history, Greek philosophy, and English literature. (Courtesy Oakland History Room, Oakland Public Library.)

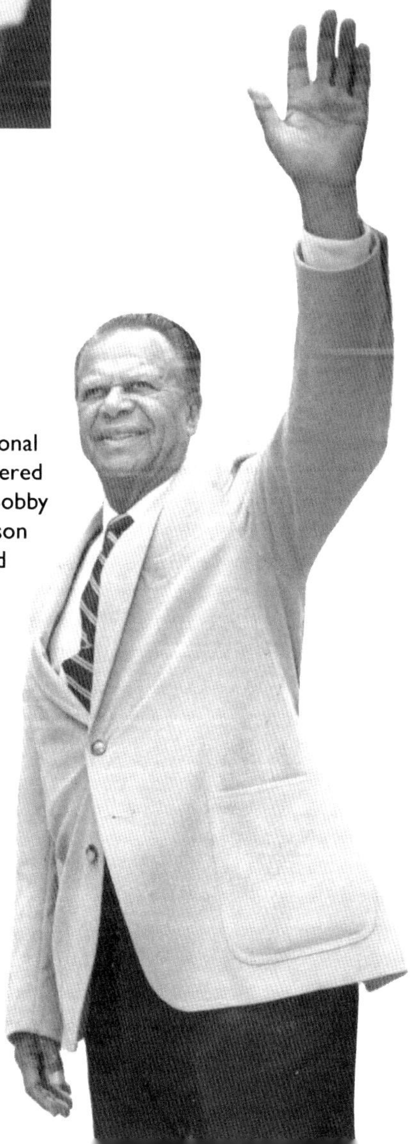

First Black Mayor of Oakland
Although he was a lawyer and judge and played semiprofessional baseball for the Oakland Larks, Lionel Wilson is best remembered as the first black mayor of Oakland. After Black Panther Bobby Seale lost a runoff against mayoral candidate John Reading, Wilson was seen as a moderate (pro-business and pro-growth) and was more accepted by the existing political powers. Wilson served three terms from 1977 to 1991. (Courtesy Oakland History Room, Oakland Public Library.)

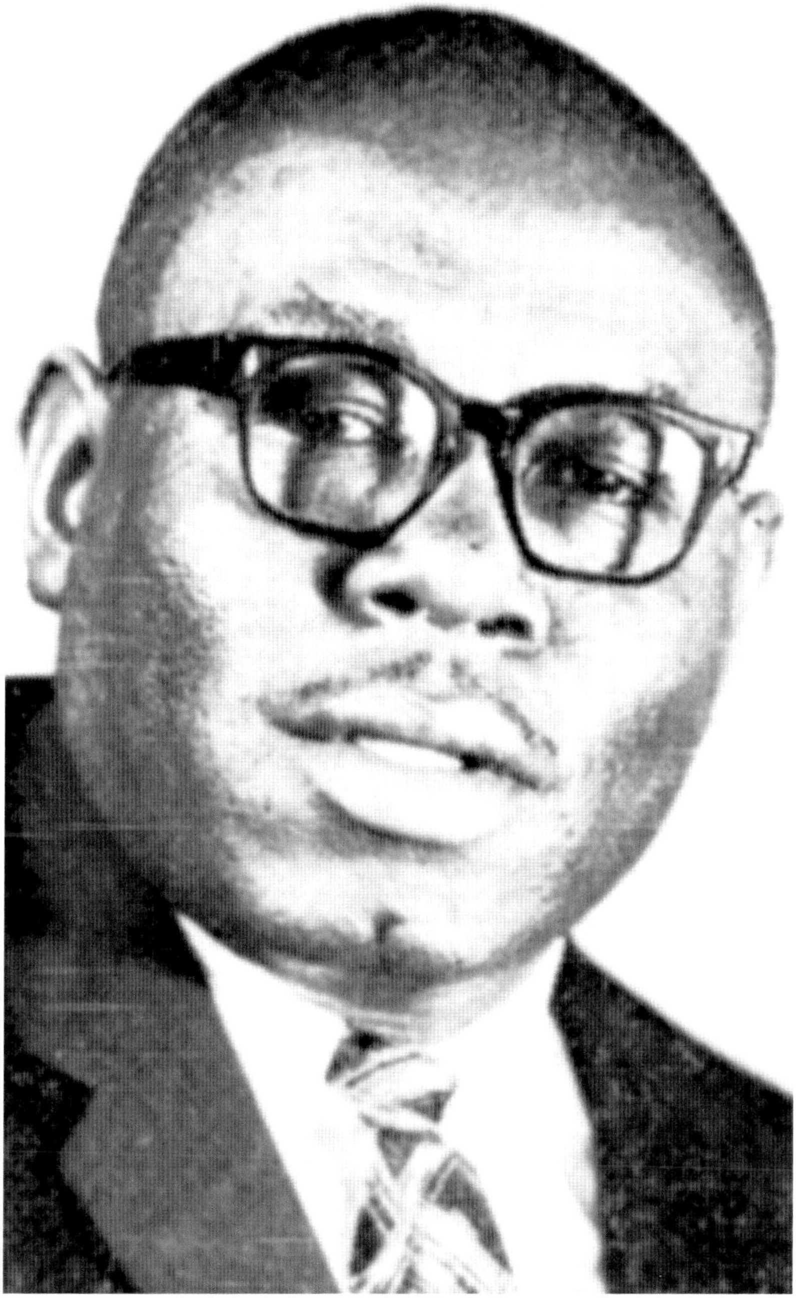

"Mayor" of West Oakland

Ralph Williams never held political office and only had a ninth grade education through night classes at McClymonds High School, but he was known as a force to be dealt with on community matters in West Oakland. As head of the West Oakland Planning Council, Williams oversaw the new alignment for the Cypress Freeway replacement and the creation of the West Oakland Health Center and a recreation center in Poplar Park. (Courtesy Oakland Post Photograph Collection, MS 169, African American Museum & Library at Oakland.)

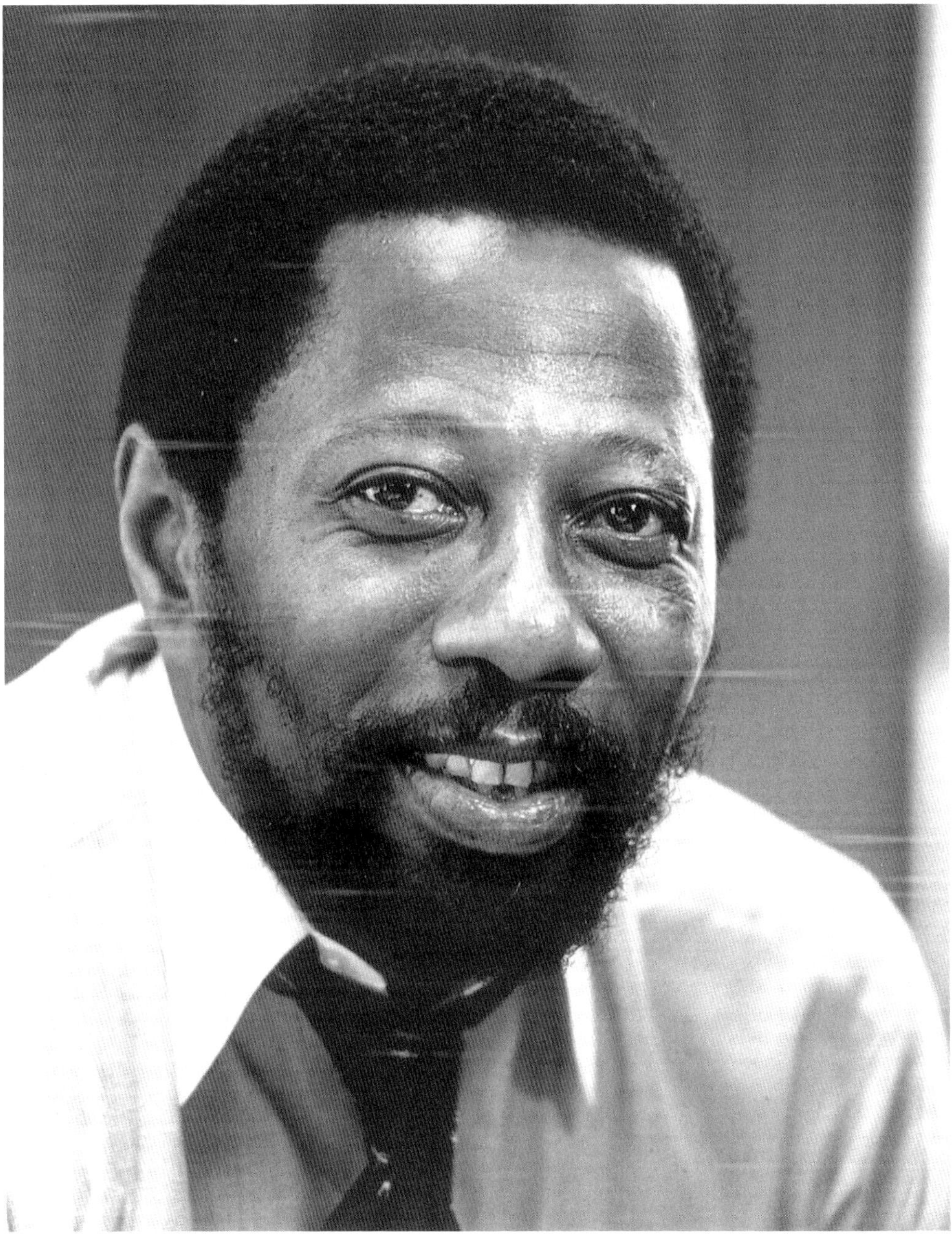

Pioneering Journalist

Robert Maynard dropped out of high school to take his first reporting job and went on to become a nationally known journalist. At the *Washington Post*, he was the first African American national newspaper correspondent. In 1977, he left to cofound the Institute for Journalism Education to help address inequality in newsroom coverage. He was named editor of the *Oakland Tribune*, becoming the first African American to head a major daily newspaper, and in 1983, the Maynards bought the paper and led it to a 1990 Pulitzer Prize. Sadly, cancer forced Maynard to sell the paper, and he died at age 56. (Courtesy Maynard Institute for Journalism Education.)

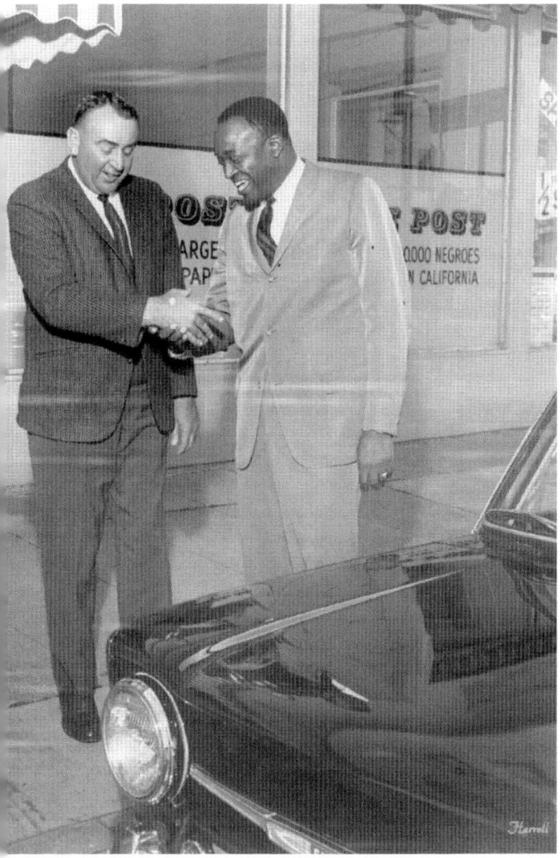

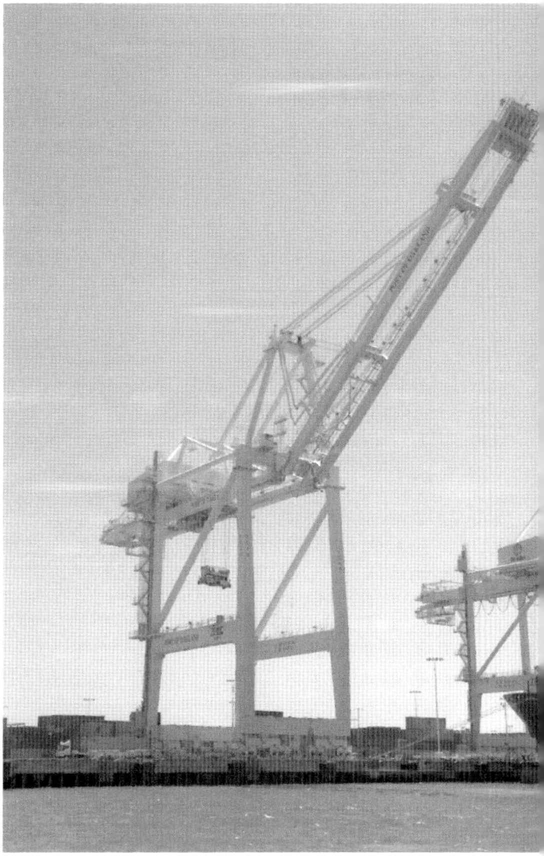

Lawyer, Publisher, Port Commissioner, Athlete

Thomas L. Berkley (right) was a world-class athlete. He studied economics at the University of California, Los Angeles, where his track coach rated him the best hurdler in the world in 1938. When the 1940 Olympics were canceled, Berkley joined the Army and rose to the rank of second lieutenant.

Returning to Oakland, Berkley formed the largest racially integrated law firm in the United States and started the Post Publishing Company. Berkley also served as the first black port commissioner and was twice president of the board, helping oversee improvements in the port to make it the first major container port on the West Coast.

After his death, a section of Twentieth Street was renamed Thomas L. Berkley Way. Congresswoman Barbara Lee said, "The world has lost a giant of a man. A brilliant leader. A champion for justice." (Left, courtesy Oakland Post Photograph Collection, MS 169, African American Museum & Library at Oakland; right, author's collection.)

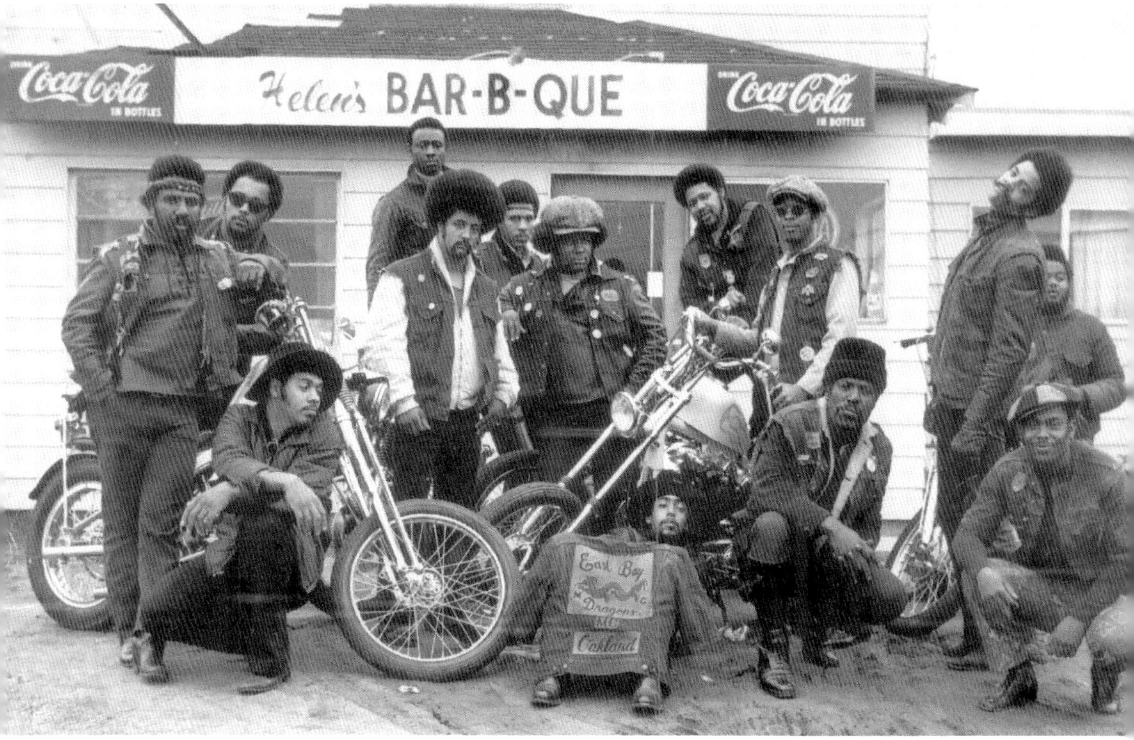

Soul on Bikes
When Tobie Gene Levingston, known as "Prez" (crouching to the right of the jacket), started the East Bay Dragons car club in 1959, he may not have envisioned it becoming one of the nation's most prominent all-black, all-Harley, all-chopper motorcycle clubs. And he probably did not imagine he would still be club president today, more than 50 years later. "Outlaw" motorcycle club or not, in 2014, the Oakland City Council recognized the club for being a "symbol of positive community activism and pride within Oakland and within the African American community." (Courtesy East Bay Dragons Motorcycle Club.)

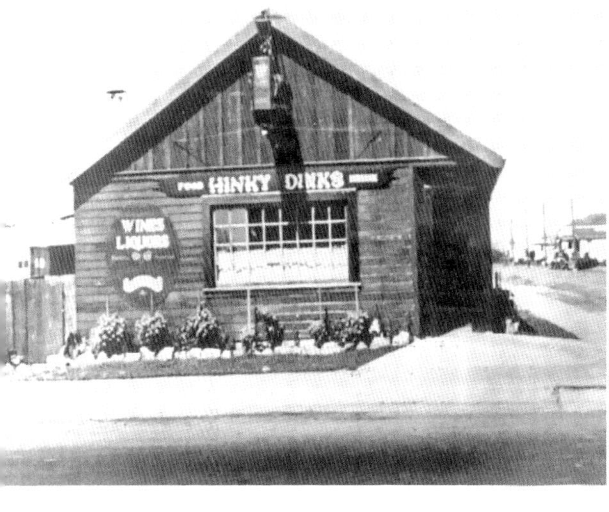

Mai Tai—Roa Ae!
Victor Jules Bergeron, better known as Trader Vic, started Hinky Dink's restaurant on San Pablo Avenue with $500 in capital. With an increasingly Polynesian menu, Hinky Dink's was renamed Trader Vic's and became one of the first tiki bars. It was there that Bergeron invented the mai tai. After an initial taste, two of Bergeron's friends from Tahiti are said to have exclaimed, "Mai Tai—Roa Ae!" which means "Out of This World." (Courtesy Trader Vic's.)

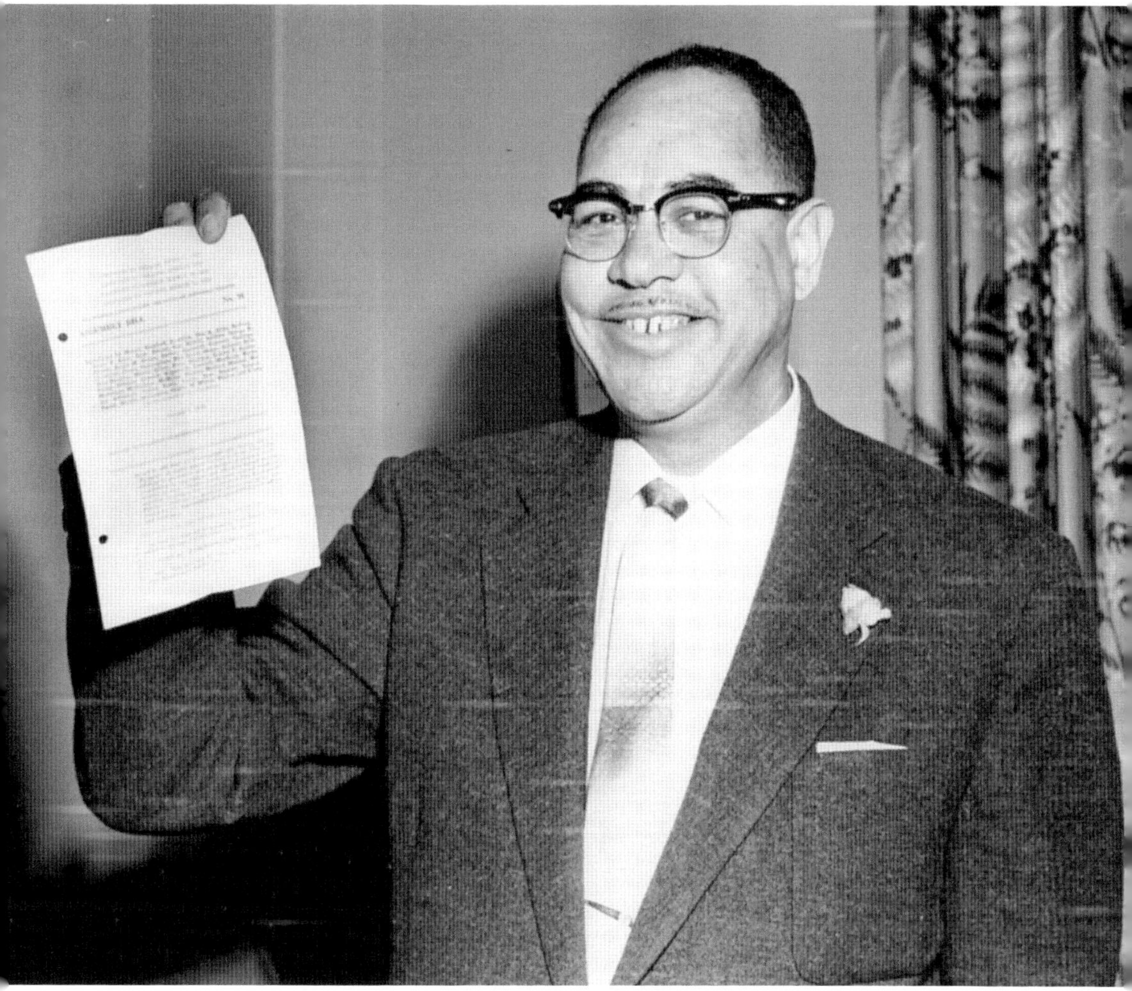

Pharmacist, Community Leader, Politician

After working his way through pharmacy school at the University of California, San Francisco, William Byron Rumford applied to work for the state of California. He was repeatedly rejected during oral exams, where he was asked irrelevant questions, but he won an appeal and was hired. In the 1930s, Rumford was hired as an assistant pharmacist at Highland Hospital.

Later, Rumford ran a pharmacy in Berkeley and also worked as director of the Red Cross Oakland chapter and as president of the East Bay Health Association. In 1944, Gov. Earl Warren (see page 56) appointed him to the Rent Control Board, which was dedicated to keeping wartime rents affordable.

Rumford served in the California State Assembly from 1948 to 1966, working for fair employment, control of air pollution, and fair housing. In 1963, the legislature passed the Rumford Fair Housing Act, which outlawed restrictive covenants and the refusal to rent or sell property on the basis of race, ethnicity, gender, marital status, or physical disability. (Courtesy Oakland Post Photograph Collection, MS 169, African American Museum & Library at Oakland.)

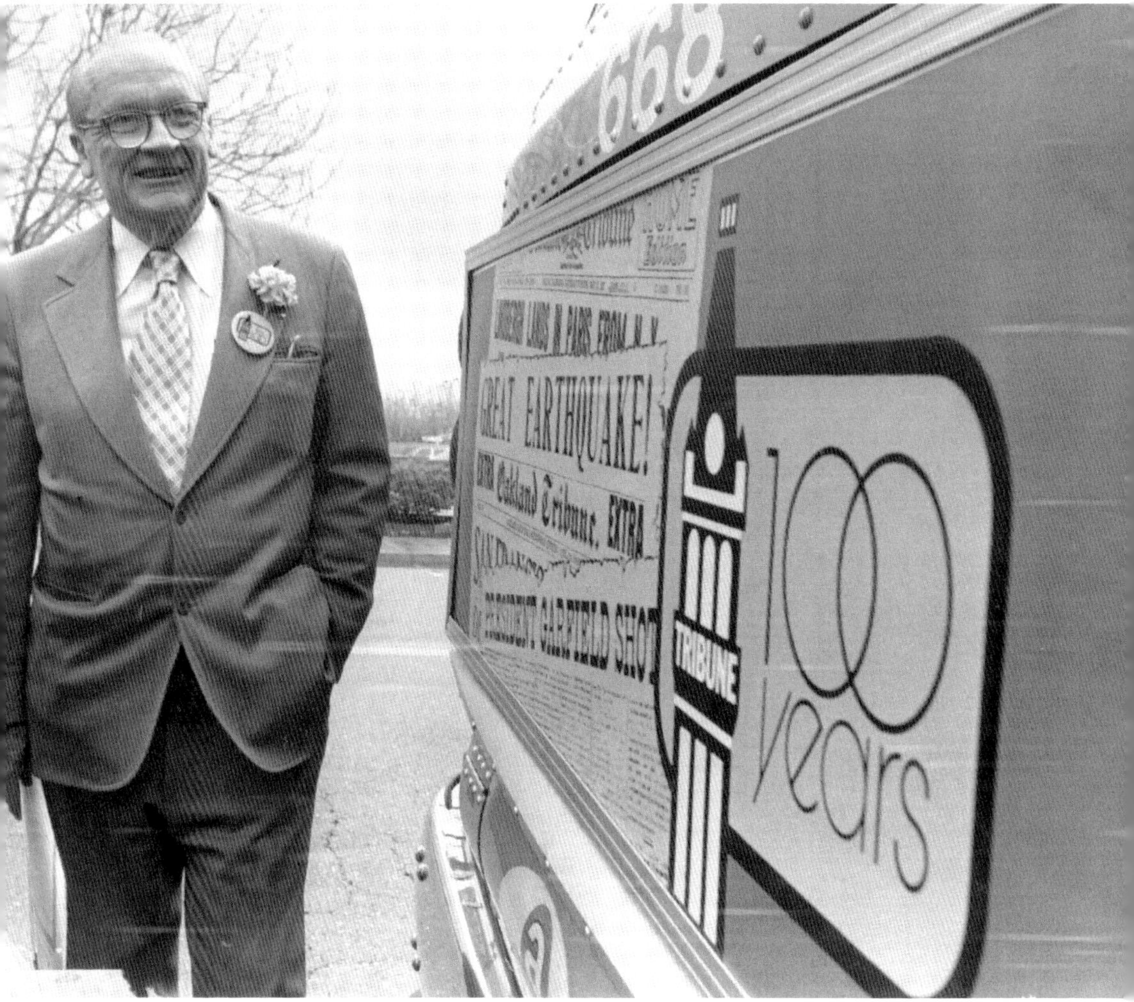

Newspaper Publisher, Senator

After terms in the state assembly and senate, William F. Knowland was appointed US senator for California by Gov. Earl Warren (see page 56) to fill the seat of Hiram Johnson. Knowland says he found out about his appointment in *Stars and Stripes* while he was serving in the US Army in Europe. Knowland served as senator from 1945 through 1958, when he made a failed bid for governor of California.

When Knowland's father, Joseph R. Knowland, died in 1966, he took over running the *Oakland Tribune*. He kept the paper firmly Republican. Knowland's personal life was not so tidy. He and his wife of 46 years divorced because of his affairs, and then, in 1972, he briefly married again. He had over $900,000 in gambling debts. On February 23, 1973, just two days after celebrating the 100th anniversary of the *Oakland Tribune*, Knowland died of a self-inflicted gunshot wound. The Knowland family sold the *Tribune* a few years later in 1977. (Courtesy Oakland Public Library, Oakland History Room.)

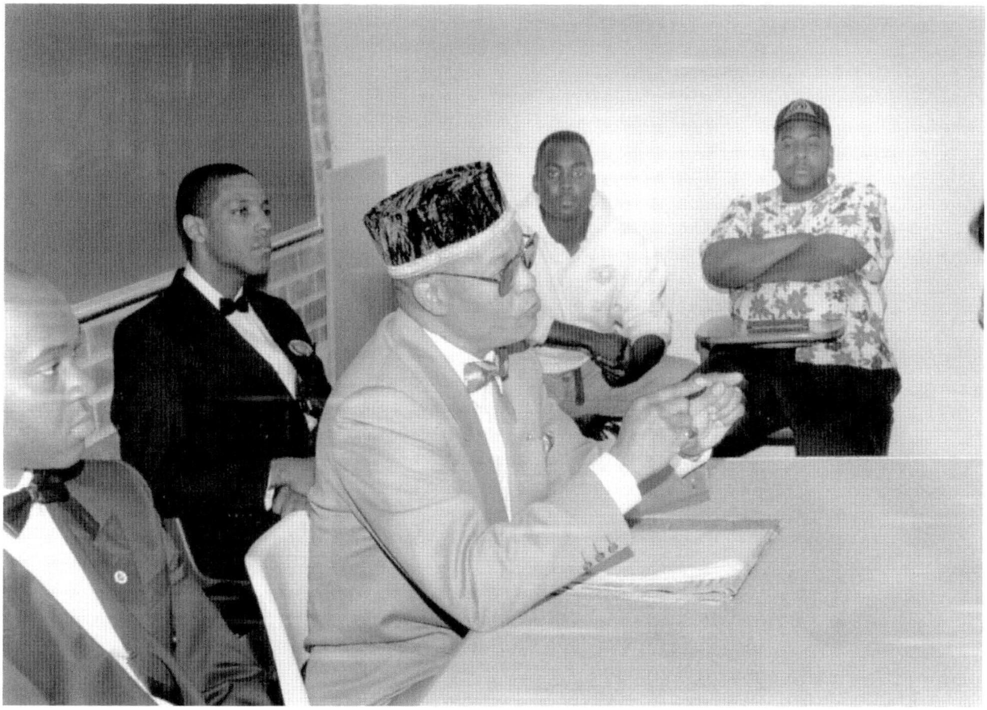

Your Black Muslim Bakery

Joseph Stephens, better known as Yusuf Bey, founded Your Black Muslim Bakery in the early 1970s. Bey and his brother also started Nation of Islam Mosque No. 26B, but split off from it by 1972. In the 1980s, Bey broadcast *True Solutions* on Soul Beat Television, hour-long sermons preaching economic self-reliance and self-knowledge for African Americans. Controversy swirled around Bey and the bakery, and numerous charges were filed against him in 2002, but Bey died in 2003 before the case went to trial. (Courtesy Oakland Post Photograph Collection, MS 169, African American Museum & Library at Oakland.)

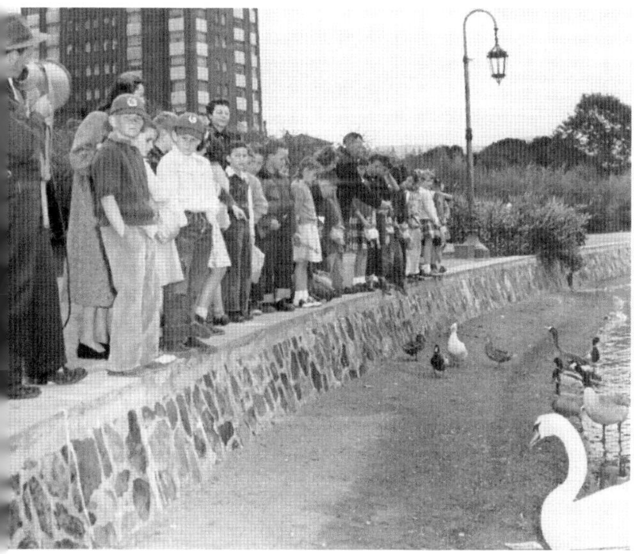

People are for the Birds

Paul Covel spent his whole life caring for animals; as a teenager, he pestered the San Diego Zoo until they gave him a job as a bird keeper. In 1948, Covel was hired as the first municipal naturalist in the United States and designed the Rotary Nature Center in 1953. Covel managed the Lake Merritt Wildlife Refuge for more than 20 years, but people from all over the Bay Area would call him with questions about animals, wild or not. (Photograph by Burton Weber, courtesy Jim Covel.)

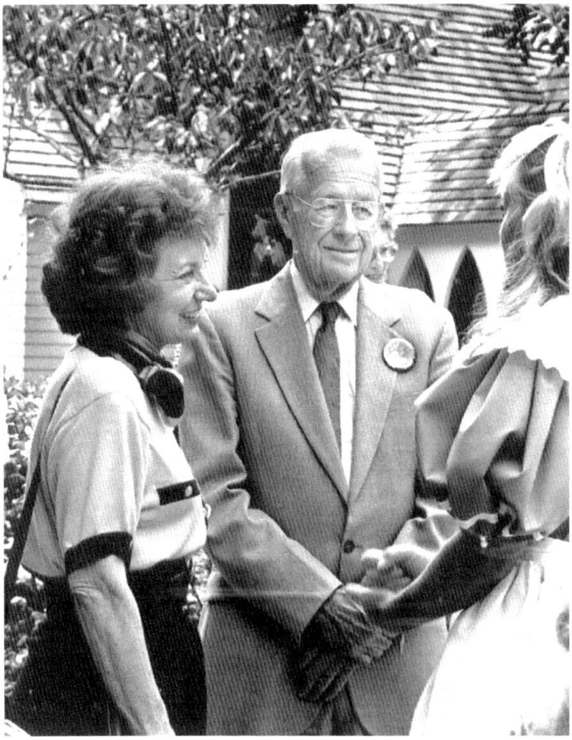

Parks in His Blood

William Penn Mott Jr. spent his life working with parks. While Mott was superintendent of Oakland parks, he was the main force behind creating Children's Fairyland in 1950, working with the Lake Merritt Breakfast Club. The Oakland Zoo was also expanded and moved to its current home in Knowland Park. Mott went on to work for the East Bay Regional Park District (where he tripled the number of parks), California State Parks, and the National Park Service. (Courtesy Children's Fairyland.)

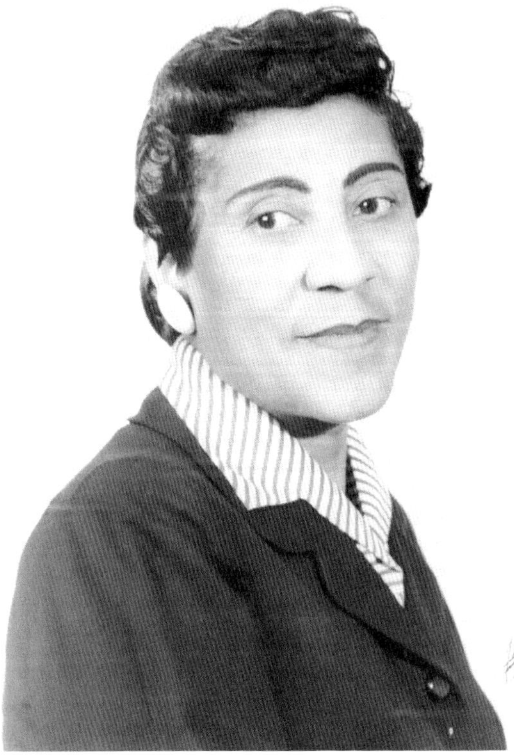

Civil Rights Leader

Tarea Hall Pittman was a civil rights leader who worked to abolish segregation in the Oakland Fire Department and was active in the NAACP. Pittman was the host of the radio program *Negroes in the News*, which was on KDIA radio in Oakland for 45 years. (Courtesy Oakland Post Photograph Collection, MS 169, African American Museum & Library at Oakland.)

CHAPTER FIVE

Home Field

"All I ever wanted to be was a ballplayer, and my dad found Oakland . . . thank God!"

—John Brodie, former National Football League MVP

For a variety of reasons, Oakland has been home to more than its share of great athletes and sports teams—you could fill a book with them. That's exactly what longtime sports journalist and author Paul Brekke-Meisner has done with *Home Field Advantage: Oakland, CA—The City that Changed the Face of Sports* (2013). With decades of research, Brekke-Meisner gives the stories of hundreds of famous (and some not-so-famous) athletes who have called Oakland home. While sports with nationwide leagues like football, baseball, and basketball get the most attention these days, Oakland has also been home to outstanding golfers, boxers, race car drivers, and even sports announcers.

But Oakland's sports heroes were not just great athletes; they also helped make great changes in sports. Don Barksdale was the first black NBA all-star, and Jim Hines was the first person to break the 10-second barrier in the 100-meter dash. Bill Russell's jumping and shot-blocking forever changed the game of basketball, and Don Budge is considered the father of the modern game of tennis. And after refusing to be traded, Curt Flood helped bring about free agency in professional sports.

There is no single answer to why so many great athletes have come from Oakland, but part of it has been great coaches like the legendary George Powles, who coached numerous future college and professional athletes, and lesser-known coaches like Lucius Bateman, who helped golfer Tony Lema fine-tune his game. Part of it is Oakland's blue-collar, immigrant roots, with people who worked hard because their parents expected it of them.

Regardless of the reasons why there are so many, Oakland loves its hometown sports heroes, whether their athletic careers keep them in Oakland or not. Despite the sense of betrayal when the Oakland Raiders moved to Los Angeles in 1982, most fans welcomed them back with open arms when they returned in 1995. Win or lose, Oakland loves its sports teams with a passion that often belies a team's record that season.

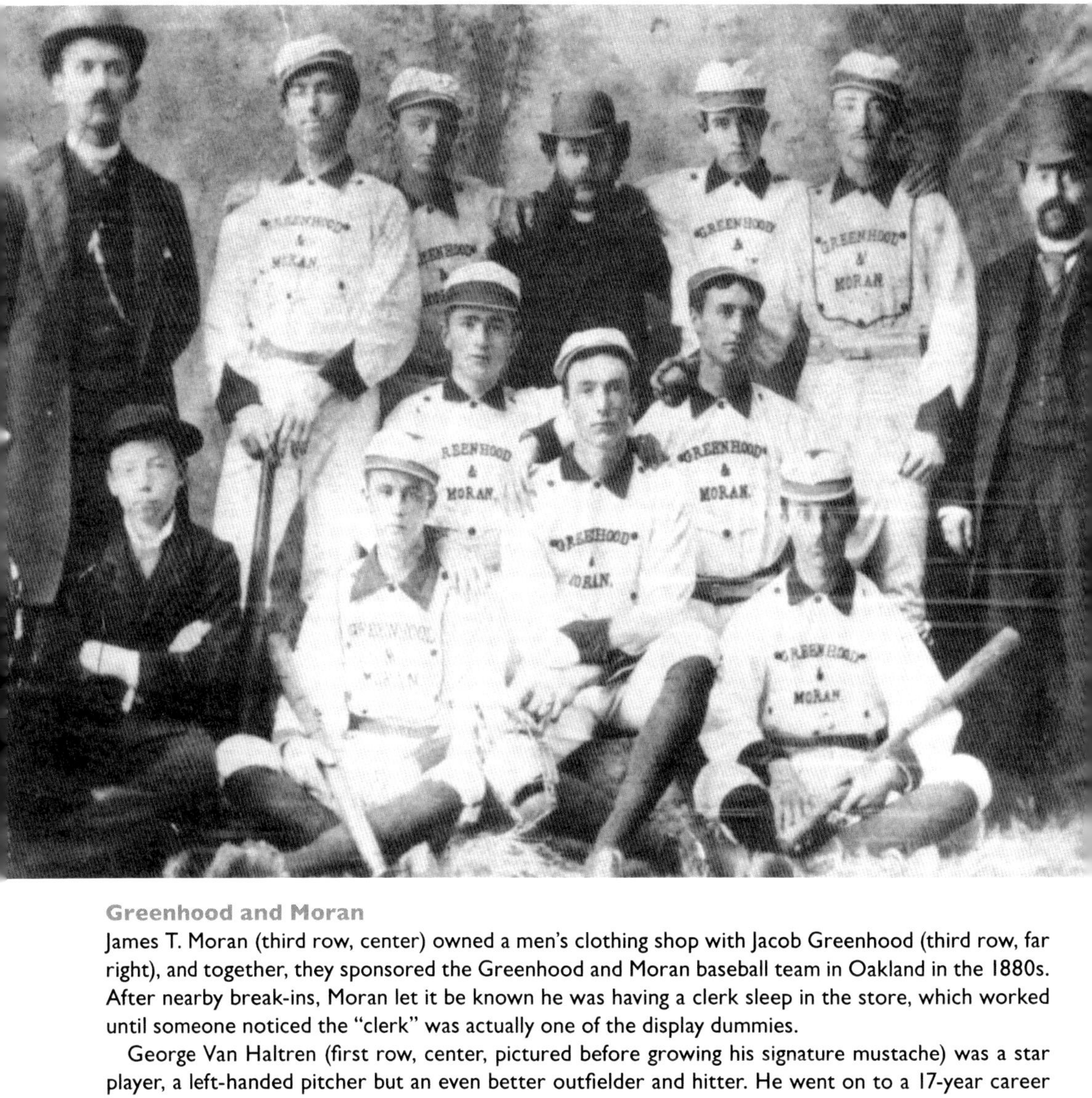

Greenhood and Moran

James T. Moran (third row, center) owned a men's clothing shop with Jacob Greenhood (third row, far right), and together, they sponsored the Greenhood and Moran baseball team in Oakland in the 1880s. After nearby break-ins, Moran let it be known he was having a clerk sleep in the store, which worked until someone noticed the "clerk" was actually one of the display dummies.

George Van Haltren (first row, center, pictured before growing his signature mustache) was a star player, a left-handed pitcher but an even better outfielder and hitter. He went on to a 17-year career in the major leagues, then returned to Oakland as a player-manager for the Oakland Oaks. By various measures, Van Haltren is one of the top three baseball players who has not yet been elected to the Hall of Fame. Players with similar career stats include Hall of Famers Ty Cobb, Honus Wagner, and Lou Brock.

Col. Thomas P. Robinson (third row, far left) was the team manager and promoter. He was known for a variety of publicity stunts involving his Oakland teams over the years, including hiring controversial player Norris "Tip" O'Neill and saying he was going to make him manager, burning a championship pennant to rid the team of a hex, and, in 1891, hiring and firing more than 40 players during the season. (Courtesy Bill Weiss collection.)

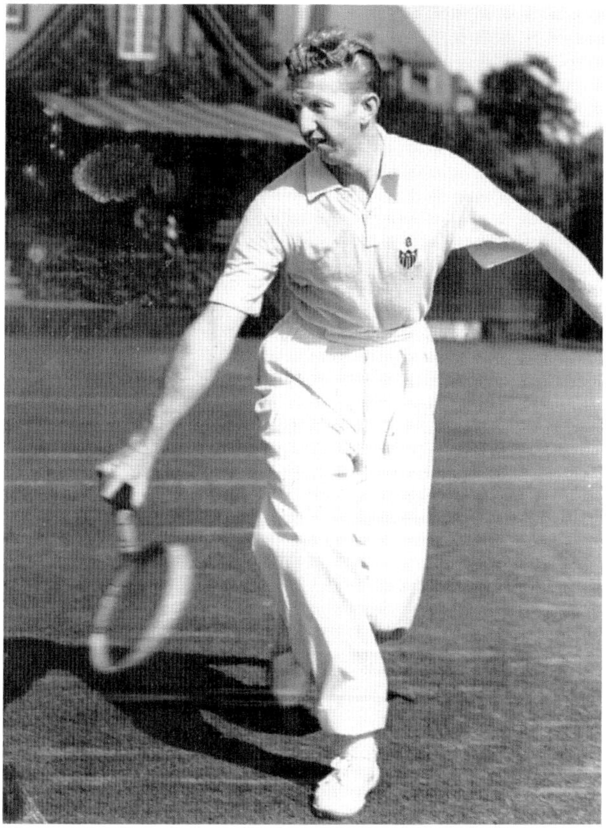

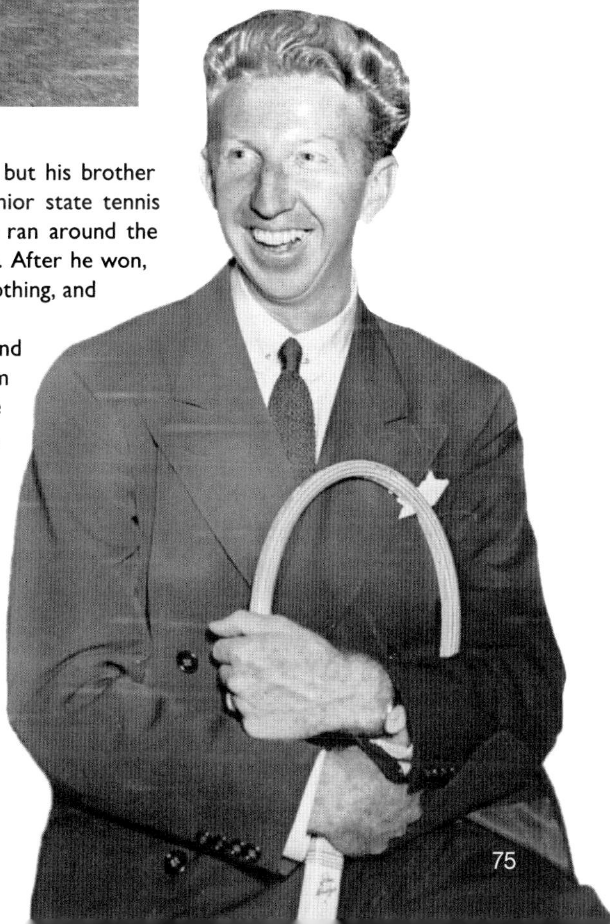

Father of Modern Tennis

Don Budge's first love in sports was baseball, but his brother Lloyd goaded him to play in the upcoming junior state tennis championship. In his first-round match, Budge ran around the court in dirty sneakers and tan corduroy pants. After he won, his father bought him more suitable all-white clothing, and Budge went on to win the tournament.

In 1938, Budge dominated amateur tennis and became the first person to win the Grand Slam of Tennis, winning the Australian Open, the US Open, the French Open, and Wimbledon. Budge's professional career was curtailed by an injury he sustained while in the Army, but he is the consensus pick for one of the greatest tennis players of all time. (Both, courtesy Jeff Budge.)

Passionate, Controversial Raiders Owner

Al Davis applied "Just win, baby!" to most everything he did. He started as head coach and general manager with the Oakland Raiders in 1963 and went on to own the team, keeping a firm hand in management. His challenge to the NFL from the younger AFL helped force the merger of the two leagues.

Davis broke some hearts when he moved the Raiders to Los Angeles in 1982, then broke some more when he moved them back to Oakland in 1995. He was known for taking misfit players and crafting them into winning teams. Davis also made some notable hires, including the second Latino head coach, Tom Flores, in 1979, and the first African American coach, Art Shell, in 1989. He also promoted Amy Trask, making her the first woman team CEO in 1997. (Courtesy Oakland Post Photograph Collection, MS 169, African American Museum & Library at Oakland.)

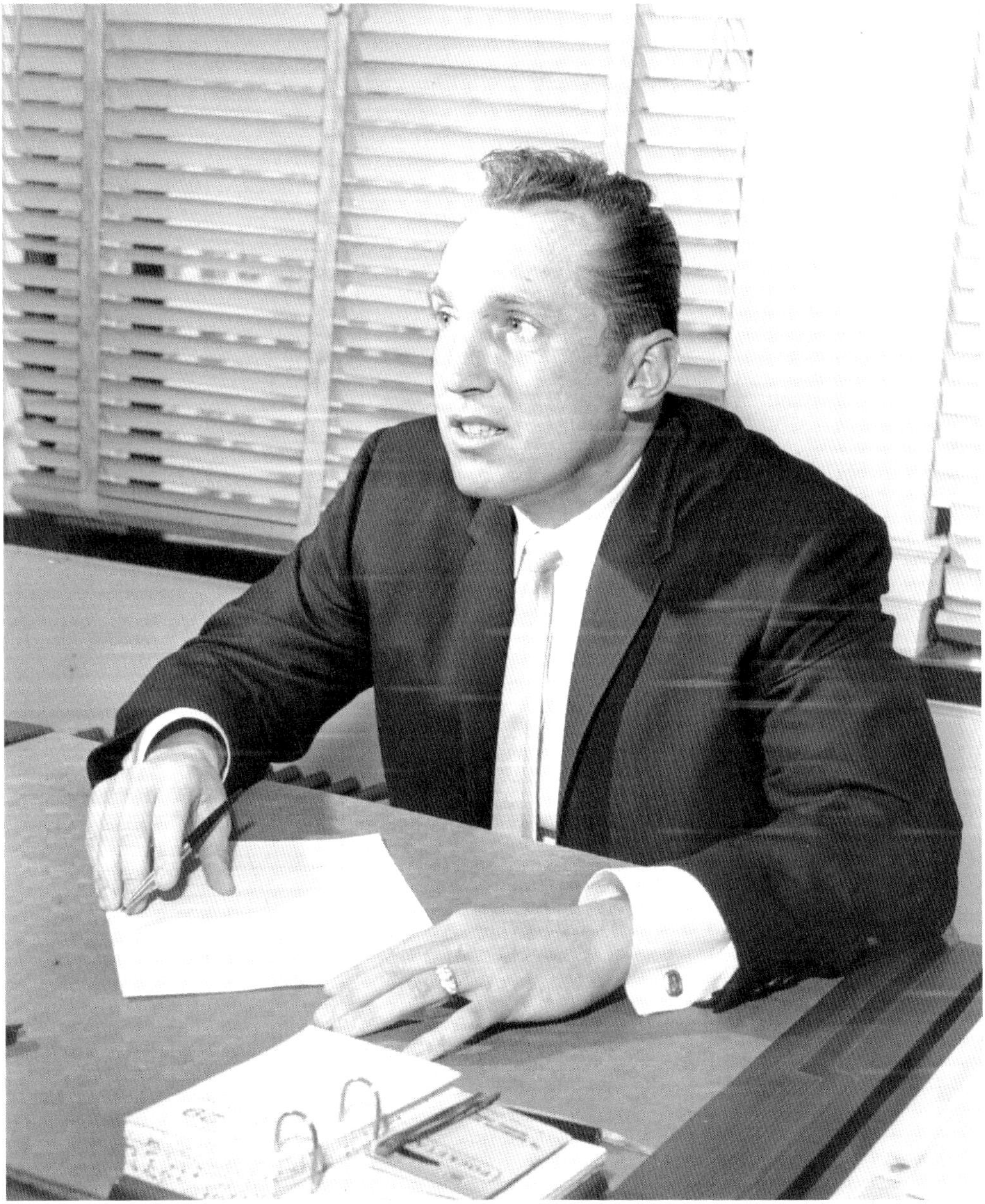

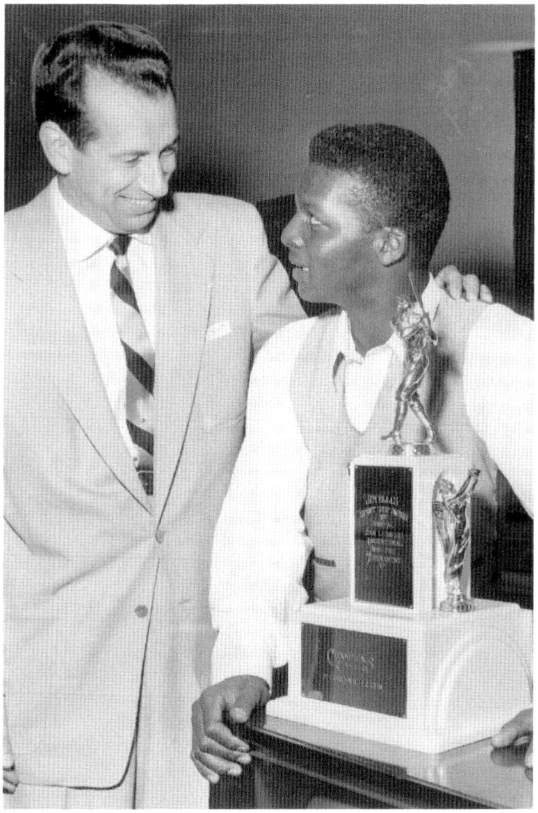

Sports Humanitarian, Game-Changing Athlete

Sam Bercovich (left) was never much of an athlete, but following a tradition begun by his father, he supported thousands of Oakland kids by sponsoring local youth sports teams. Many of the participants went on to become professional athletes, including Curt Flood (right), Willie Stargell, Kevin Maas, Rickey Henderson, Vada Pinson, Dave Stewart, Randy Johnson, Joe Morgan, Tommy Harper, and Frank Robinson. Hundreds more played at the collegiate level.

Sam's family was originally from Austria-Hungary but planted broad Oakland roots. His father, Edward Bercovich, started Bercovich Furniture in 1906, and his uncle Abraham Bercovich ran a scrap metal business in Oakland and was one of the founders of Congregation Beth Jacob. In 1907, Temple Beth Abraham was named in Abraham's honor. Sam was born in Oakland on March 3, 1916. At age five, he saw the KKK marching through the streets of Oakland, something he never forgot.

Bercovich Furniture was a longtime supporter of sports in Oakland. In 1978, there was uncertainty about whether the Oakland Athletics might move from Oakland, and none of the major radio stations in the Bay Area wanted to bid on the broadcast rights. To keep the A's on the air, Bercovich Furniture bought the rights and struck a deal to get local country station KNEW to broadcast the games, with Curt Flood as color commentator. Sam was also a big fan of the Oakland Raiders and traveled with the team for 40 years.

McClymonds High School and Oakland Technical High School alumnus Curt Flood was a fast, talented baseball player. But he is most famous for helping bring about free agency in professional sports. After 12 years of playing for the St. Louis Cardinals, Flood was unexpectedly traded to the Philadelphia Phillies. Rather than continue with pay negotiations where owners had all the leverage, Flood retired and filed a lawsuit. The case went all the way to the US Supreme Court, where Flood lost, but three years later, free agency became a reality and professional sports changed forever. (Courtesy Oakland Museum of California, gift of ANG Newspapers.)

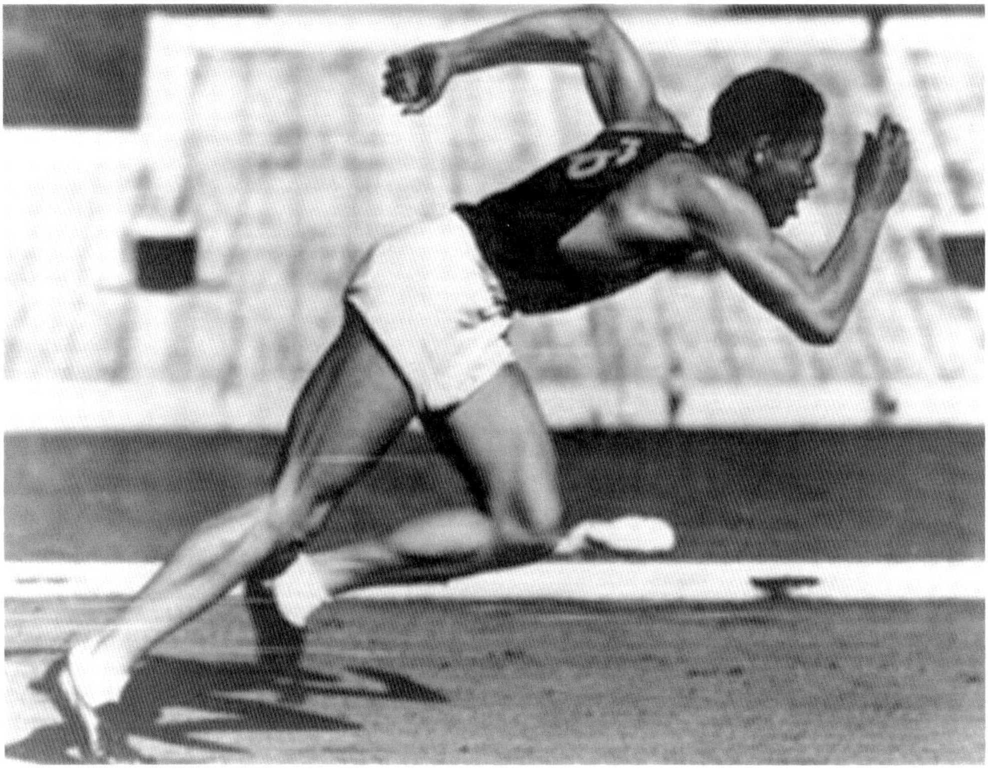

Airman, Athlete, Teacher

Less famous than Jesse Owens, Oakland native Archie Williams also won gold in track at the 1936 Olympics, and Adolph Hitler did not shake Williams's hand, either. Williams joined the Army Air Corps during World War II and trained at Tuskegee. He was active in the US Air Force for 22 years, retiring as a lieutenant colonel. He then taught in California schools for 21 years, where his love for teaching and helping students was legendary. (Courtesy US Air Force archives.)

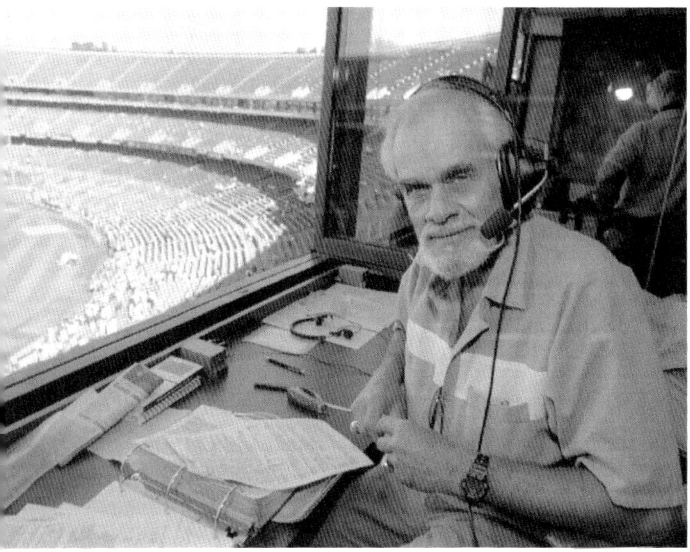

Holy Toledo!

In a profession where many focus on a single sport, Bill King announced for three different Oakland sports teams. In addition to the Golden State Warriors and Oakland Raiders, King was the lead announcer for the Oakland Athletics, where his dry sense of humor and phrases like "Holy Toledo!" made him a fan favorite. The broadcast booth at the Coliseum was named in his memory. (Courtesy *San Jose Mercury News.*)

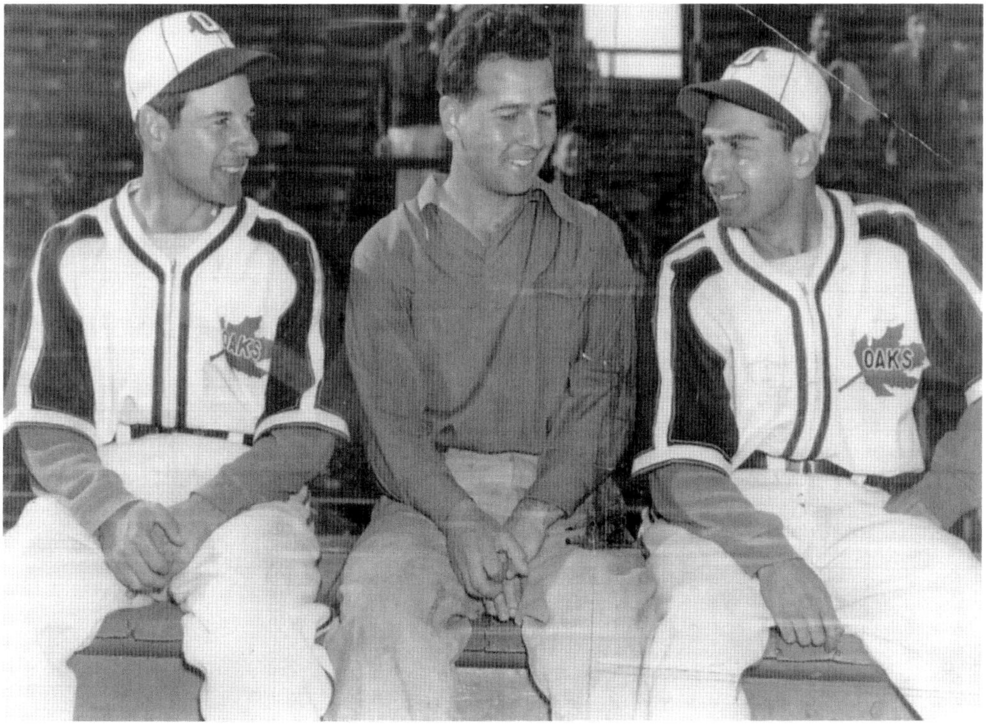

West Oakland's First Family of Baseball

Ernie Raimondi (on left, with brothers Al and Billy) came from a large Italian immigrant family with a lot of baseball talent. At various times, four of the Raimondi brothers played for the Oakland Oaks, but Ernie made headlines when the San Francisco Seals recruited him out of McClymonds High School at age 16. After his semiprofessional career, Raimondi played on the company team at the Moore Dry Dock Company where he worked. Raimondi was drafted in World War II and died in battle in France in 1945. Raimondi Park was named in his honor. (Courtesy Gary Bedingfield.)

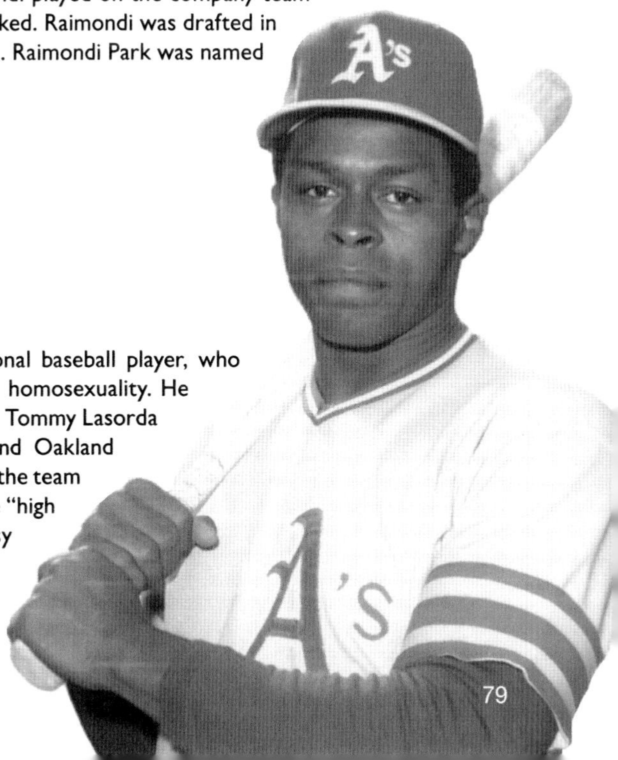

First Openly Gay Professional Athlete

Glenn Burke was the first openly gay professional baseball player, who suffered discrimination both for his race and his homosexuality. He drew the wrath of Los Angeles Dodgers manager Tommy Lasorda for befriending Lasorda's estranged gay son, and Oakland Athletics manager Billy Martin introduced him to the team as a "faggot." Burke is credited with inventing the "high five" along with teammate Dusty Baker. (Courtesy Oakland Athletics.)

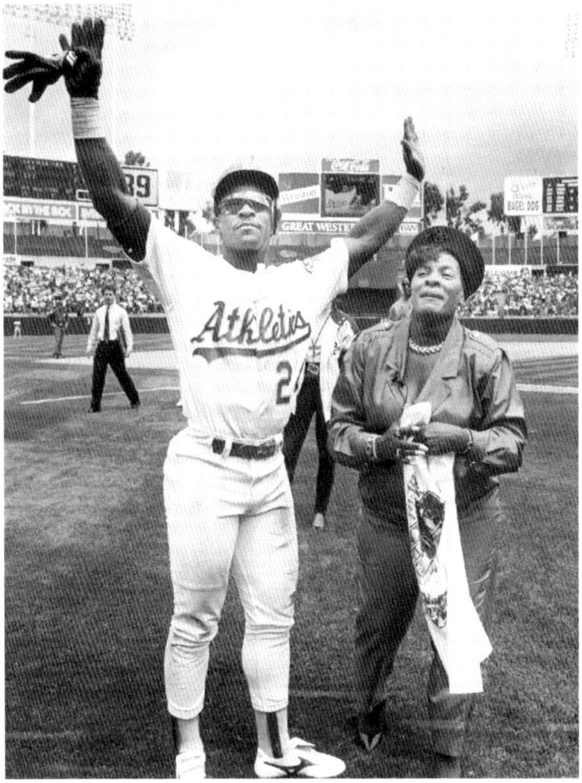

"The Man of Steal"
Oakland Technical High School graduate Rickey Henderson, pictured here with his mother, was a multisport athlete, running track, playing basketball, and playing as an all-star in football. However, baseball was his sport. Henderson's amazing professional career started with the Oakland Athletics in 1979 and led to numerous awards, including induction to the National Baseball Hall of Fame in 2009. Certainly one of the highlights is Henderson's reputation as "The Man of Steal" for his amazing base-stealing ability. (Photograph by Michael Macor, courtesy Oakland Tribune Collection at the Oakland Museum of California, gift of ANG Newspapers.)

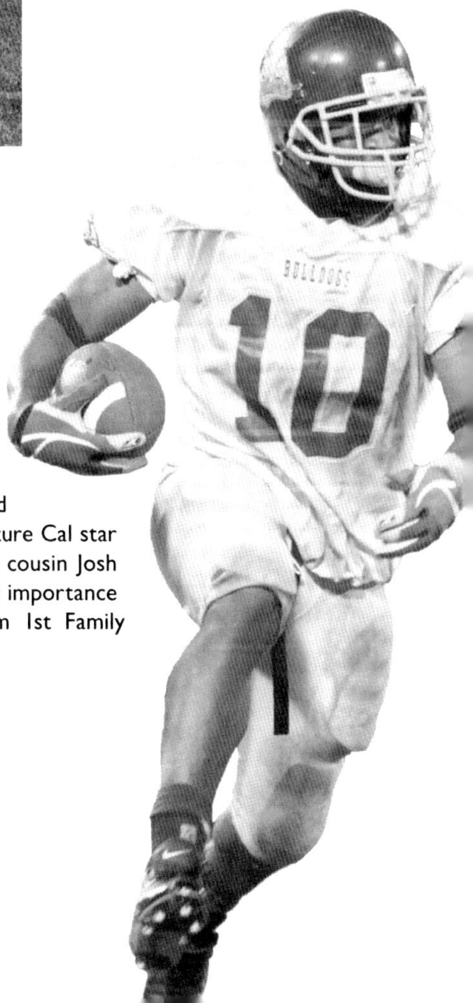

"Beast Mode"
Nicknamed "Beast Mode" for his aggressive running style and penchant for breaking tackles, Marshawn Lynch did not cut his Oakland ties when he was drafted into the NFL. Lynch was a four-sport athlete at Oakland Technical High School and played basketball alongside future Cal star and NBA player Leon Powe. Since 2006, Lynch and his cousin Josh Johnson have supported Oakland youth and stressed the importance of education, literacy, and self-esteem with their Fam 1st Family Foundation. (Courtesy *San Jose Mercury News*.)

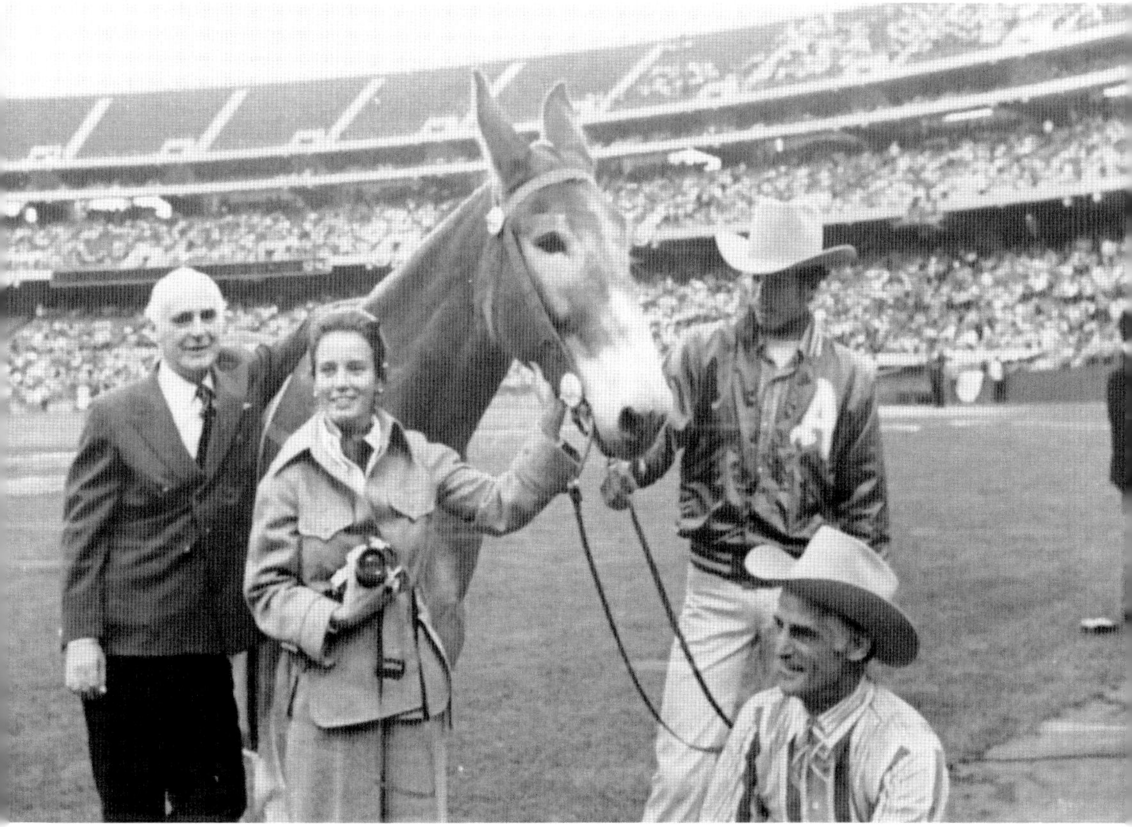

Charlie O

The current generation of Oakland Athletics fans may not remember him, but "Charlie O" Finley (left) owned the A's even before they moved from Kansas City in 1968. Finley was a showman and a hands-on owner who some people found difficult to work with. But with his cousin Carl Finley as his right-hand man, Finley built a dominant team that won three straight World Series in 1972, 1973, and 1974.

Finley should also be remembered for innovations in baseball like helping bring about the designated hitter rule in the American League and advocating for night games in the World Series. Some of his innovations are lesser known, like the bright green, gold, and white uniforms that were a sensation in baseball when introduced and the introduction of ball girls (including Debbi Fields, later of Mrs. Fields Cookies fame) to handle out-of-play baseballs. He even hired Stanley Burrell (better known as MC Hammer; see page 98) as a batboy and later vice president to be his spy in the clubhouse.

Some of Finley's gimmicks did not stick, like orange baseballs and a mechanical rabbit named Harvey to bring a new baseball to the umpire. But every Oakland A's fan in the 1970s should remember team mascot Charlie-O the Mule. Finley not only had the mule brought out before home games but sometimes took Charlie-O to bars and restaurants, all in the name of promotion. (Courtesy Nancy Finley.)

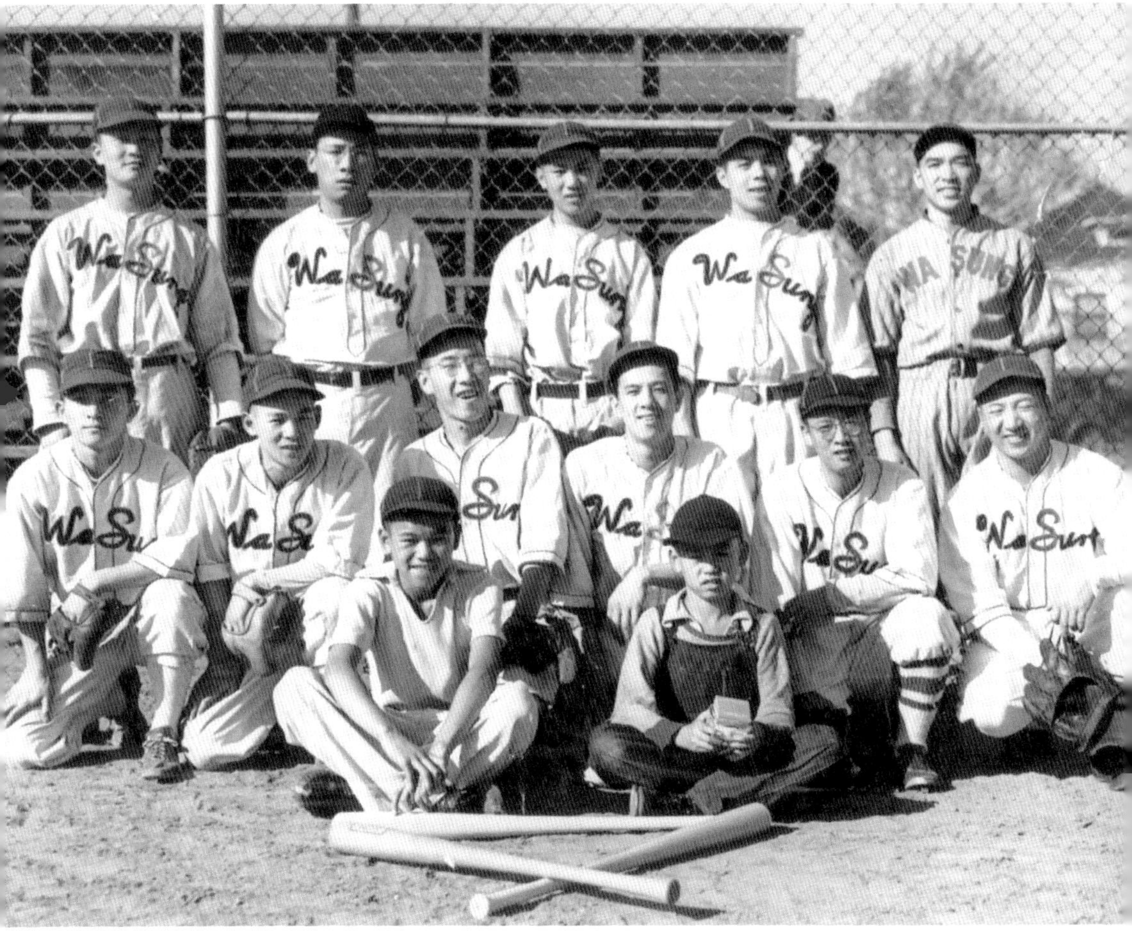

Community Service Club President

The Wa Sung Athletic Club was formed in the 1920s and played a variety of area baseball teams but disbanded in the 1930s. In 1953, it was reformed as the Wa Sung Community Service Club, with Joseph Lee (second row, third from left; see page 52) as its first president. Its accomplishments include the Junk Boat play structure in Lincoln Park and decades of scholarships. From left to right are (first row) batboys Bill and Bob Chinn; (second row) Sung Wong, Key Chinn, Joseph Lee, Al Bowen, Eddie Hing, and Tommie Hing; (third row) Hector Eng, Ben Chan, Al Wong, George Bowen, and Robert Chow. (Courtesy Betty Wong via William Gee Wong.)

CHAPTER SIX

Artists, Builders, and Makers

I learned to make my mind large, as the universe is large, so that there is room for paradoxes.

—Maxine Hong Kingston

Painters, poets, dancers, writers, musicians, sculptors, architects—all artists have a creative spark. Long before the 2006 Art Murmur started bringing crowds on First Fridays to Oakland's art studios and galleries, Oakland was home to a variety of creative people.

Immigrants from other parts of the country, arriving on the transcontinental railroad, or from other parts of the world, arriving by ship, have all brought their cultural and artistic roots. The natural beauty of the Bay Area has been an inspiration to many in Oakland.

Oakland is a special place for music. Once known as the "Harlem of the West" because of the numerous jazz and blues clubs in West Oakland, it has been home to many musicians and has created some new musical sounds. In 1969, The Pointer Sisters got their start in Oakland, and native MC Hammer pioneered pop-rap and has created and produced numerous other acts on his record label. In 1994, Oakland-based rapper Keak da Sneak created the term "hyphy."

Countless beautiful buildings and parks around Oakland were designed by well-known architects like Julia Morgan and lesser-known ones like Charles W. Dickey. Oakland's growth means the work of newer architects is being added on a regular basis.

Today, Oakland is known for countless galleries and studios and hundreds of murals on the sides of buildings, freeway underpasses, and fences, as well as being a hub for graffiti artists. Mosaics grace trash cans all over the city. Oakland has a burgeoning do-it-yourself and "maker" scene of people, who create things from jewelry and clothing to robots and electronics. And for the time being at least, there are more affordable former industrial spaces in Oakland that make great studios for artists moving to the area. This all means that Oakland's creative community will continue to grow as the city does.

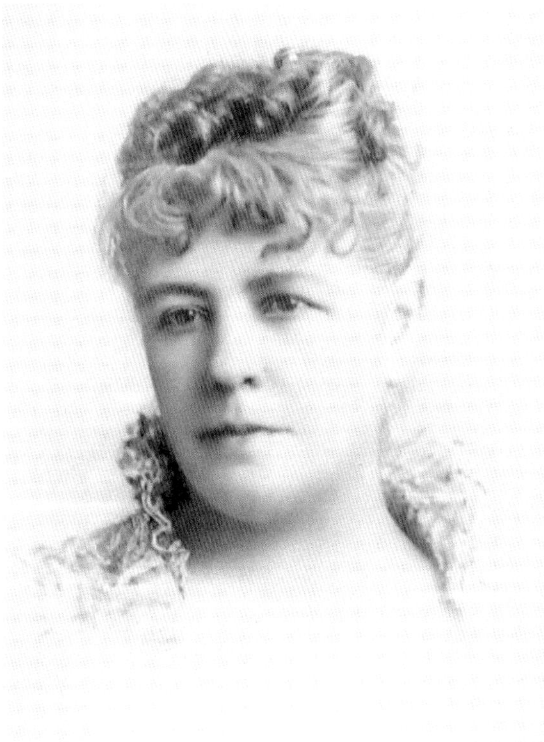

Oakland's First Librarian

Ina Coolbrith came to California with her family, led over the Sierra Nevada by African American mountain man Jim Beckwourth. Coolbrith is best known as California's first poet laureate. But she was also the first librarian of the Oakland Free Library, where she befriended and mentored 10-year-old Jack London in 1886. (Courtesy Oakland History Room, Oakland Public Library.)

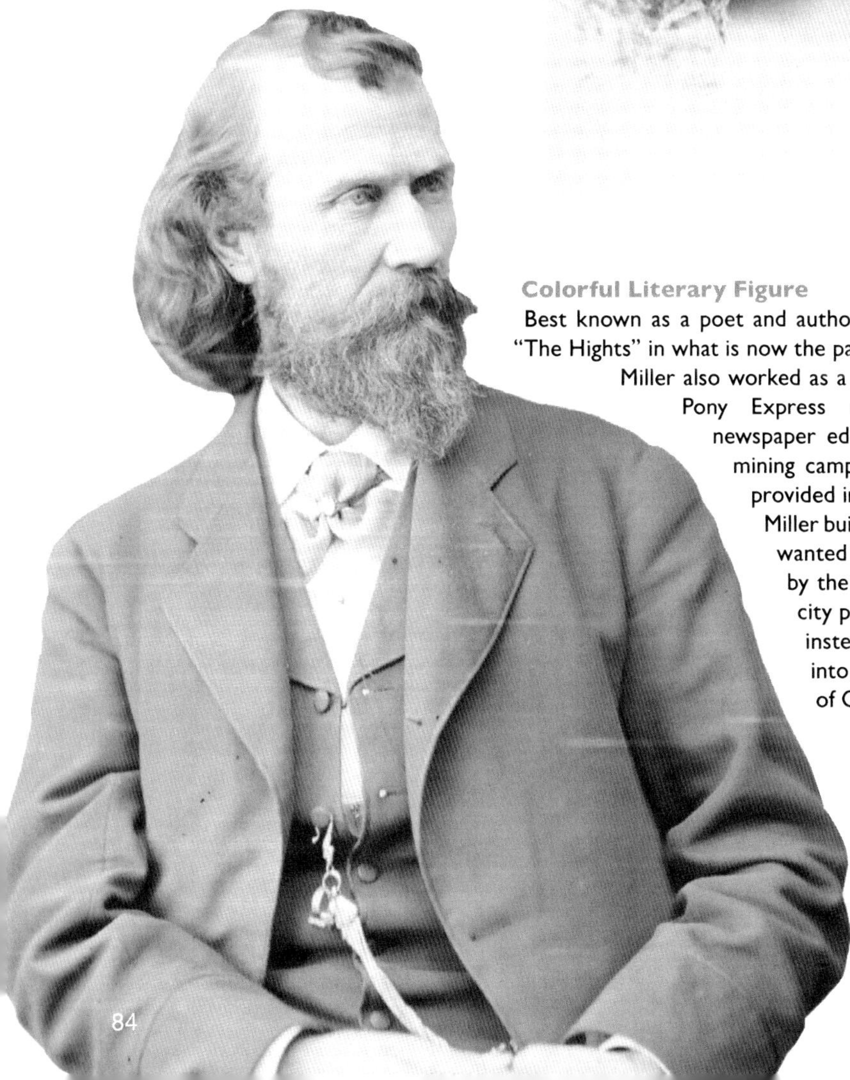

Colorful Literary Figure

Best known as a poet and author, Joaquin Miller lived at "The Hights" in what is now the park bearing his name. But Miller also worked as a surveyor, schoolteacher, Pony Express rider, attorney, judge, newspaper editor, and cook in a gold mining camp, all of which doubtless provided inspiration for his writing. Miller built a funeral pyre where he wanted his body cremated, but by the time he died it was in a city park, and the city refused; instead, his ashes were cast into a fire. (Courtesy Library of Congress.)

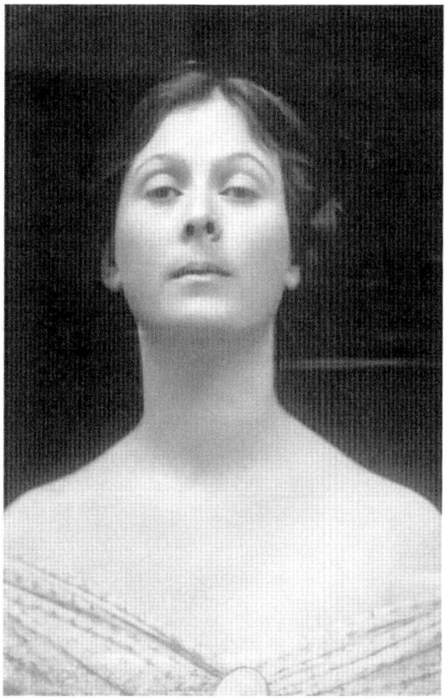

Mother of Modern Dance

Dancer Isadora Duncan wasn't born in Oakland, but her family moved to Oakland when she was a toddler. She found school too restrictive to her individuality but was mentored by librarian Ina Coolbrith. It has been speculated that the affections of Duncan's father for Coolbrith may have led to the divorce of her parents. One of Duncan's first dance recitals was at the First Unitarian Church. (Photograph by Arnold Genthe, courtesy Library of Congress.)

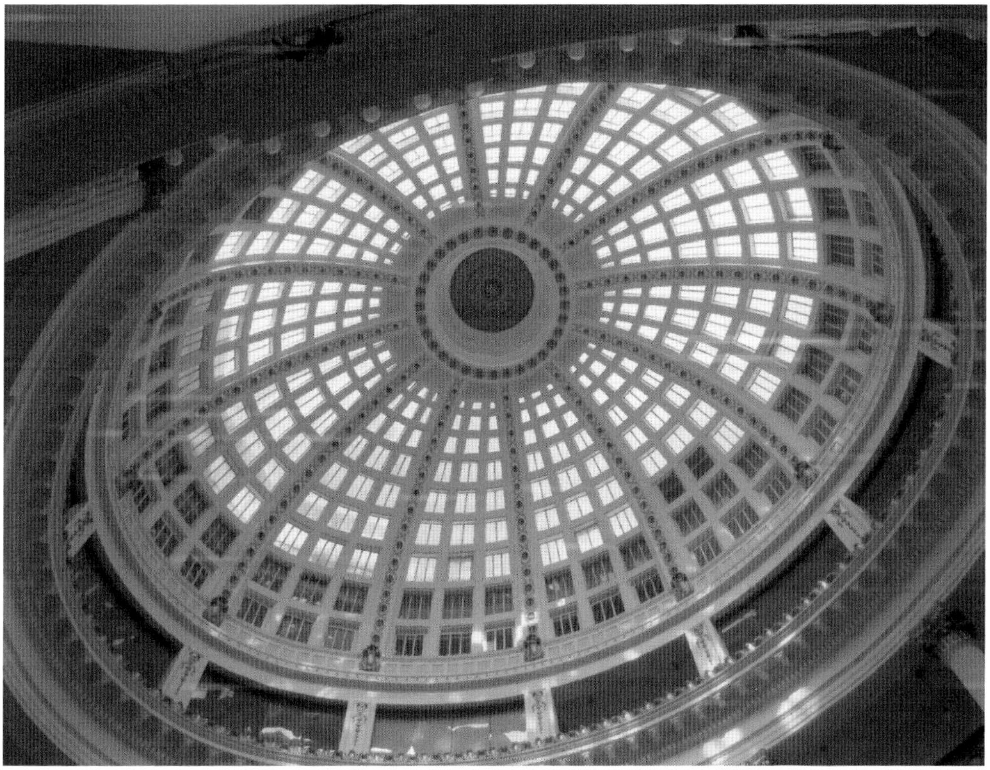

Designer of the Claremont Hotel

Most Oaklanders today will not recognize the name Charles W. Dickey, but they will recognize some of the buildings he designed. In addition to the Claremont Hotel, Dickey also designed Kahn's Department Store (now known as the Rotunda Building; interior shown here), the Temescal, Golden Gate, and Miller Avenue branch libraries, and University High School. (Author's collection.)

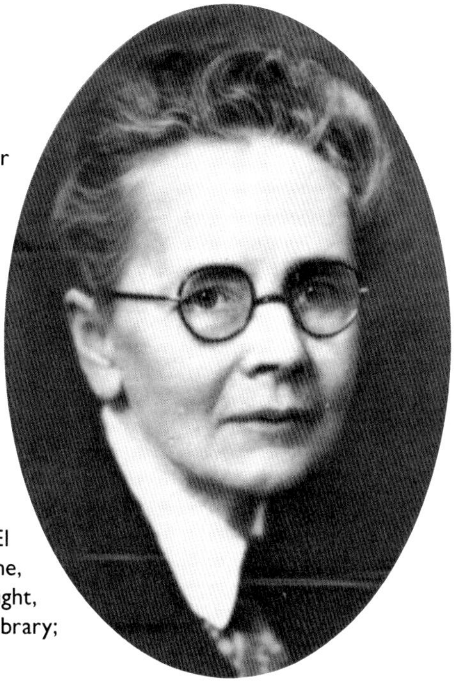

Pioneering Architect

Oakland's Julia Morgan was one of the first major woman architects; she designed over 700 buildings in California.

After graduating from Oakland High School, she attended the University of California, Berkeley, where she was mentored by noted architect Bernard Maybeck. She graduated with a degree in civil engineering and then applied to the prestigious École nationale supérieure des Beaux-Arts in Paris, the national fine arts school of France. After initially being rejected because she was a woman, she was finally accepted, and in 1902, became the first woman to receive a certificate in architecture from the school.

In Oakland, Morgan designed the YWCA building, El Campanil at Mills College, The King's Daughters Home, several churches, and a number of residences. (Right, courtesy Oakland History Room, Oakland Public Library; below, author's collection.)

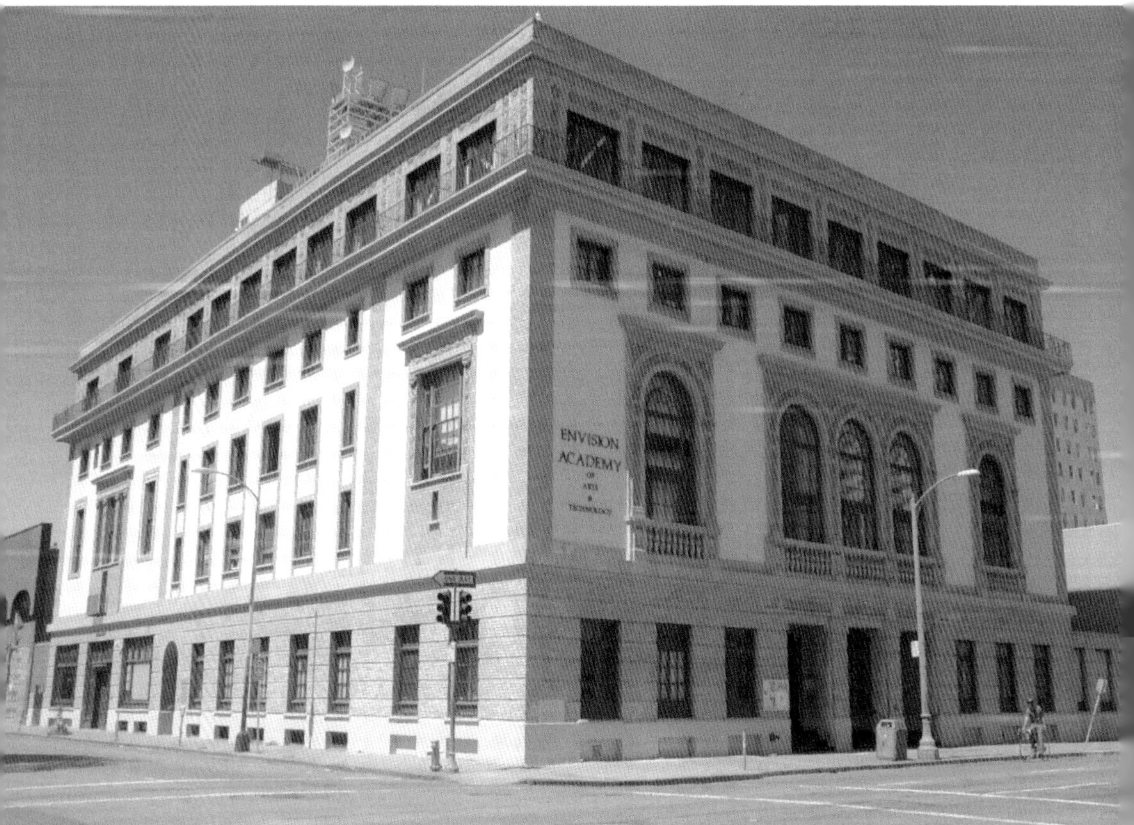

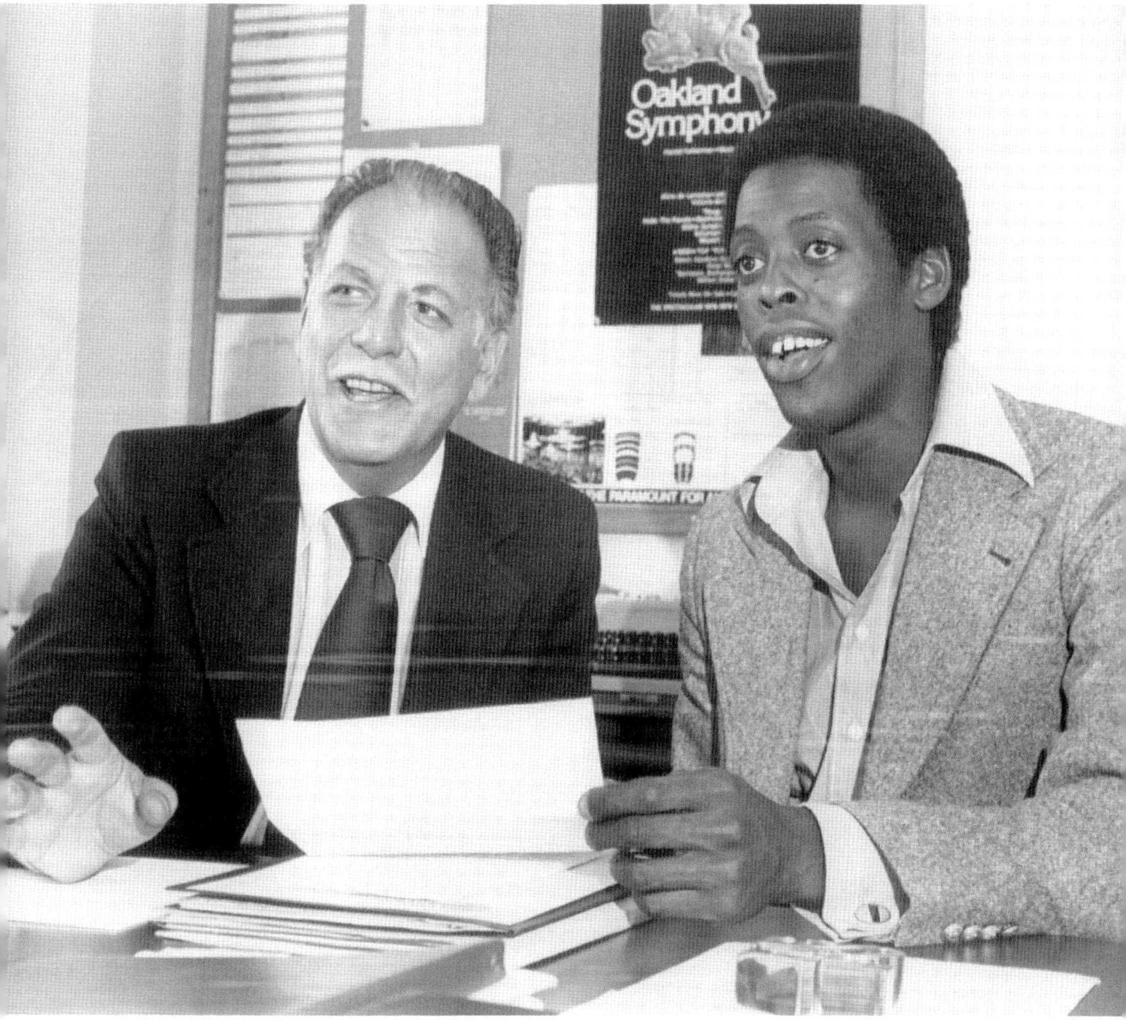

Career Cut Short

Calvin Simmons (right) was the first black conductor of a major symphony at age 29 and a frequent guest conductor with some of the nation's best-known opera companies and orchestras. Simmons became director of the Oakland Symphony Orchestra in 1978, but sadly, he died just four years later in a canoeing accident.

The man who had the vision to hire Simmons was Harold Lawrence (left), a world-renowned classical music producer and the general manager of the Oakland Symphony Orchestra. Lawrence had previously managed the London Symphony Orchestra (where he recruited Andre Previn to the podium) and the New York Philharmonic. Lawrence was a member of the Lake Merritt Breakfast Club and was instrumental in the restoration of Lake Merritt's necklace of lights. (Courtesy Barbara Stack.)

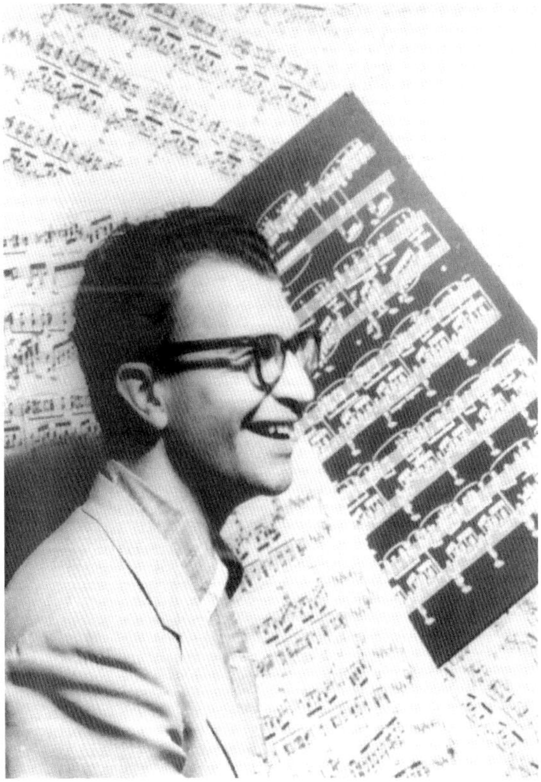

Take Five

Following military service during World War II, Dave Brubeck enrolled at Mills College and studied composition with Darius Milhaud. In 1947, Brubeck and other students formed the Dave Brubeck Octet but found it difficult to book such a large jazz group. Brubeck struggled until he was hired as a pianist at the Burma Lounge in Oakland. After hearing Brubeck play, DJ Jimmy Lyons was inspired to start the Monterey Jazz Festival. (Photograph by Carl Van Vecthen, courtesy Library of Congress.)

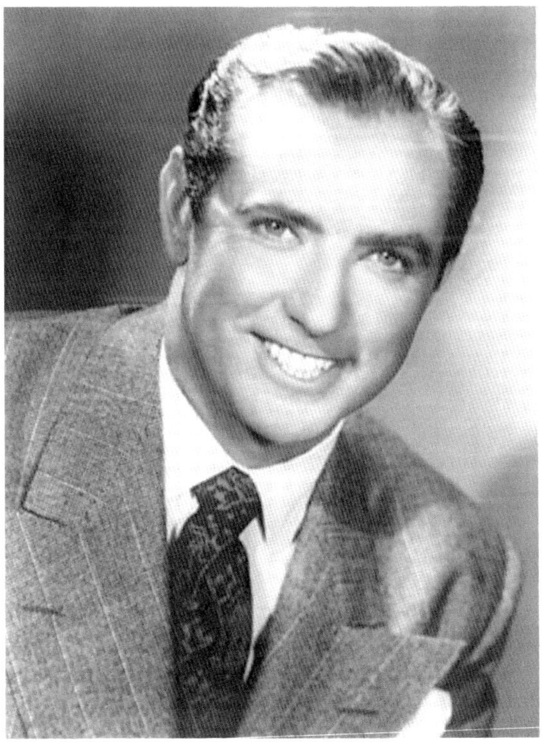

"The Old Smoothie"

Oakland native Del Courtney formed his first big band and started playing at the Claremont Hotel in 1933. Courtney had his own radio show and later hosted a variety show on KPIX TV. From 1959 to 1978, Courtney was the band leader for the Oakland Raiders and conceived the idea of the Raiderettes cheerleading squad. (Courtesy Oakland History Room, Oakland Public Library.)

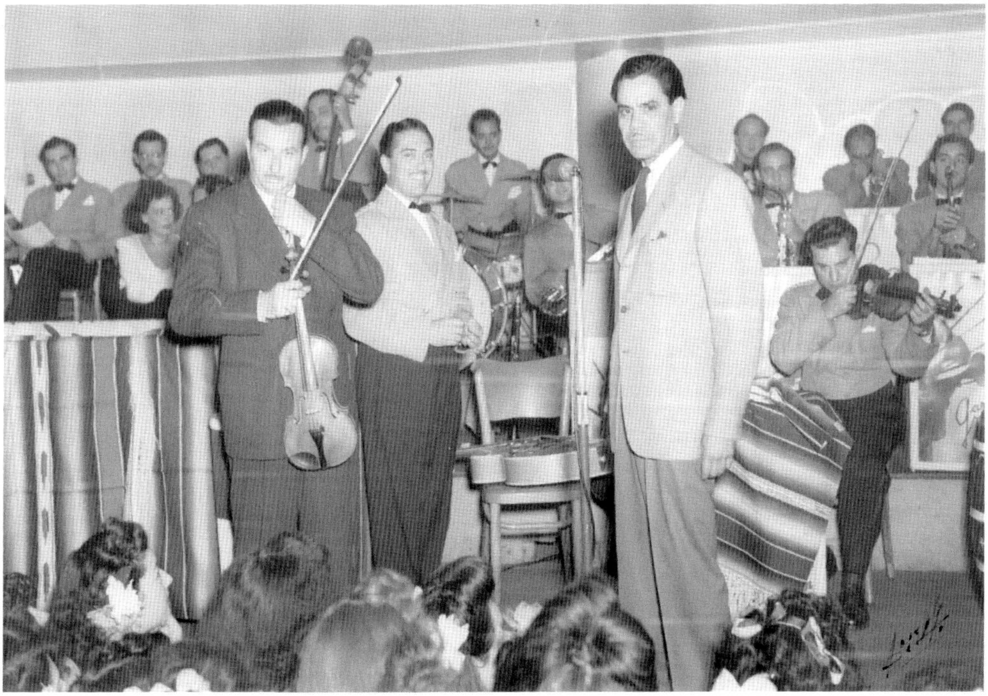

Latino Music Icon

After fleeing the Mexican Revolution, Guadalupe Carlos (right; Xavier Cugat on left with violin) settled in West Oakland and went to work in the shipyards. In the 1930s, he began organizing *tardeadas*, Sunday afternoon dances, at Sweet's Ballroom. The dances became a major social gathering for the Latino community. Carlos even traveled to Mexico to book acts, including the legendary Pedro Infante. (Photograph by E.F. Joseph, courtesy Oakland Museum of California, gift of Charles Hector Carlos.)

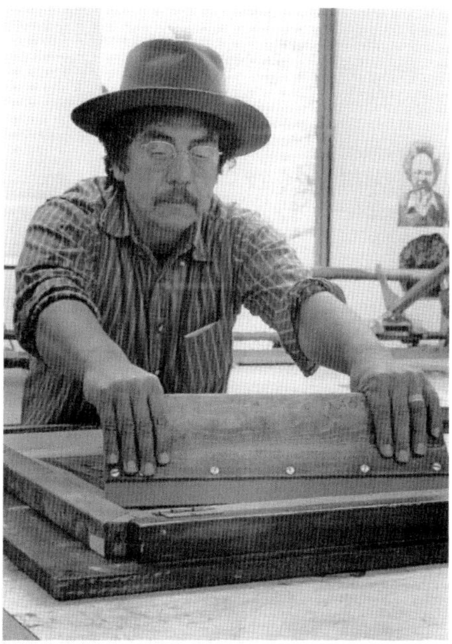

La Nueva Raza

Chicano artist Malaquias Montoya, along with other artists, founded the Mexican American Liberation Art Front with the goal of organizing artists who wanted to integrate art into the burgeoning Chicano social revolution that was sweeping the country in the 1960s. Montoya taught at the California College of the Arts for 12 years, and while many of the works have disappeared over time, Montoya and his students also painted distinctive murals around Oakland including *En El Libro Tu Libertad* on the building at Clinton Square Park. (Courtesy Malaquias Montoya.)

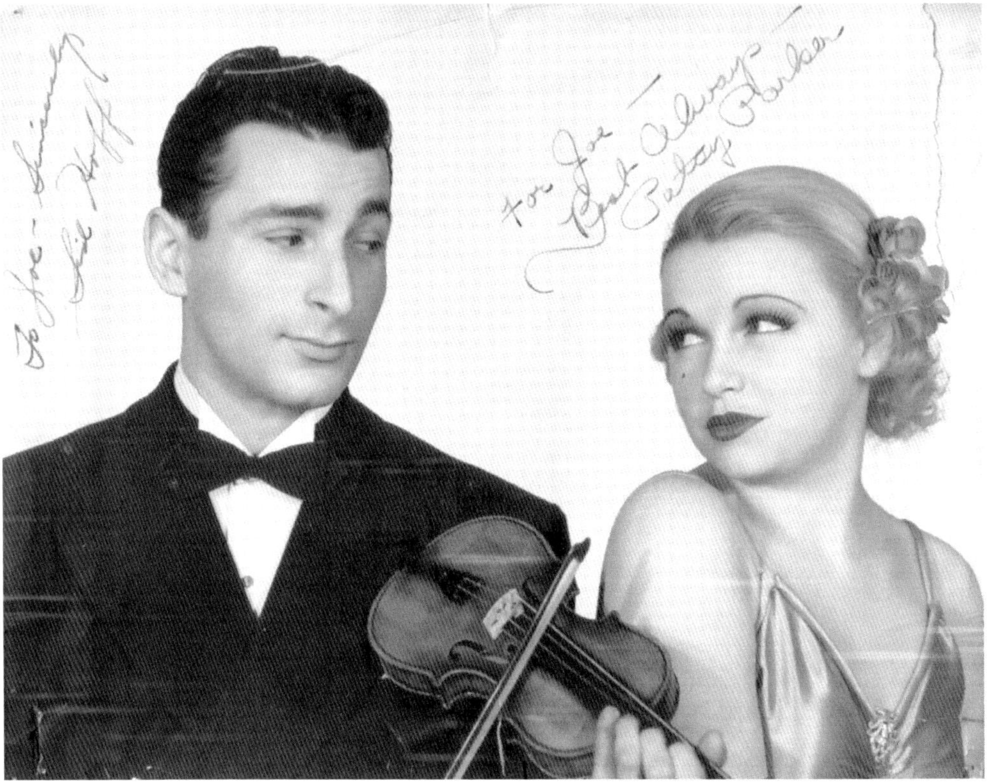

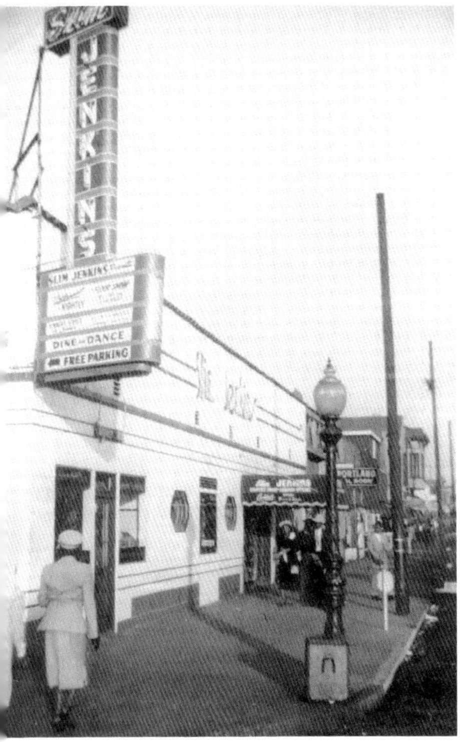

Ali Baba Ballroom

Bandleader and musician Sid Hoff grew up in Oakland with music in his life, even playing the violin with the San Francisco Symphony when he was 16. Hoff is best remembered for his orchestra, the house band at the Ali Baba Ballroom for 21 years. In the summer, when Sid Hoff and his orchestra were not playing at the Ali Baba, they would play at the Camp Curry Ballroom in Yosemite National Park. Hoff also played on the hotel circuit for nine years, including stints at the Claremont Hotel and the Lake Merritt Hotel. (Author's collection.)

Harlem of the West

Oakland was once known as the Harlem of the West, and Harold "Slim" Jenkins's namesake club was the start of it. Jenkins opened his club on December 5, 1933, the day Prohibition was repealed. Over the years, black music icons like B.B. King, Earl "Fatha" Hines, and Aretha Franklin performed at the Slim Jenkins Café. Visitors included Pres. Franklin D. Roosevelt, and *Oakland Tribune* owner and publisher William Knowland was a regular. (Courtesy Harold Jenkins Photograph Collection, MS 11, African American Museum & Library at Oakland.)

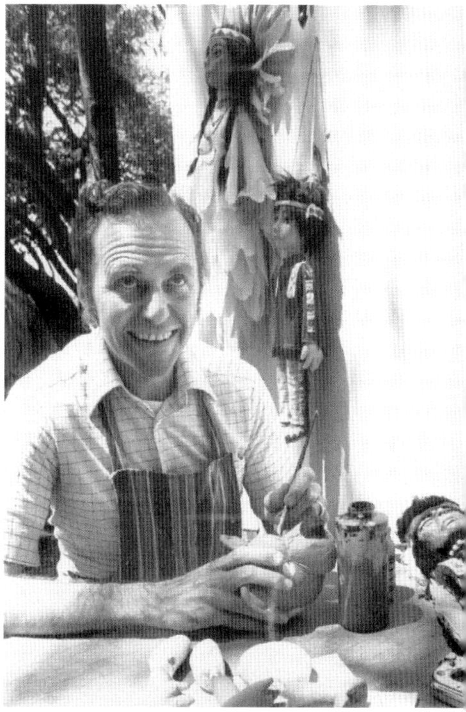

Master Puppeteer

Lewis Mahlmann and his handmade puppets entertained children for decades at Children's Fairyland. He believed children should never be talked down to and, in addition to more traditional folk tales, created versions of ballets and operas like *The Magic Flute* and *The Nutcracker* to present in his puppet shows. Mahlmann was twice president of the Puppeteers of America, where he met Jim Henson. (Courtesy Children's Fairyland.)

The Puppeteering Is Strong . . .

Richard Frank Oznowicz, better known as Frank Oz (right, along with Bert and Lewis Mahlmann) of Muppets and *Star Wars* fame, grew up in Oakland and went to Oakland Technical High School. More important to his future career, he joined Lettie Schubert's traveling Vagabond Puppets team, which performed regularly at Children's Fairyland. Oz was a close collaborator with Muppets creator Jim Henson; he was Bert to Henson's Ernie and Miss Piggy to Henson's Kermit the Frog. (Courtesy Children's Fairyland.)

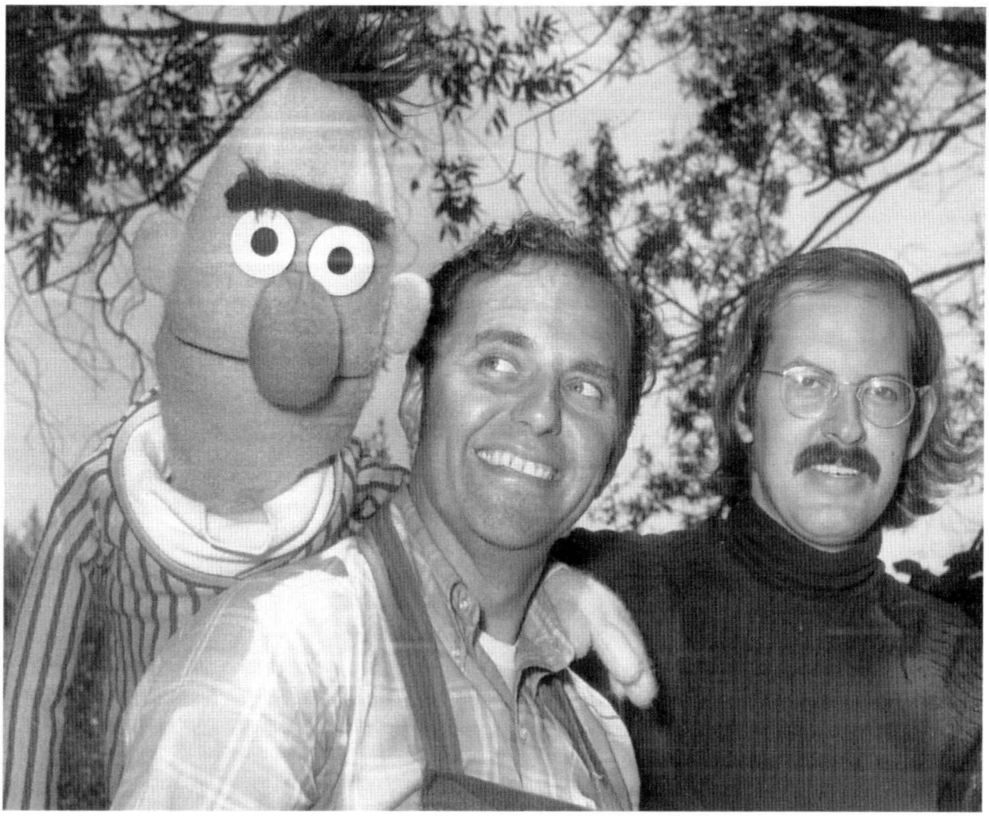

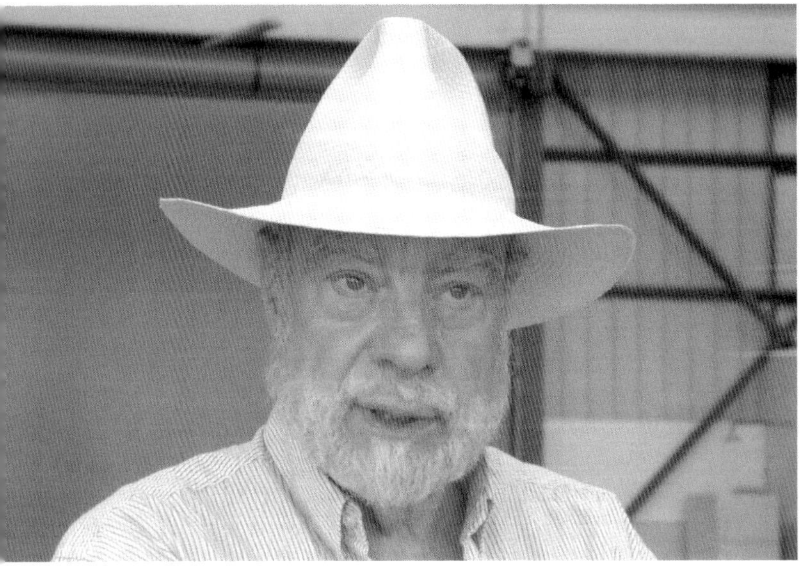

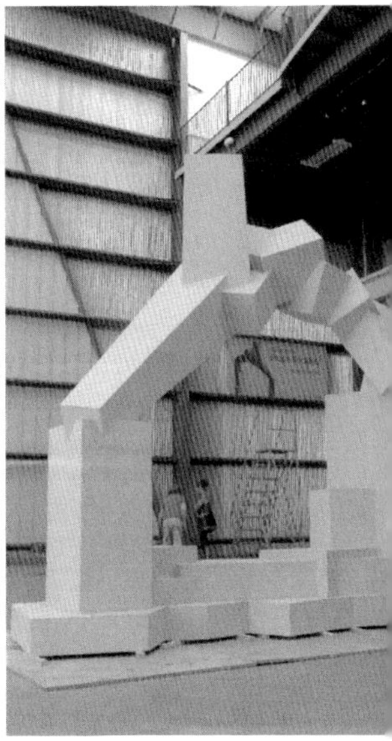

World-Renowned Sculptor

Young artist and University of California, Berkeley graduate Bruce Beasley moved to West Oakland in 1962 because he could not afford any place else. Over the last 50 years, Beasley has been active in improving and promoting the area. In 2014, Beasley bequeathed his West Oakland studios and sculpture gardens to the Oakland Museum of California. (Both, author's collection.)

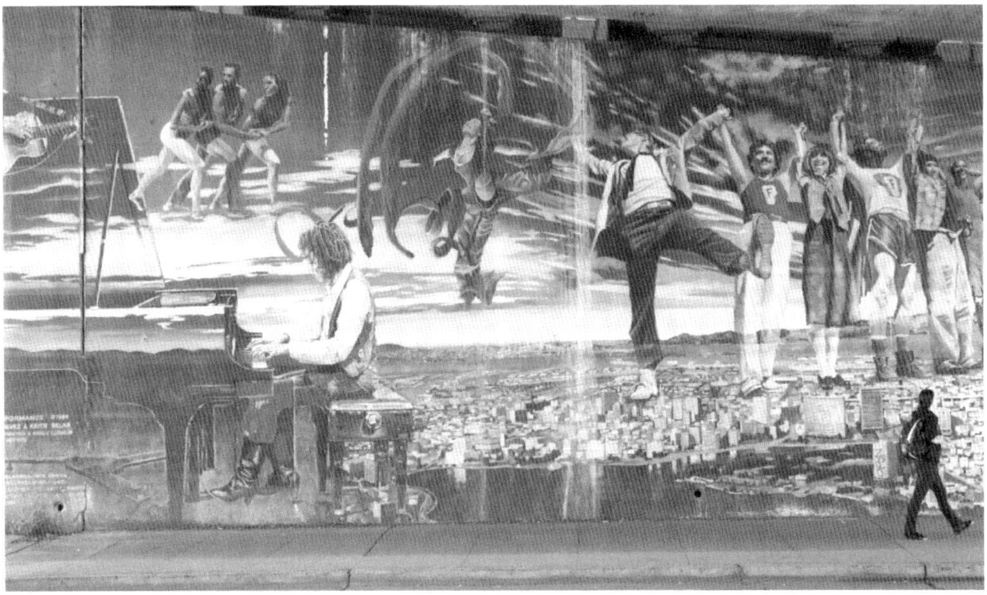

Grand Performance

California College of the Arts graduate Daniel Galvez has painted and collaborated on some of the biggest murals around Oakland. One of the newest and largest murals graces the outside of the East Oakland Sports Center. One of the oldest outdoor murals still visible is *The Grand Performance* along Grand Avenue under I-580, which features creative people of Oakland, including Calvin Simmons, Jack London, and Julia Morgan. (Author's collection.)

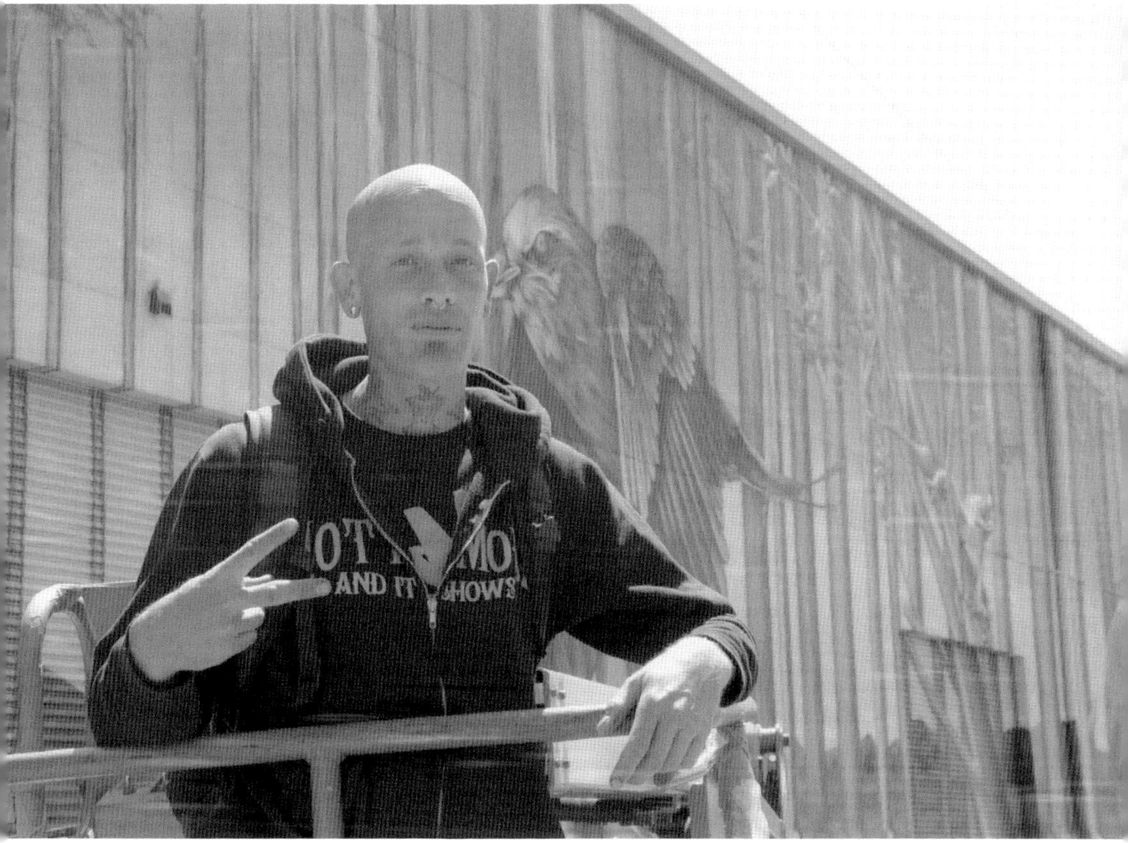

Prolific, Passionate Artist

Ernest Doty's murals can be seen all over Oakland and all over the world. A frequent collaborator with artists Griffin One and Vogue TDK, Doty uses a distinctive style as seen in this mural adorning the Oakland Museum of California's White Elephant Sale warehouse. Doty's work often contains elements of nature, mysticism, and political statements. (Author's collection.)

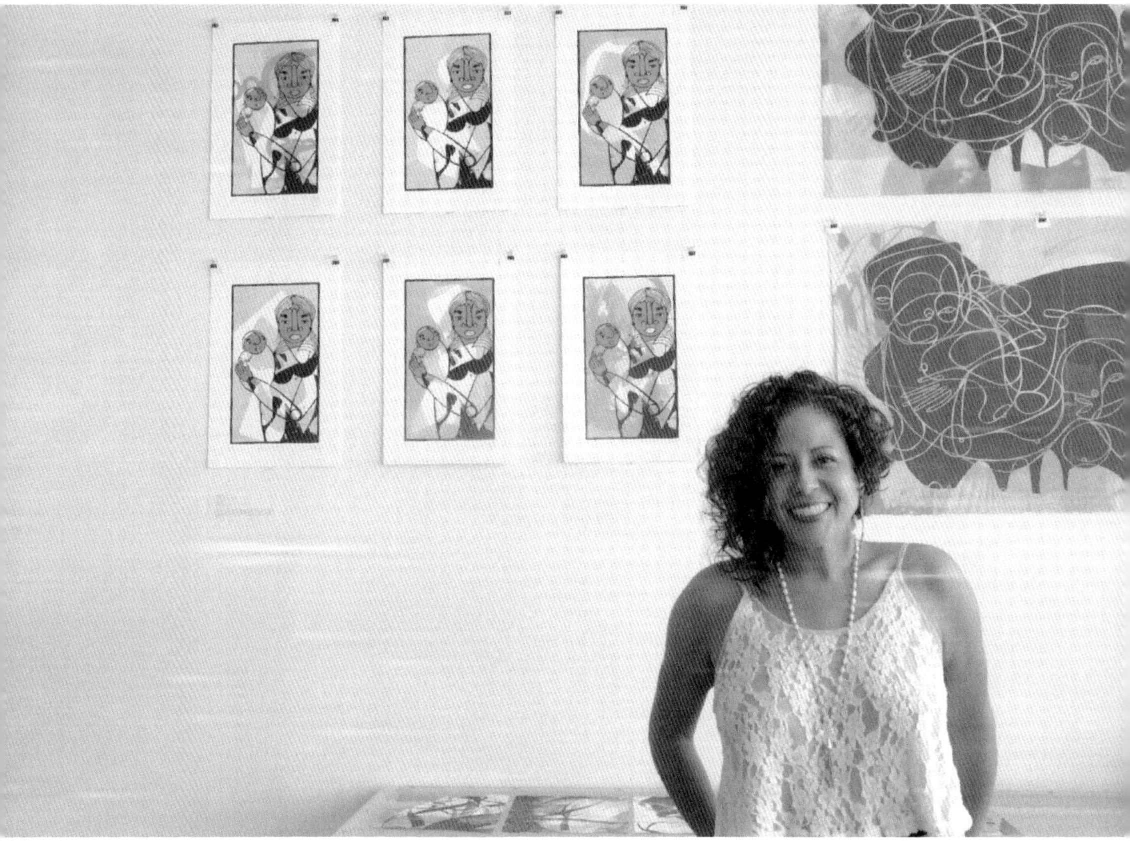

Artist and Activist

Known for creating art with strong lines and bright colors, artist Favianna Rodriguez has long used her art for social activism. Born and raised in the Fruitvale district, Rodriguez cofounded the Eastside Arts Alliance, the Visual Element youth mural program, the Taller Tupac Amaru printing studio, and presente.org. She continues to use her art for social change. (Author's collection.)

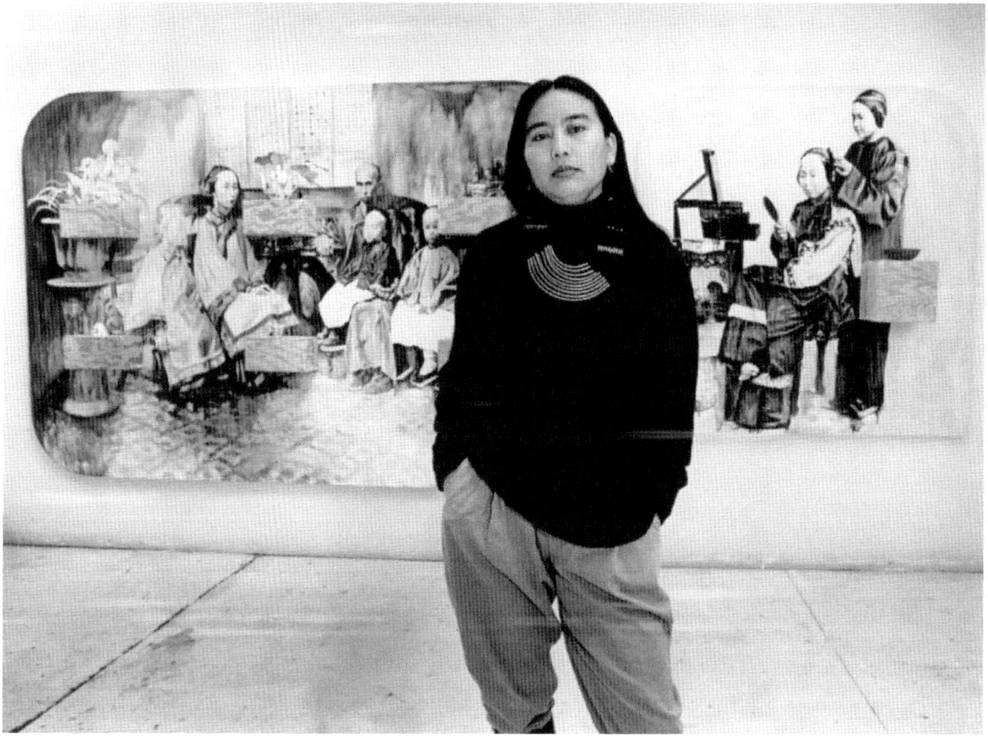

Summoning Ghosts
The artwork of American-born Chinese artist Hung Liu frequently makes use of anonymous historic photographs and sometimes includes representations of her own ancestors. Dripped linseed oil blurs the images the way our memory blurs into history. Liu was trained both in Maoist China and in the United States, and her art is a bridge between the times and cultures. Liu is a professor emerita of studio art at Mills College. (Photograph by Michael Macor, courtesy Oakland Tribune Collection at the Oakland Museum of California, gift of ANG Newspapers.)

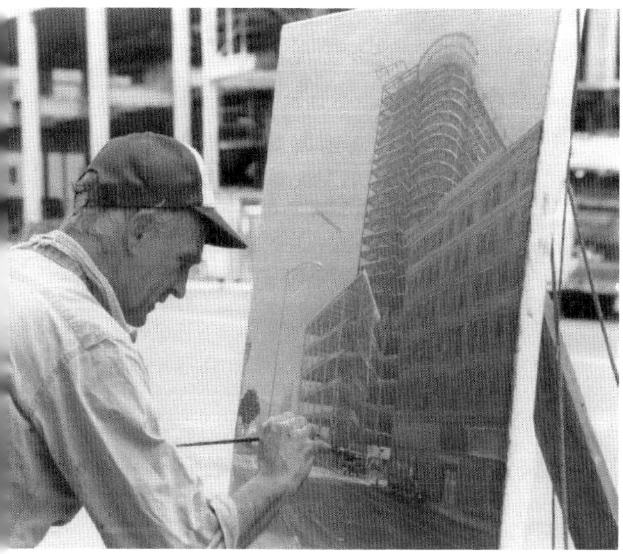

Urban Landscapes
Urban landscape artist Anthony Holdsworth was born in England and started painting in Italy, but it was not until he lived in Oakland that he started focusing on urban landscapes: "The urban landscape is an accurate and disquieting testament to our common condition," he says. His paintings show both what is seen and what is unseen. Federal officials in San Francisco refused to display some of his work that shows the future effects of global warming. (Courtesy Anthony Holdsworth.)

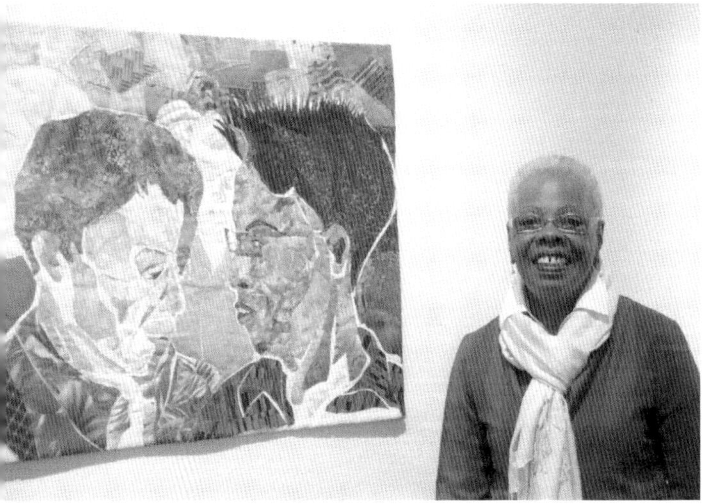

Founding Member of Art Murmur

While many of Oakland's more recent art galleries are in Uptown, Joyce Gordon has had her namesake gallery downtown for more than 10 years. "She invested in downtown Oakland before it was fashionable," said Samee Roberts, Oakland's cultural arts and marketing manager. The Joyce Gordon Gallery features innovative exhibits showing cultural and ethnic diversity, from both local and international artists. (Author's collection.)

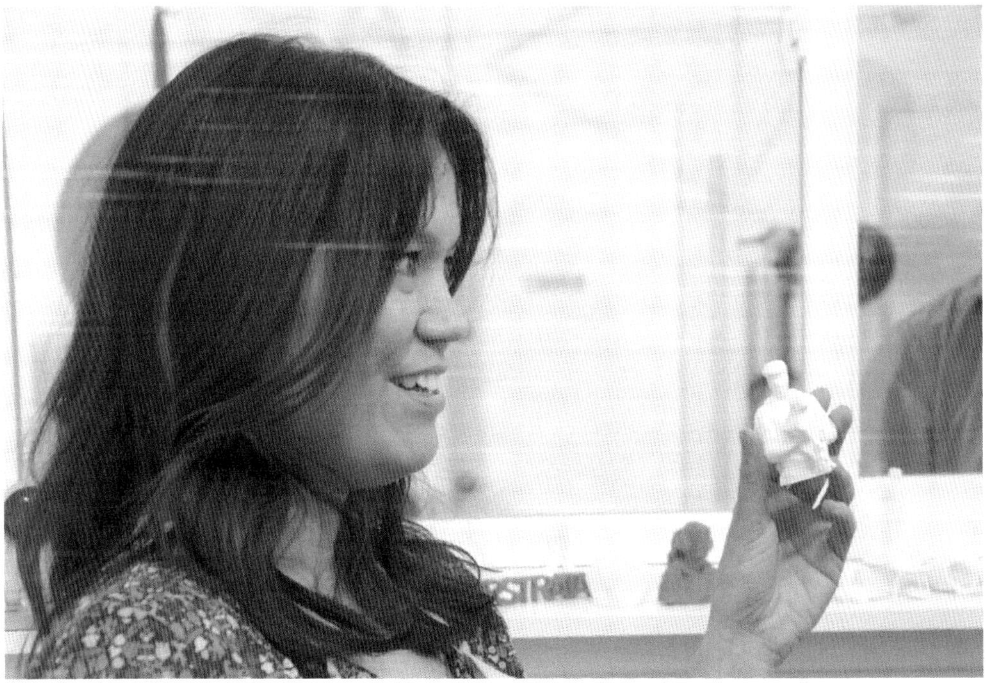

A Passion for Art

Lena Verderano Reynoso is the cofounder of the Compound Art Gallery, an artist-run gallery and art space in North Oakland. While she studied mathematics, astrophysics, folklore, and anthropology in school, Reynoso followed her heart and now creates art and runs a space where others can create art too. (Author's collection.)

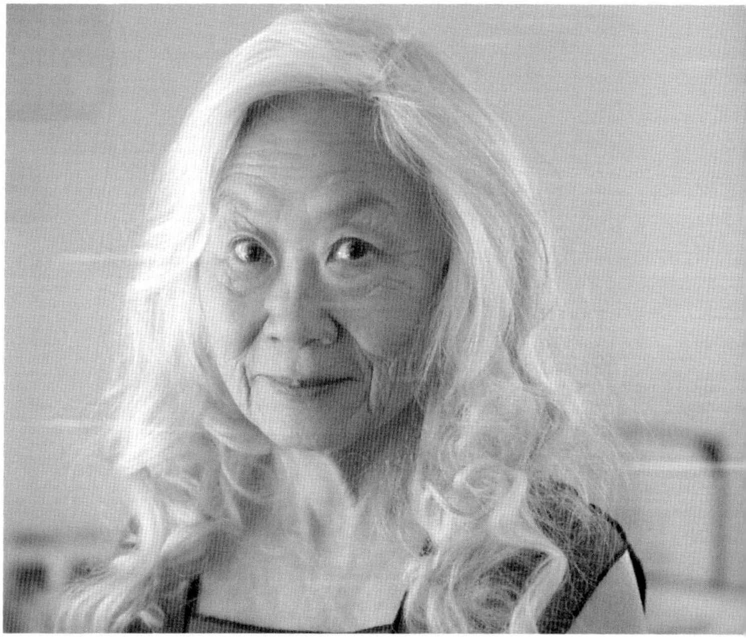

The Woman Warrior
Drawn to writing at an early age after she won $5 for an essay titled "I Am An American," Maxine Hong Kingston taught for many years at Oakland Technical High School and the University of California, Berkeley. Her books and poetry about the experiences of Chinese immigrants living in the United States have won numerous awards, and in 2014, Kingston was awarded a National Medal of Arts by Pres. Barack Obama. (Photograph by David Shankbone.)

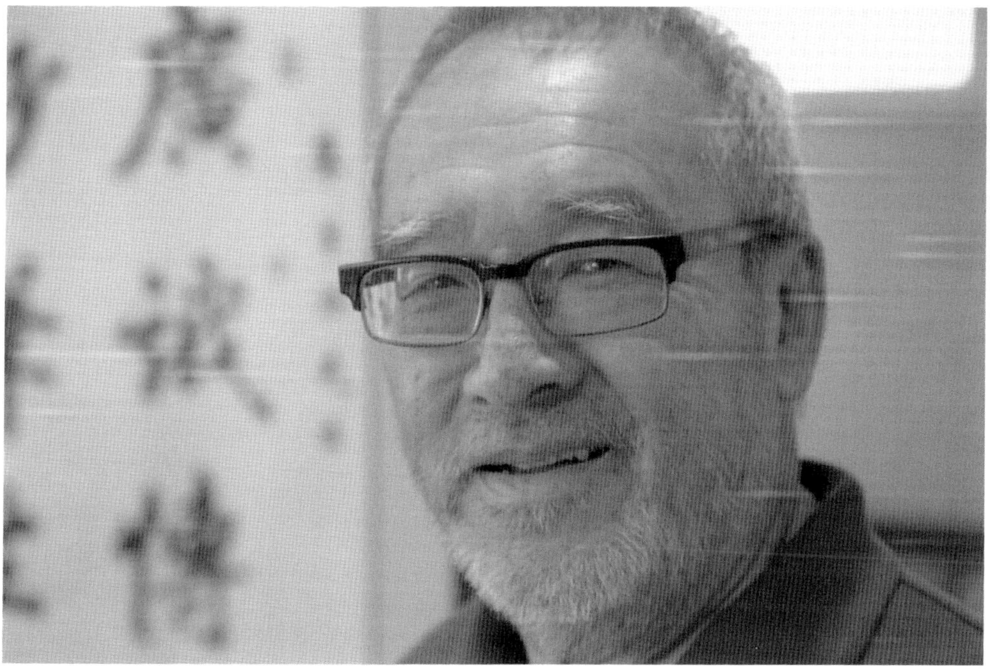

Elder Son of Asian American Journalism
Journalist and author William Gee Wong was born and raised in Chinatown. In 1962, he became the first Asian American reporter for a mainstream San Francisco newspaper and eventually wrote for various publications, including the *Oakland Tribune*, *San Francisco Chronicle*, *Wall Street Journal*, and *Asian Week*. Wong is also the author of *Yellow Journalist: Dispatches from Asian America* (2001) and *Oakland's Chinatown* (2004). He is currently working on a book about his father, who emigrated from China in 1912 during the Chinese Exclusion era. (Courtesy Joyce Mende Wong.)

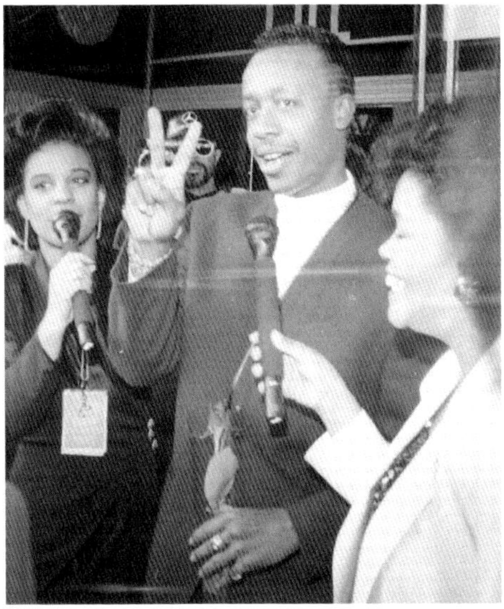

You Can't Touch This
Better known as musical artist MC Hammer, Stanley Burrell got his start as a batboy for the Oakland Athletics. Hall of Famer Reggie Jackson gave him the nickname "Hammer" because he reminded Jackson of the legendary Hank Aaron. Now, Burrell is involved in high tech and other interests. He is the spokesman for Visit Oakland, the Oakland Convention Center and Visitors Bureau. (Courtesy Oakland Tribune Collection at the Oakland Museum of California, gift of ANG Newspapers.)

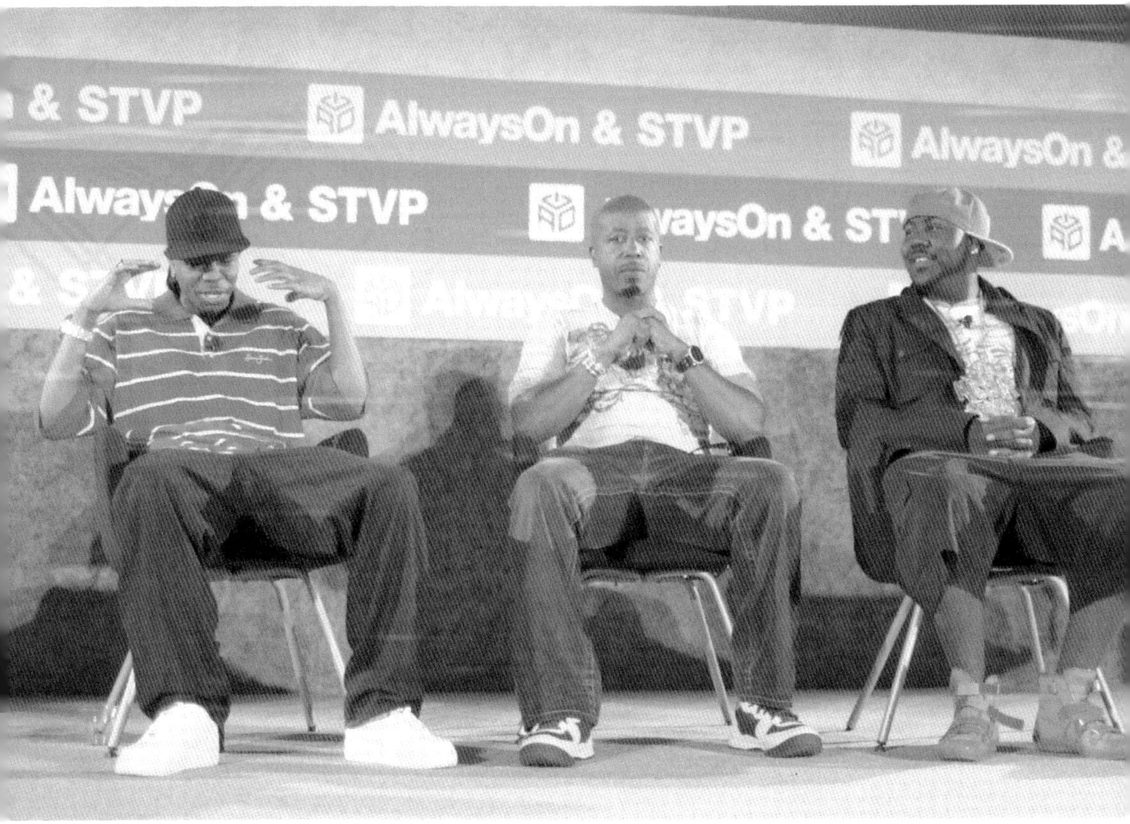

Down to Earth
Oakland-born Mistah F.A.B. (on right; MC Hammer in center; and Chamillionaire on left) may be more widely known for his music, but in Oakland, he has been honored for his charity work. He holds an annual back-to-school backpack giveaway and other events. Although his name is an acronym for Money Is Something To Always Have, FaEva After Bread, F.A.B. is down to earth. (Photograph by Brian Solis.)

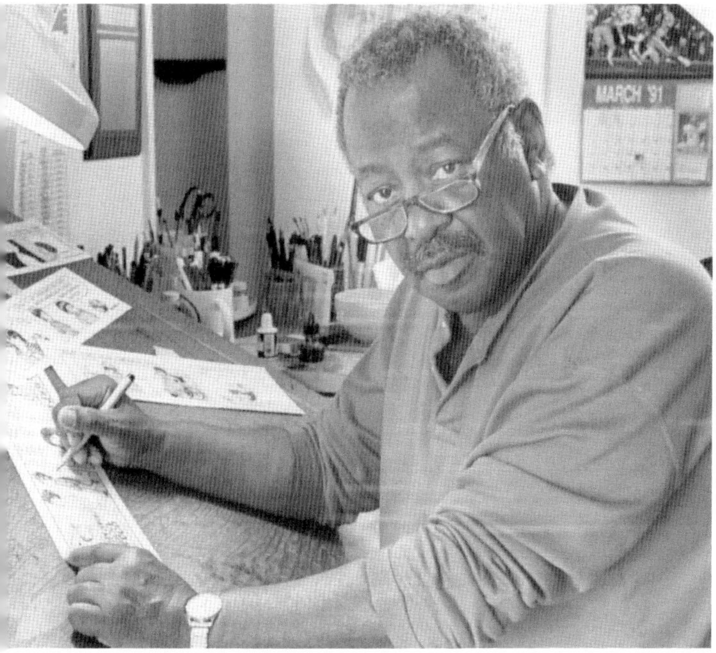

Keeping the Faith
Son of a Pullman porter and a nurse, cartoonist Morrie Turner was inspired by his diverse West Oakland neighborhood and created the first nationally syndicated cartoon strip with a diverse ethnic cast. His intention in drawing *Wee Pals* was to "portray a world without prejudice, a world in which people's differences—race, religion, gender, and physical and mental ability—are cherished, not scorned." (Courtesy Morrie Turner Papers, MS 24, African American Museum & Library at Oakland.)

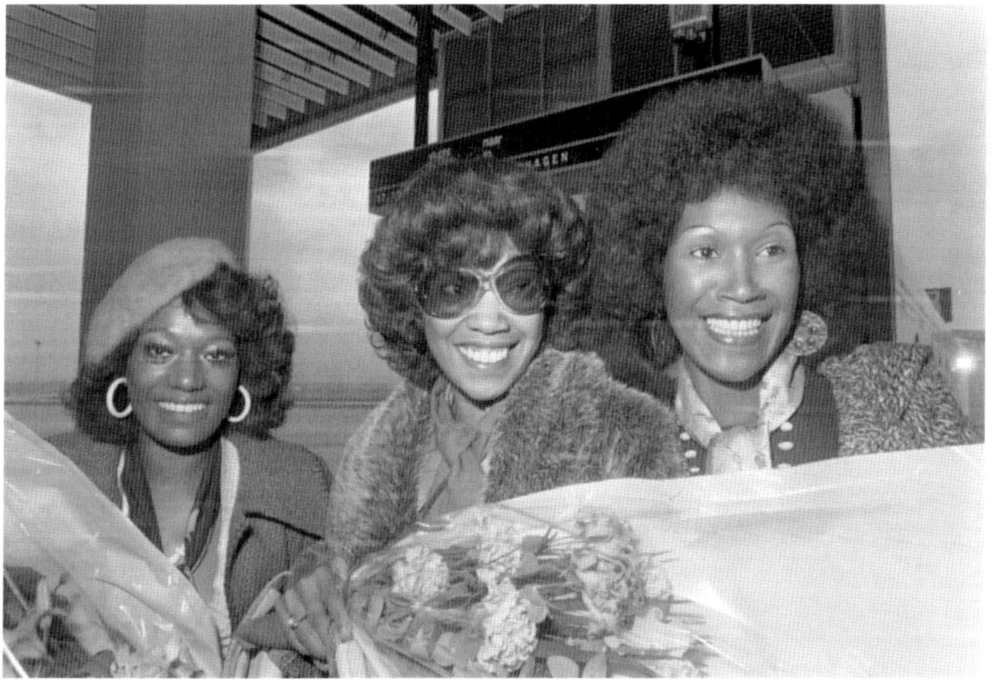

Yes We Can Can
The Pointer Sisters are a hugely successful R&B group from Oakland. Despite their parents, Sarah and Rev. Elton Pointer, telling them rock and the blues were "the devil's music," June, Bonnie, Anita, and later Ruth Pointer formed a group that combined jazz, bebop, and the blues. The group is still active today, consisting of Anita, Ruth, and Ruth's granddaughter Sadako Pointer. (Courtesy National Archives of the Netherlands.)

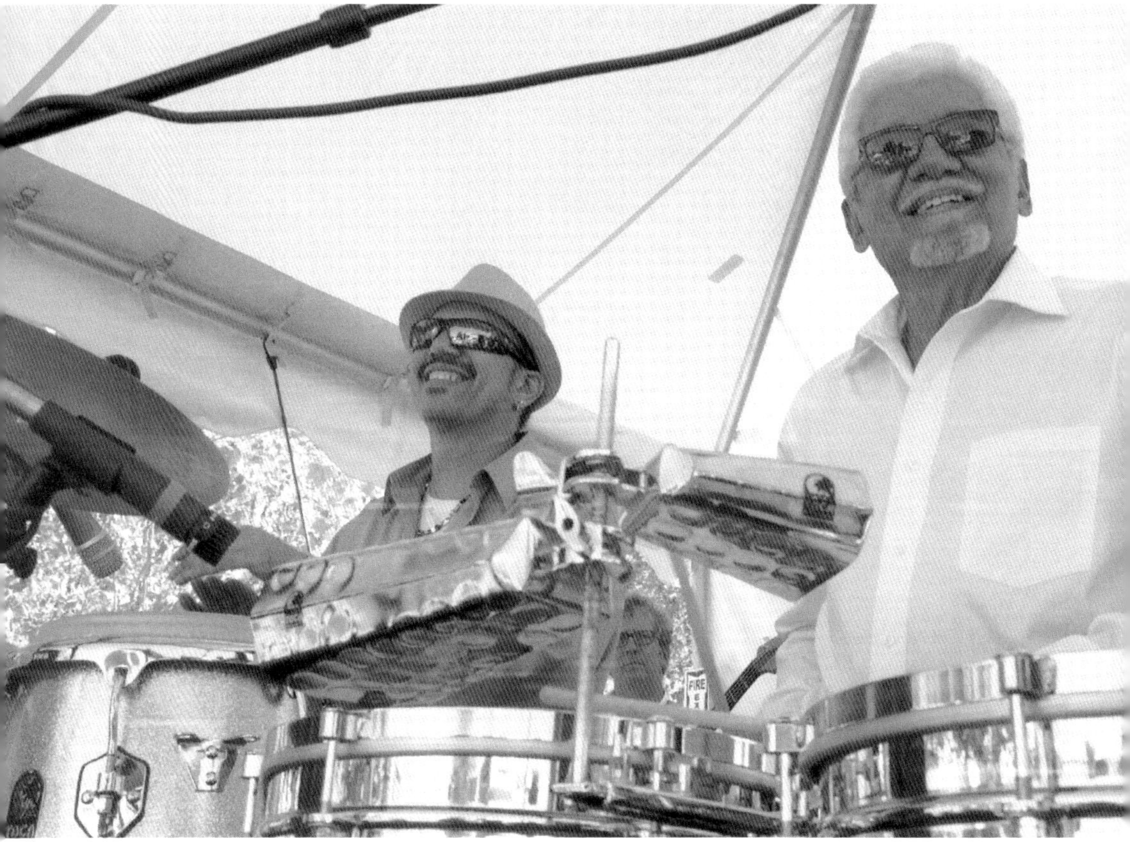

Music in Their Blood

Latin jazz percussionist Pete Escovedo (right) grew up in Oakland exposed to music. His father sometimes sang with Latin big bands, and Escovedo would spend evenings sitting on the steps of nightclubs, watching the musicians perform. Escovedo played in a group with his brothers until Carlos Santana hired him and his brother Coke in 1967. After a stint leading the Latin big band Azteca, Escovedo played with many notable musicians, including Herbie Hancock, Tito Puente, and Lionel Richie.

The music continues to the next generation of the Escovedo family. Sons Juan (left) and Peter Michael regularly perform with Escovedo, and daughter Sheila E. (see page 104) is a star in her own right, working with notable musicians including Natalie Cole, Stevie Wonder, Prince, Ringo Starr, Gloria Estefan, and Beyoncé. She started playing drums at the tender age of three. (Author's collection.)

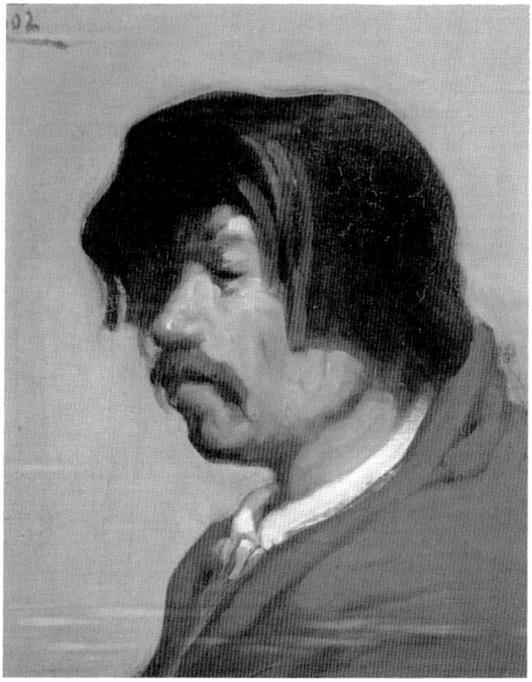

Early Latino Artist and Teacher
Xavier Timoteo Orozco Martinez came to San Francisco from Mexico in 1893, sponsored by his foster mother, Rosalia LaBastida de Coney (featured below in a bronze piece by Martinez), and her husband. Following the 1906 San Francisco earthquake, Martinez moved to the East Bay, and taught at the California College of the Arts in Oakland from 1908 to 1942. (Left, courtesy Oakland Museum of California; below, author's collection.)

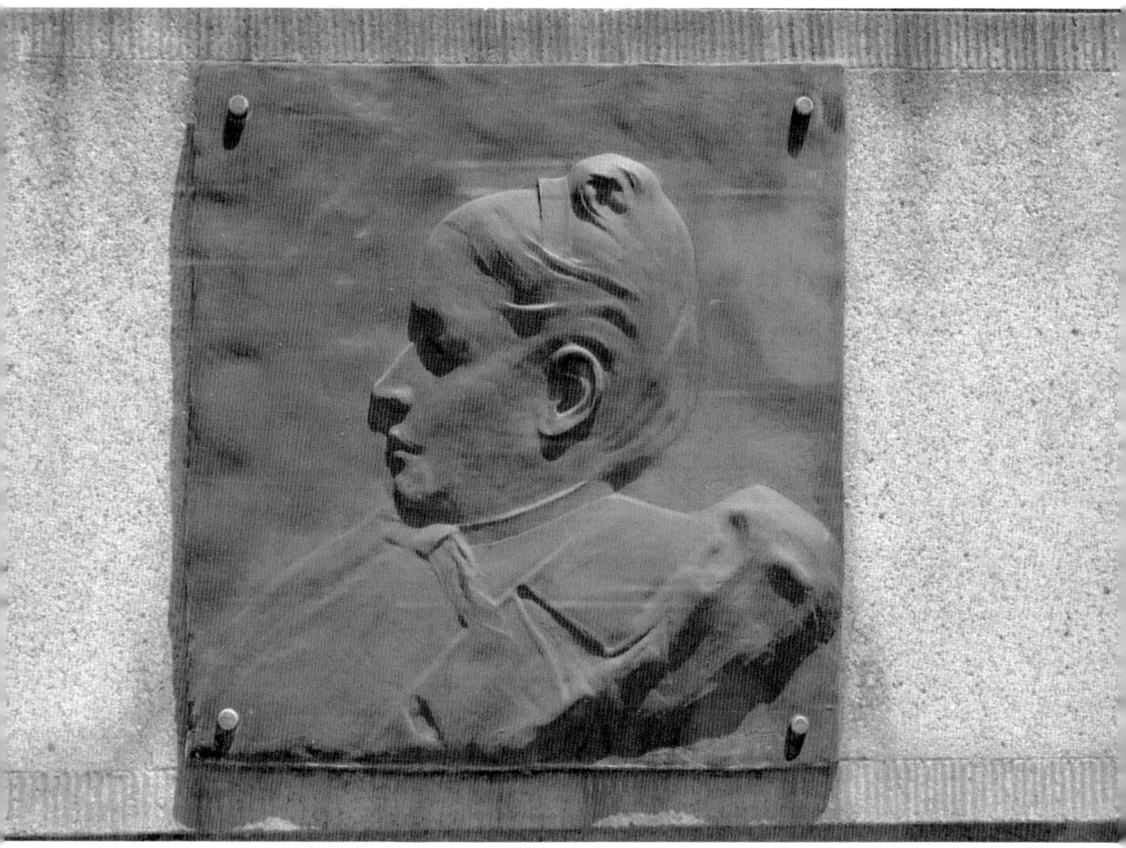

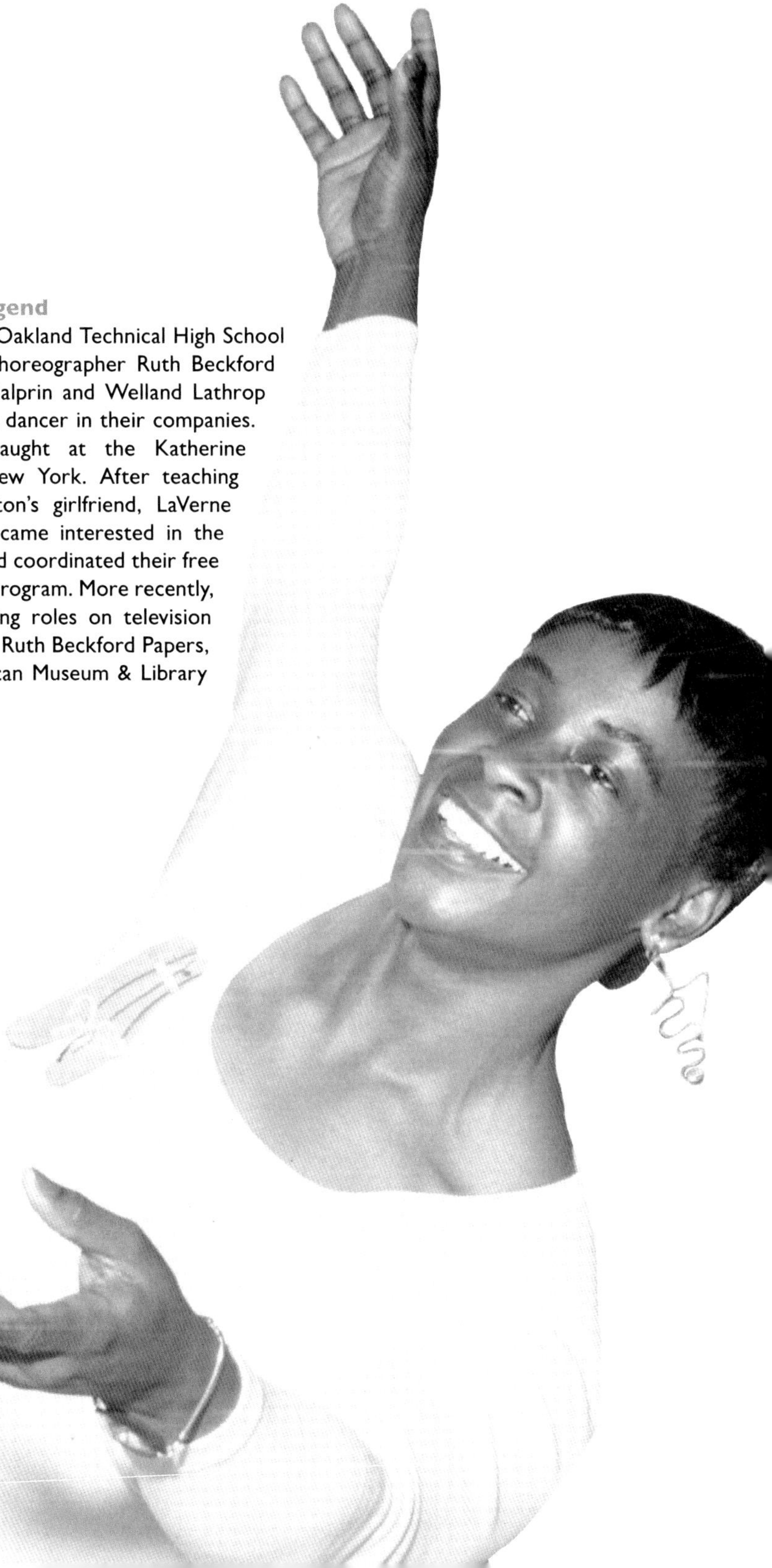

Oakland Dance Legend
After graduating from Oakland Technical High School in 1944, dancer and choreographer Ruth Beckford studied under Anna Halprin and Welland Lathrop and was the first black dancer in their companies. In 1953, Beckford taught at the Katherine Dunham School in New York. After teaching dance to Huey Newton's girlfriend, LaVerne Williams, Beckford became interested in the Black Panther Party and coordinated their free breakfast for children program. More recently, Beckford has had acting roles on television and in films. (Courtesy Ruth Beckford Papers, MS 60, African American Museum & Library at Oakland.)

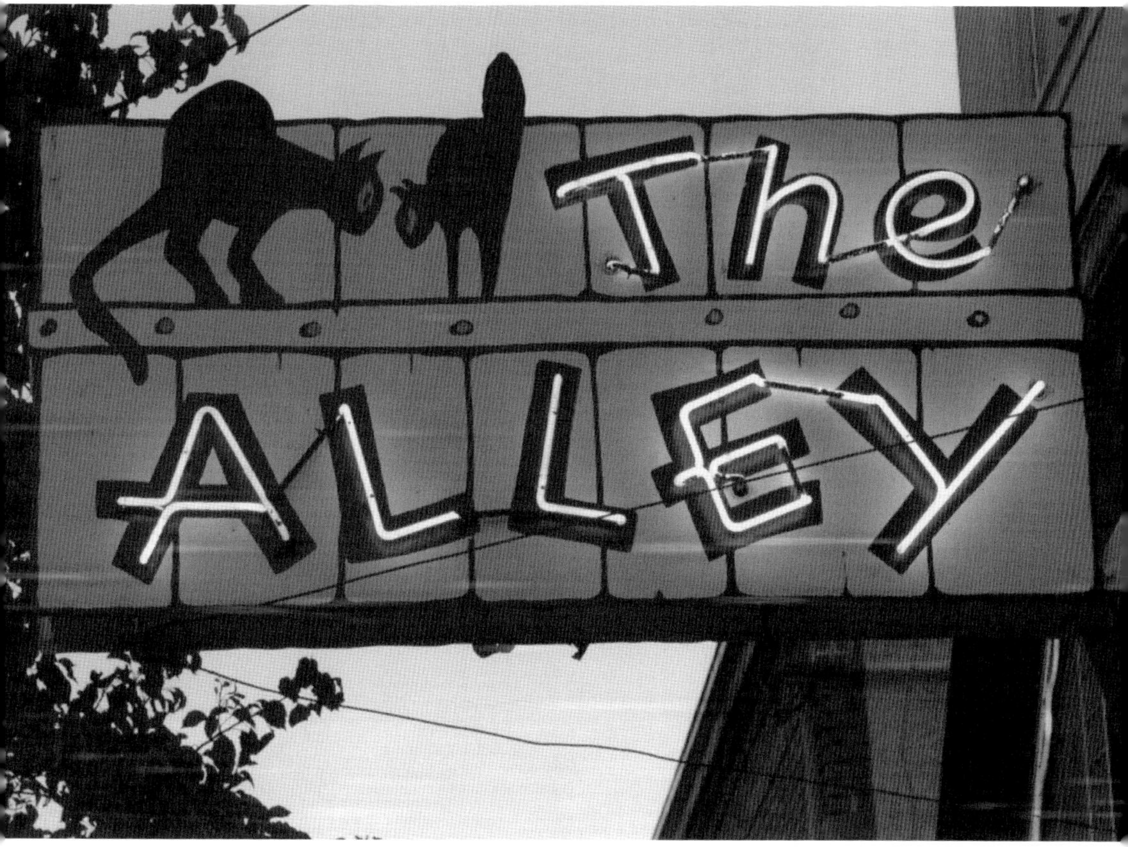

Piano Man

Anyone who has ever been to a small, dimly lit bar on Grand Avenue called the Alley has probably heard Rod Dibble on the piano. He has been banging out American standards since 1960, with patrons singing along. Dibble used to play five nights a week, but after 52 years, he slowed down to just two or three. (Author's collection.)

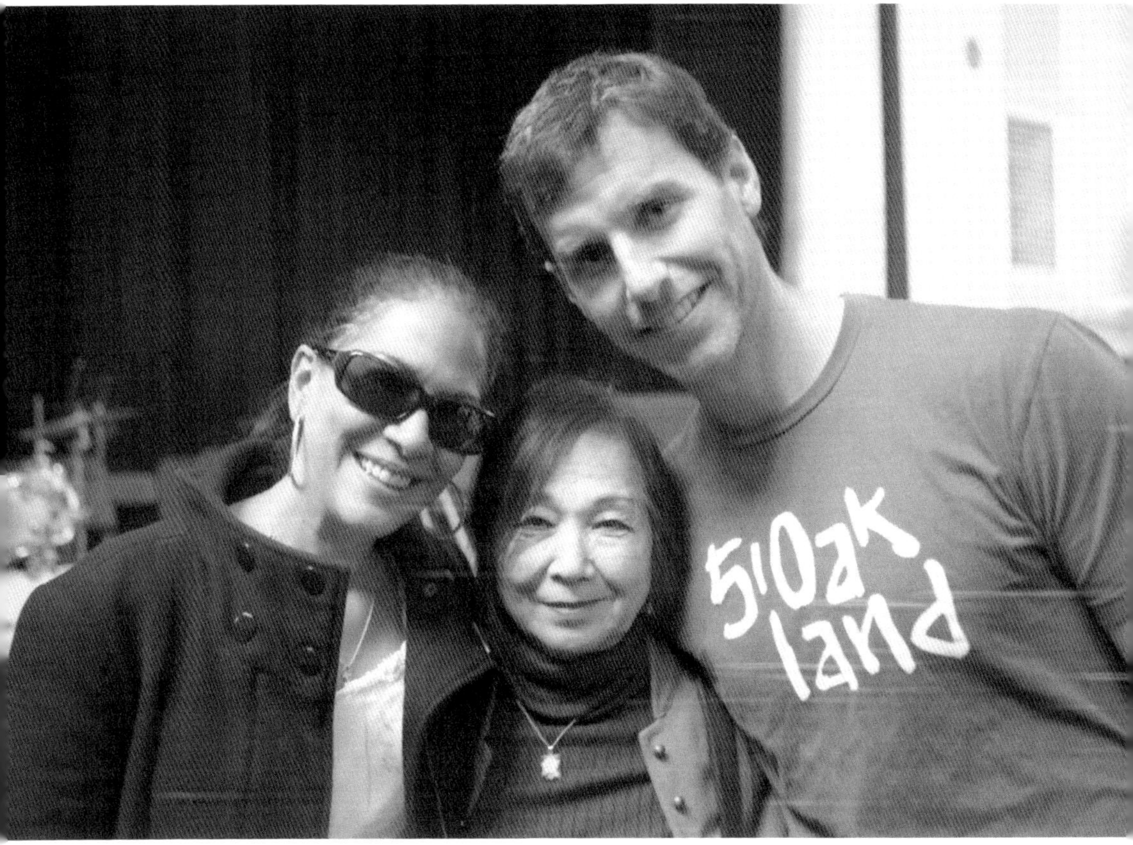

Yoshi's Jazz Club

Starting with a small sushi bar in North Berkeley in 1972, World War II orphan Yoshie Akiba (center) and two friends quickly became successful and, in 1977, moved to a converted laundromat on Claremont Avenue and introduced live music to the restaurant. Since then, Akiba has built Yoshi's into one of the world's most respected jazz venues, hosting jazz legends from Betty Carter to Branford Marsalis. Akiba is also cofounder of 51Oakland, which brings music training into Oakland schools. Also shown are Sheila Escovedo (left; see page 100) and 51Oakland cofounder Jason Hofmann (right). (Courtesy 51oakland.org.)

CHAPTER SEVEN

Oakland Today

If only it could be parades and soul trains all the time . . .

—Rebecca Bird Grigsby, via Twitter

Modern history has brought change to Oakland. It is a geographically and culturally diverse city, but some longtime residents worry it may not stay that way. Today, some of the things that made Oakland what it is also threaten its character.

While the transcontinental railroad is no longer a major source of immigration, Oakland is minutes away from San Francisco by BART and is at the hub of several Bay Area freeways. Its proximity to San Francisco, lower real estate costs, and sunnier weather have led to an influx of younger, wealthier people making Oakland their home, driving housing costs up to the point where some longtime Oaklanders can no longer afford to live here.

Others are attracted by Oakland's burgeoning food scene, the liveliness of the art scene, and the diversity of it all. While the flow of energy and new tax dollars are welcome, Oakland's aging infrastructure and housing market have struggled to keep up. As in any big city, crime can be a problem. Balancing reforms, fighting crime across the geographically and economically diverse city, and building trust with the public have challenged the police department.

But despite all these things, most people who call Oakland home love it. Oaklanders can be passionate about their city like few others and express their pride in numerous ways. Whether they have deep Oakland roots or are relative newcomers, the Oaklanders profiled here help to make Oakland the great city that it is.

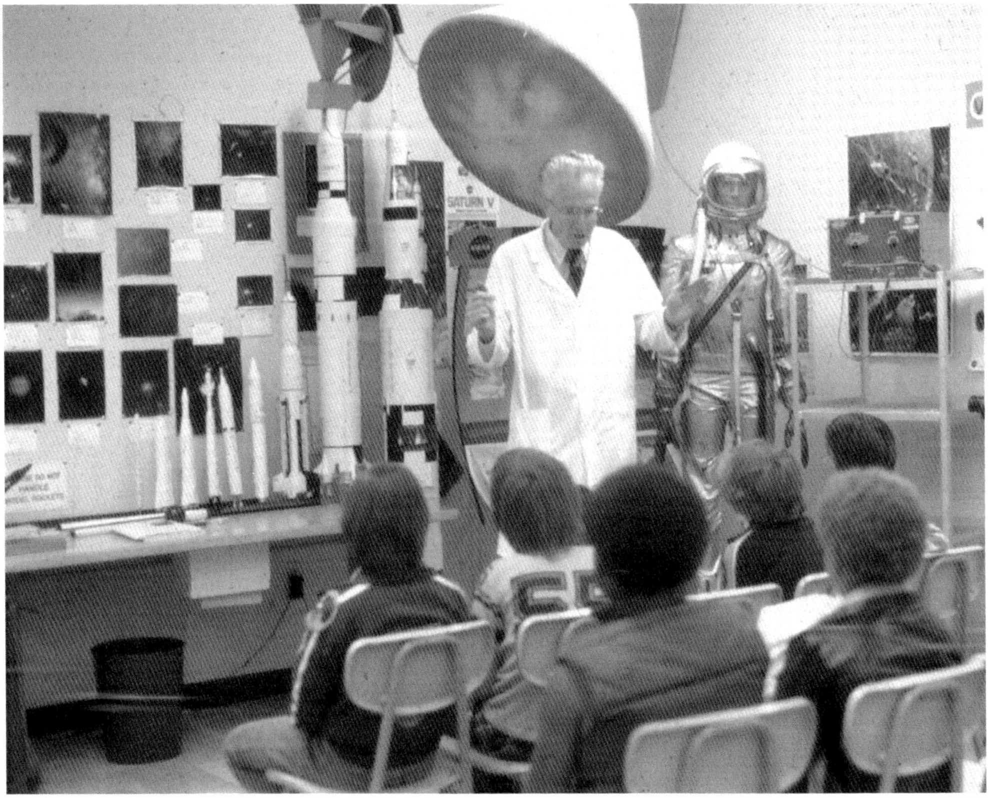

Beloved Astronomer and Teacher
Generations of Oakland schoolchildren remember trips to the old Chabot Observatory on Mountain Boulevard, where lab coat–clad astronomer Kingsley Wightman conducted unforgettable demonstrations, often involving at least one explosion. Wightman worked at the observatory for 46 years and served as its director from 1976 to 1986. (Courtesy Chabot Space & Science Center.)

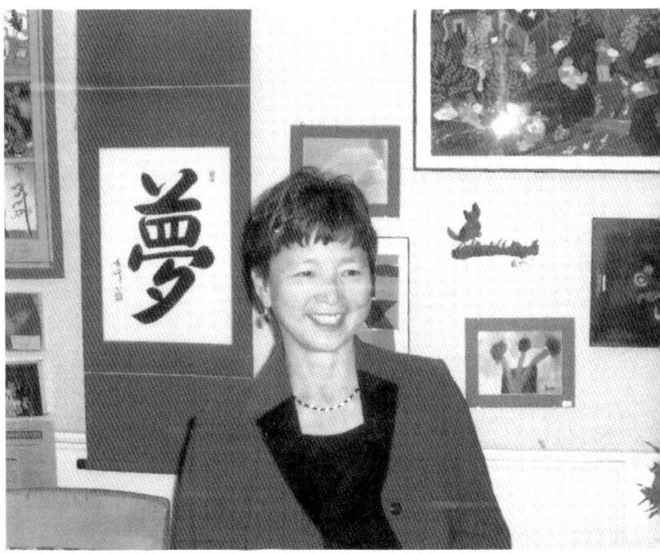

"Work Hard, Learn a Lot"
That was educator Caroline Chin Yee's message to students and teachers alike, later amended to include "Have fun." Born in Oakland's Chinatown in 1944 when it was still technically illegal for the state to hire Chinese employees, Yee moved up the ladder from teacher to principal, going full circle to become principal of Lincoln Elementary, where she had been a student herself years before. Yee died in 2013, and the new wing of Lincoln School was named in her honor. (Courtesy Dr. Gary Yee.)

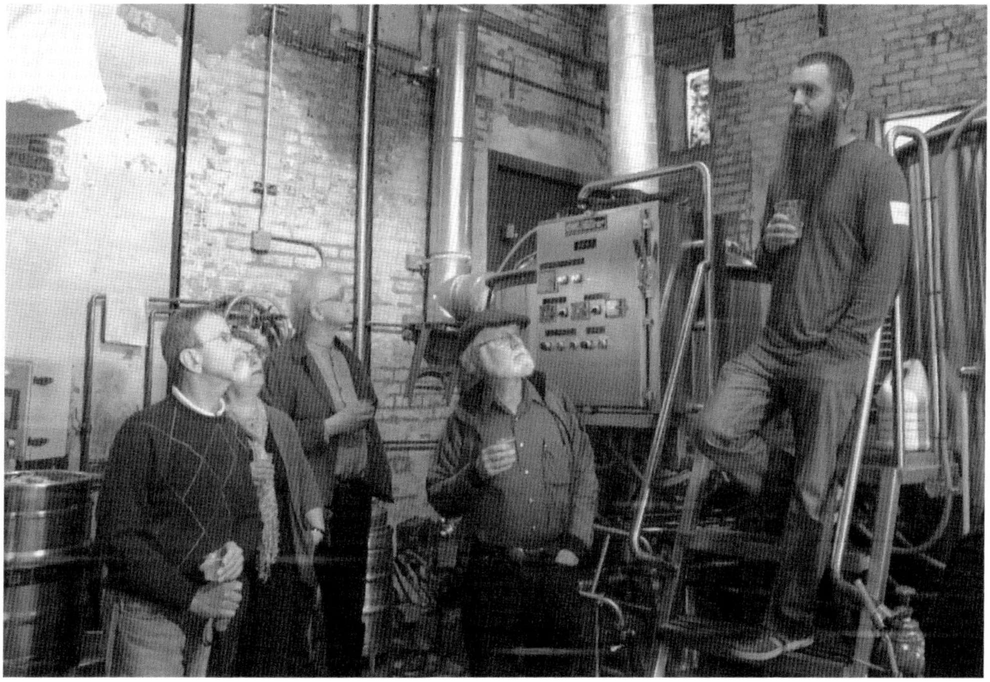

Bringing Beer Back to Oakland
Beer was once big in Oakland, with breweries like Brooklyn Brewing and Golden West Brewing producing almost as many barrels of beer each year as there were people in Oakland. Prohibition and World War II changed that, but now beer is once again becoming big, thanks in part to Adam Lamoreaux (on steps at right, speaking to members of the Oakland Heritage Alliance), founder of Linden Street Brewery. (Author's collection.)

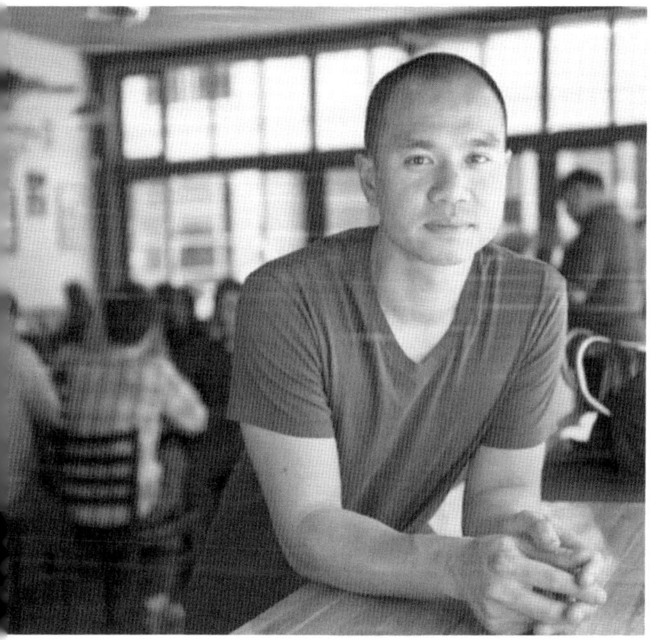

Michelin Star
Most chefs would be happy to have one successful restaurant in Oakland's burgeoning food scene, but Oakland Technical High School graduate James Syhabout has three, including the Michelin-starred Commis. Syhabout has worked in famous kitchens around the world, but when it came time to open his own restaurant, he came home to Oakland. In addition to Commis and Hawker Fare, Syhabout partnered with Lamoreaux to open the Dock at Linden Street. (Courtesy Nader Khouri.)

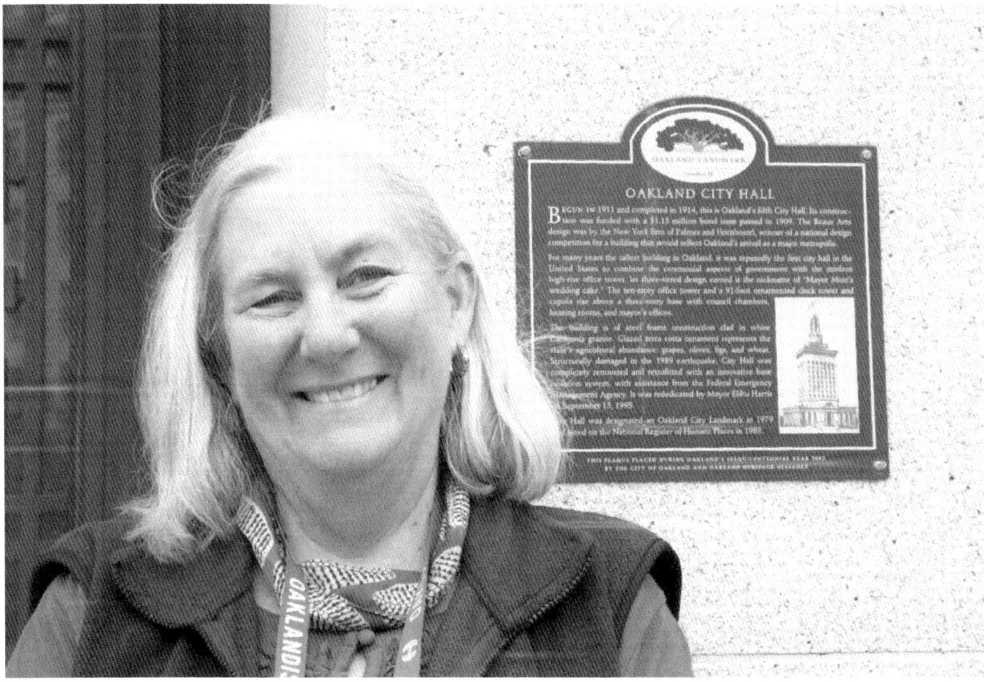

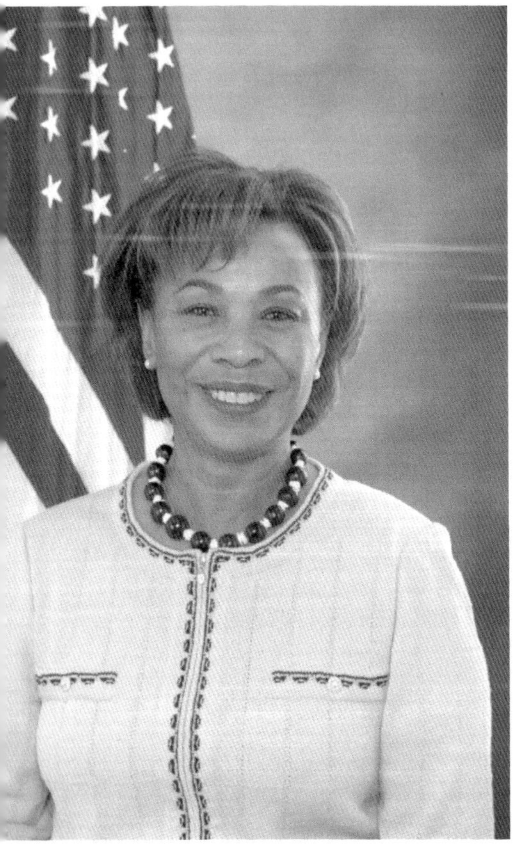

The Landmarks Lady

A resident of Oakland since 1978, historian, columnist, and author Annalee Allen is a dedicated Oakland booster. She has written two books about Oakland—*Oakland* (a postcard history) and *Selections from the Oakland Tribune Archives*—and created *Oakland Landmarks* with artist Heidi Wyckoff. Besides writing a weekly *Oakland Tribune* column about Oakland and its history, Allen is the director of the city of Oakland's downtown walking tours program. (Author's collection.)

"Barbara Lee Speaks for Me"

Barbara Lee has represented Oakland and the East Bay in the US House of Representatives since 1998. Lee was the only member of either house of Congress to vote against the authorization of use of force following the September 11, 2001, attacks, believing it gave the president overly broad powers. While Lee was attending Mills College, she volunteered with the Black Panther Party's community learning center and worked on Bobby Seale's mayoral campaign in 1973. (Courtesy US House of Representatives.)

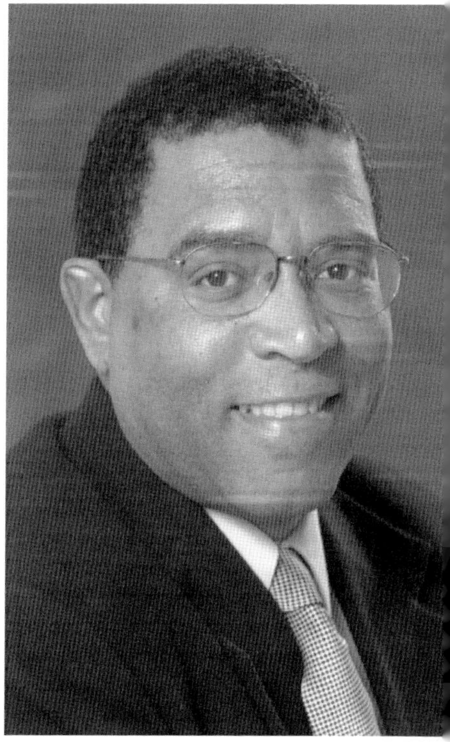

Investigative Journalist and Editor
Chauncey Bailey worked in television and print journalism, and was editor-in-chief of the *Oakland Post*. While working on a story about the possible criminal activity of Your Black Muslim Bakery, he was ambushed on Fourteenth Street and killed. Fellow journalists created the Chauncey Bailey Project, dedicated to continuing his work. Yusuf Bey IV, head of the bakery, and Devaughndre Broussard were later convicted of Bailey's murder. (Courtesy Chauncey Bailey Project.)

Faith's Story
Faith Fancher (on right, presenting an award to Betty Burrell, mother of MC Hammer; see page 98) was an inspirational and award-winning reporter for KTVU, beginning in 1983. When she was diagnosed with breast cancer in 1997, she turned her private battle into a public one to raise awareness about the disease. Over the next six years, she worked to inform people and to raise money for programs benefiting low-income women with breast cancer. Fancher lost her battle with cancer in 2003, but the Friends of Faith nonprofit continues her mission. (Courtesy Oakland Post Photograph Collection, MS 169, African American Museum & Library at Oakland.)

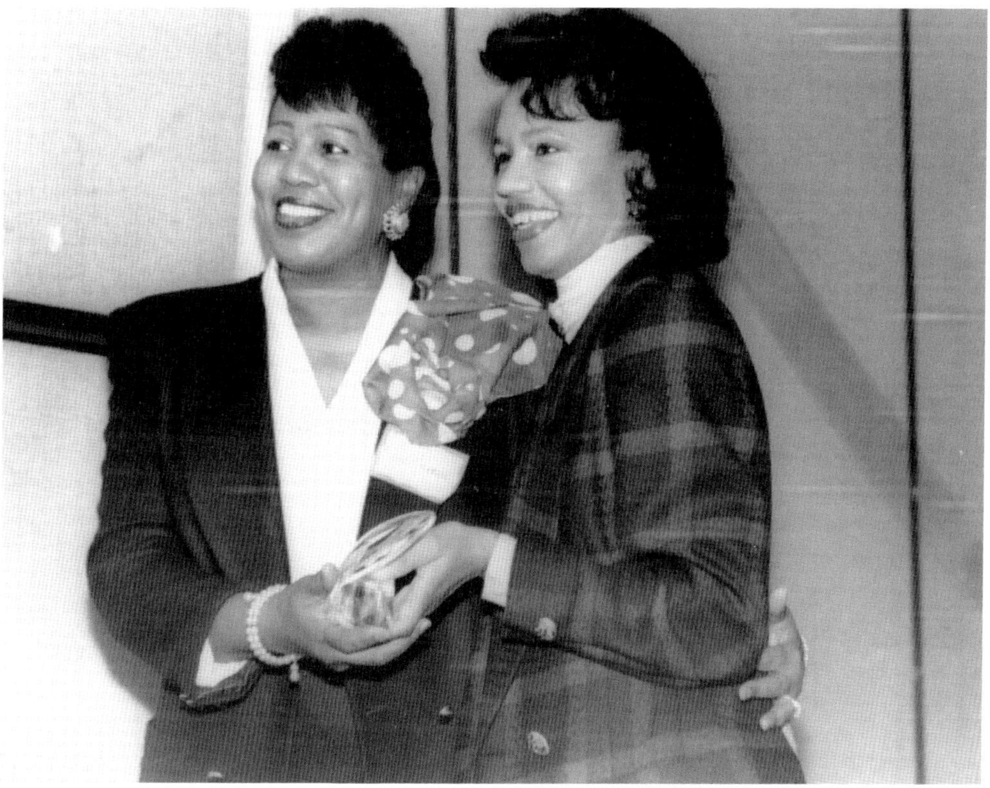

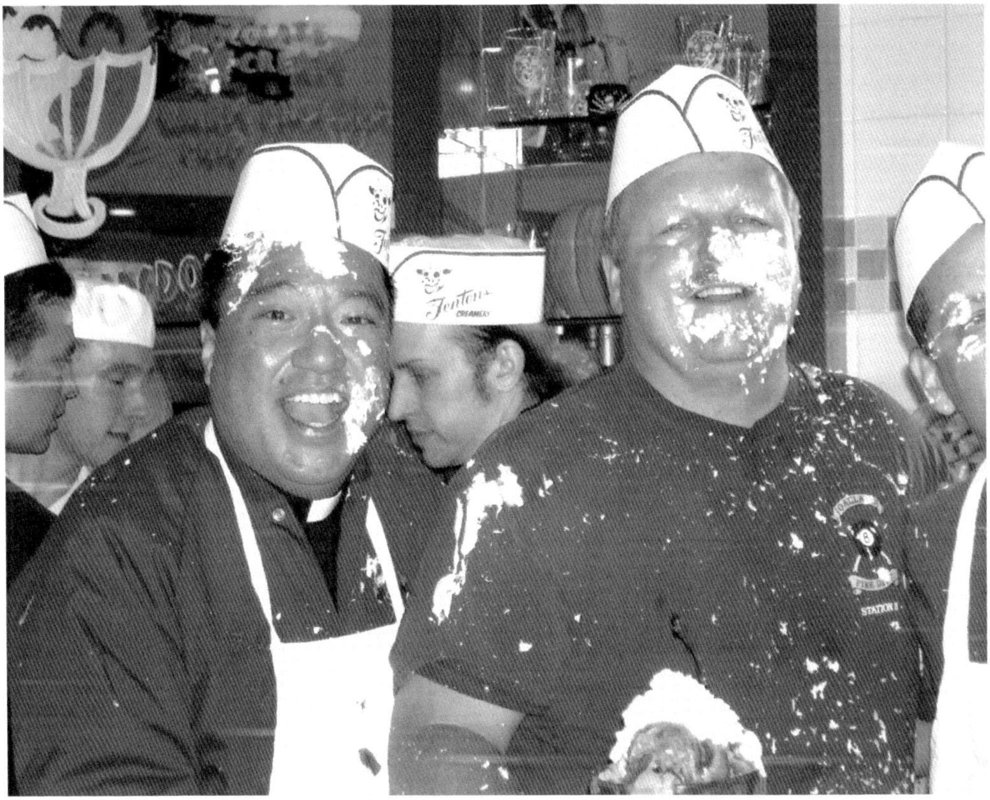

Man of Many Hats

For a priest, Fr. Jayson Landeza (on left, with Oakland firefighter Kevin Reed at a fundraiser at Fenton's) wears a lot of hats, and not just those associated with the Catholic Church. From 1999 to 2009, Landeza was the pastor at Saint Columba Church in the Golden Gate neighborhood. He also served for more than a decade as the chaplain for the Oakland Police Department and Oakland Fire Department, where he had the sometimes sad and sometimes joyful duty of remembering officers who had died, as well as comforting the friends and family of the fallen. (Above, courtesy Oakland Firefighters Random Acts; right, author's collection.)

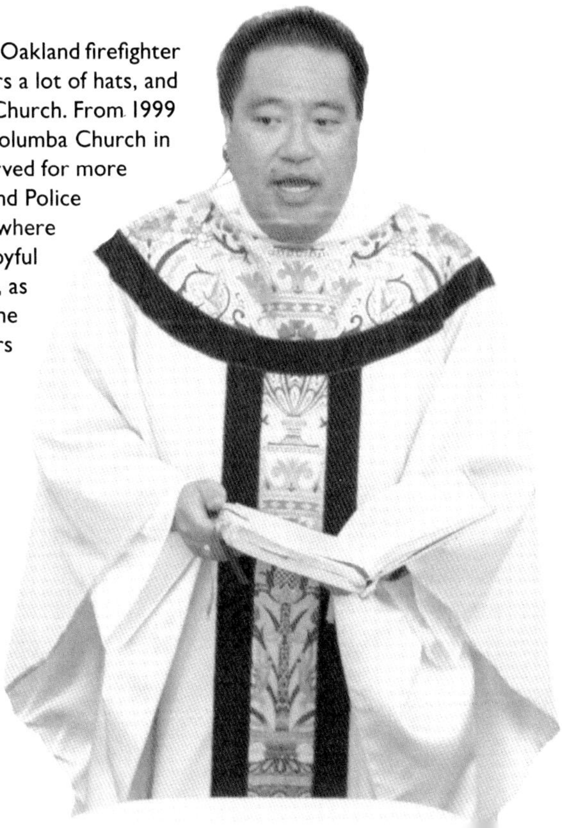

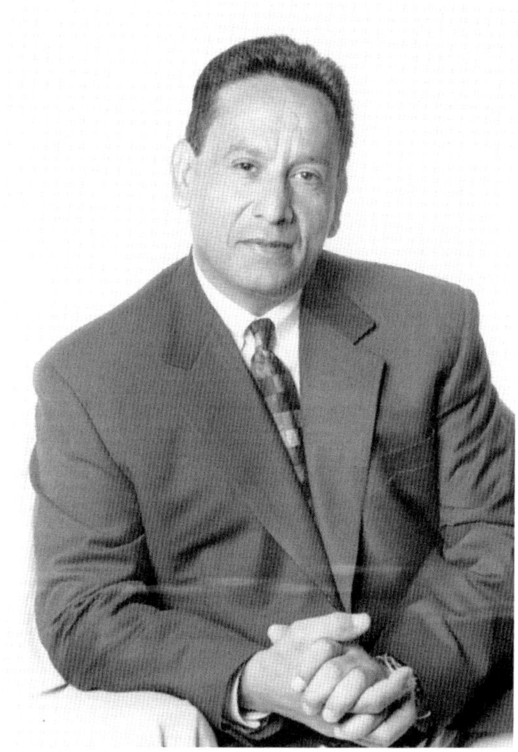

Labor Leader, Councilmember
Mexican-born Ignacio de la Fuente came to the United States in 1971, was elected a union representative in 1977, and became a citizen in 1979. In events that foreshadowed those on the national scene, detractors said he was unfit for office because he was not a citizen, but the facts proved otherwise. De la Fuente was first elected to city council in 1992 and served council district five for 20 years. He also ran for mayor in 2006 but came in second to Ron Dellums. (Courtesy Oakland Post Photograph Collection, MS 169, African American Museum & Library at Oakland.)

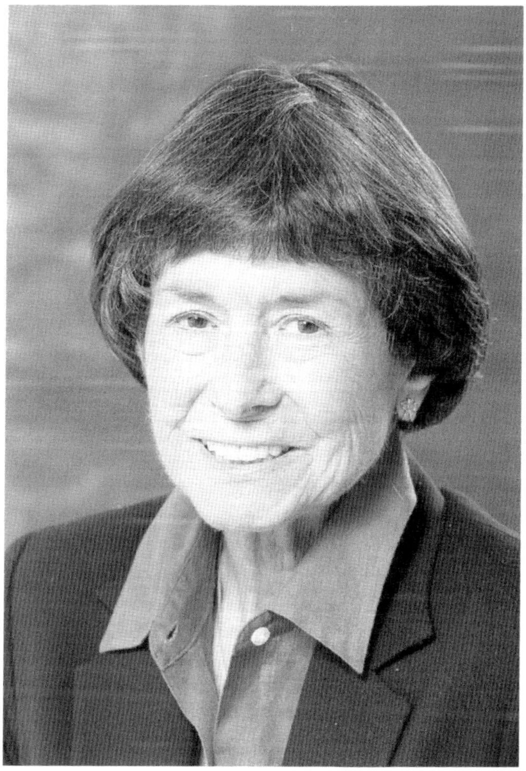

Epitome of a Journalist
Known as a city hall watchdog, Peggy Stinnett had a career of more than 50 years in journalism. Besides writing for the *Oakland Tribune* and local paper *The Montclarion*, Stinnett wrote for the *San Jose Mercury*, served as an editor for the *Oakland Tribune*, and even did television reporting for local stations KTVU and KQED. Stinnett came out of retirement to write a weekly column for the *Oakland Post*. (Courtesy *San Jose Mercury News*.)

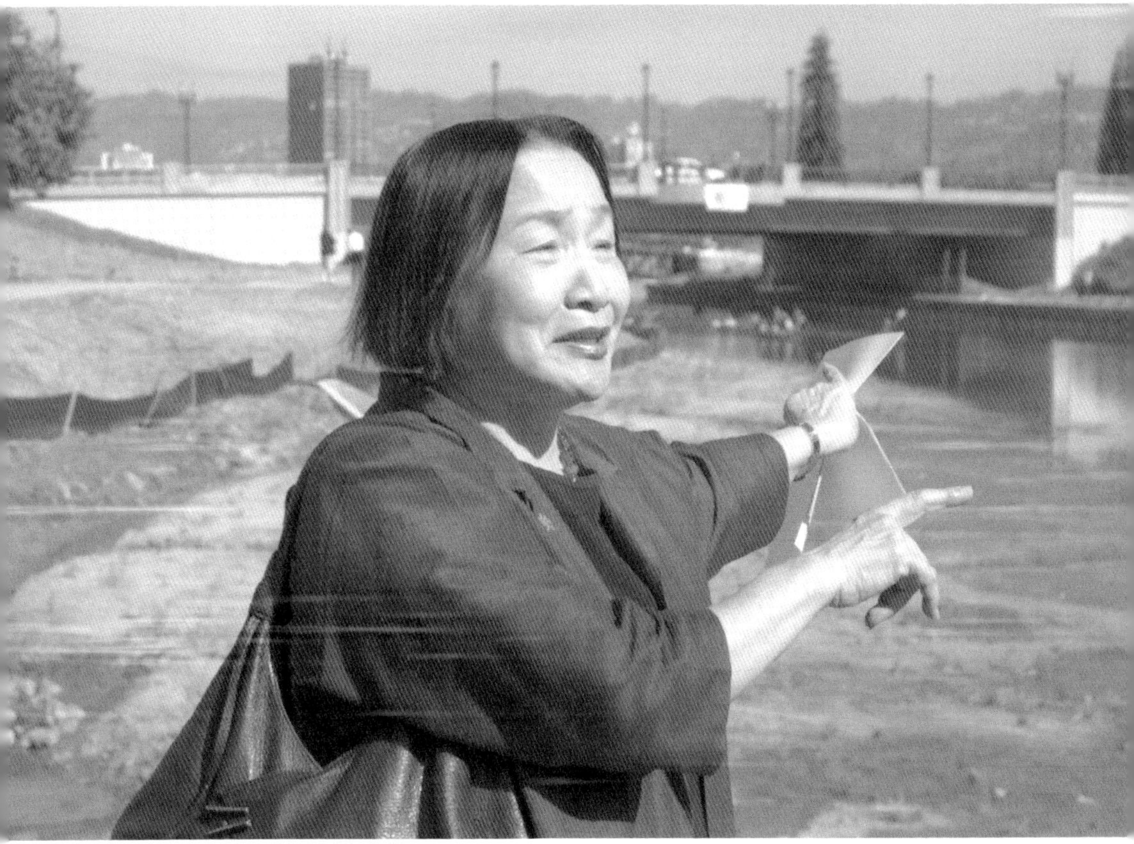

Trailblazing Mayor

Jean Quan's restaurateur father died when she was five, and she grew up poor and facing discrimination, but these circumstances helped teach her the value of hard work and connecting with people. Quan was a student activist at the University of California, Berkeley, where she met her husband, Dr. Floyd Huen. She was also an Oakland Unified School District board member and an Oakland city council member, but she is best known as Oakland's 49th mayor. In 2010, Quan became the first woman and the first Asian American to be elected mayor of Oakland, but not without some controversy. The 2010 election was the first where ranked choice voting was used. Quan trailed longtime politician Don Perata until the final round, when the remaining votes gave her the victory.

Quan's time as mayor involved controversy, too. The Oakland Police Department was undergoing reforms following the "Riders" scandal in 2000, so when the Occupy Oakland protests in 2011 were met with an overly strong response while Quan was in Washington, DC, some people felt she was too pro-police. At the same time, crime in Oakland was (and still is) a problem, and there was high turnover in police department leadership, so other people felt she did not support the police enough. Regardless, Quan was a hardworking mayor who helped bring investment to Oakland, and her commitment to the city set high expectations for future leaders. (Author's collection.)

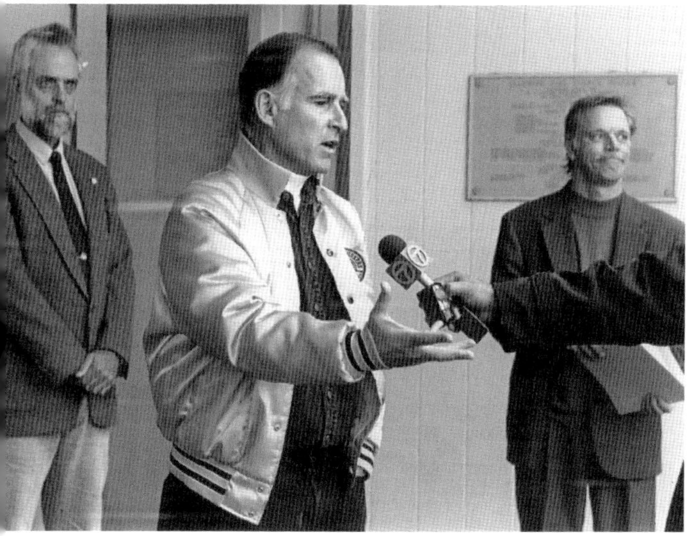

Two-Time Governor
Jerry Brown is best known as governor of California, but the Oakland resident was mayor of Oakland from 1999 until 2007 and is credited with revitalizing parts of Oakland by bringing in new residents. While Brown had dated some famous women in the past, including singer Linda Ronstadt, in 2005, he married Anne Gust, and they live in the Oakland hills with their dog, Sutter. (Courtesy Oakland History Room, Oakland Main Library.)

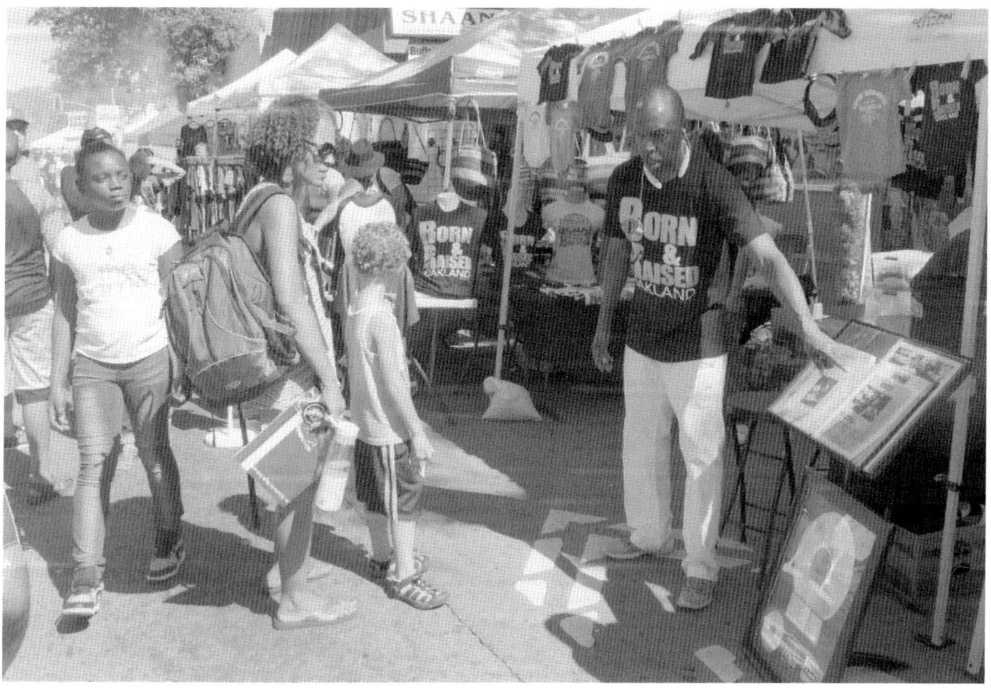

Da Mayor of Eastmont Mall
Jim Copes is a lifelong resident of Oakland and has seen a lot of its history. In the 1970s, Copes taught tennis to people of all backgrounds and sponsored the Jim Copes Tennis Classic. Rapper Too $hort dedicated his platinum-selling album *Short Dog's in the House* to Copes. In the 1990s, Copes was forced to close his t-shirt stores because of repeated break-ins, but he still sells his unique brand of Oakland love at various festivals and farmers markets. (Author's collection.)

Advocate for Neighborhoods

Part of a progressive movement in the late 1970s, when the city council was changed from the citywide system to districts, Mary Moore (on left) was only the third woman selected to city council. Moore was an advocate of affordable and fair housing and was also instrumental in the fight to keep trucks off of I-580. She inspired many Oaklanders to engage with city government. (Courtesy Alison Moore.)

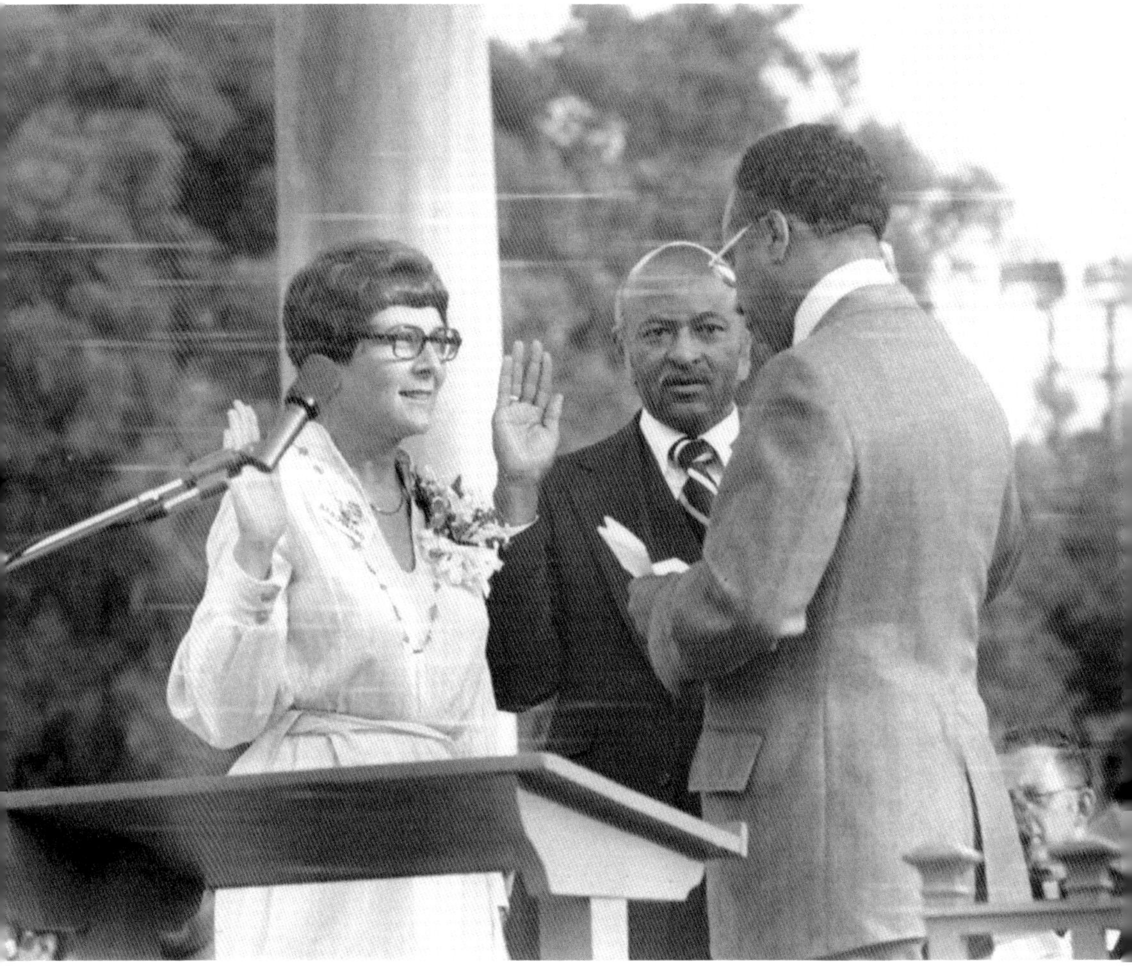

"Quiet Storm"

Carter Gilmore (center) was the first black Oaklander elected to city council. He was elected in 1977, the same year as Mary Moore. (Josh Rose was appointed to council in 1964.) Gilmore worked as a plant manager for Granny Goose snack foods and served as president of the local NAACP. He had a gentle way of talking but got things done. Gilmore is remembered for creating Oakland's anti-blight ordinance, and played a key role in organizing the citizen police review board. (Courtesy Alison Moore.)

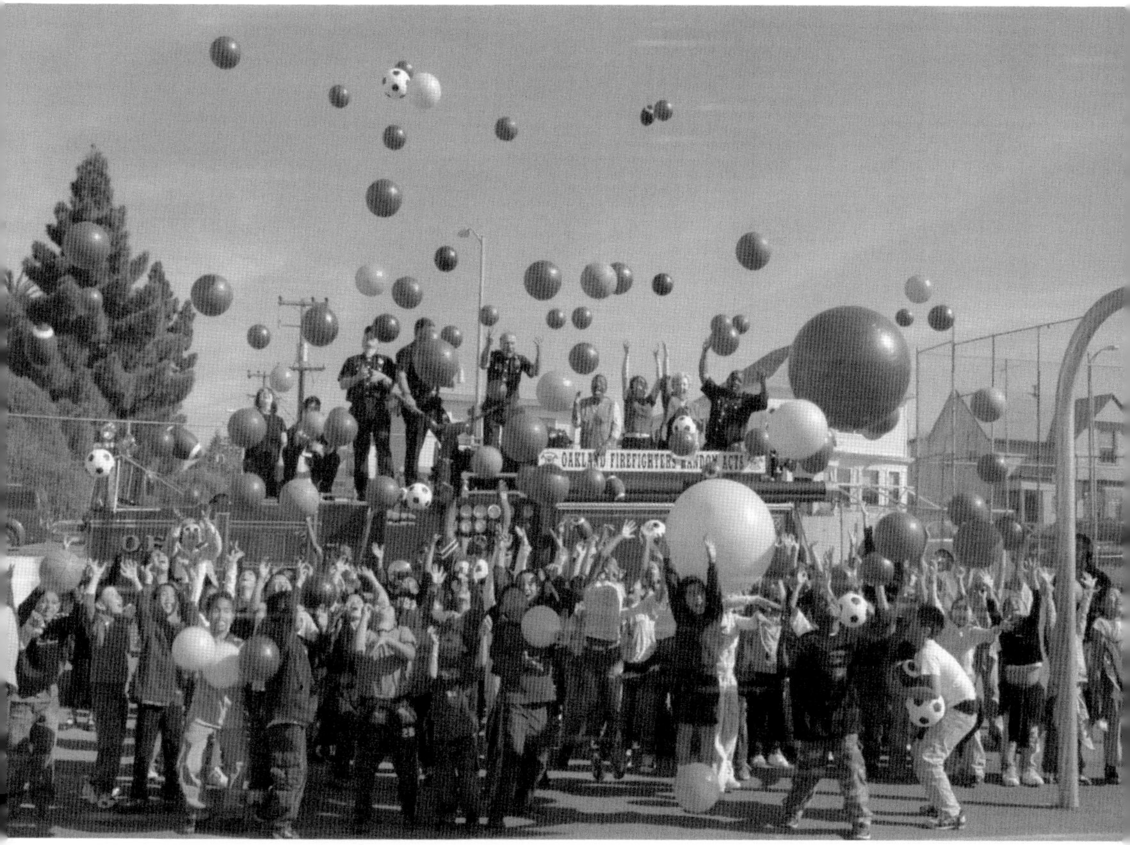

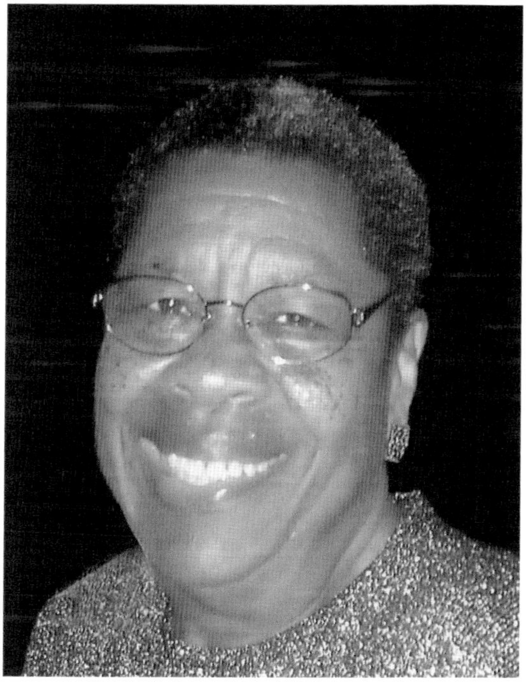

"It's Never Too Late to Do Good"
Cora "Mom" Green spent her life helping people and doing what needed to be done. Police, firefighters, teachers, and neighbors all knew they could call on her and "Pop" to help. Green received enough awards to cover a wall, but she did not do it for the recognition. "It comes back to me in so many ways. It comes in the faces of the children I help," said Green. (Above, author's collection; left, courtesy Oakland Firefighters Random Acts.)

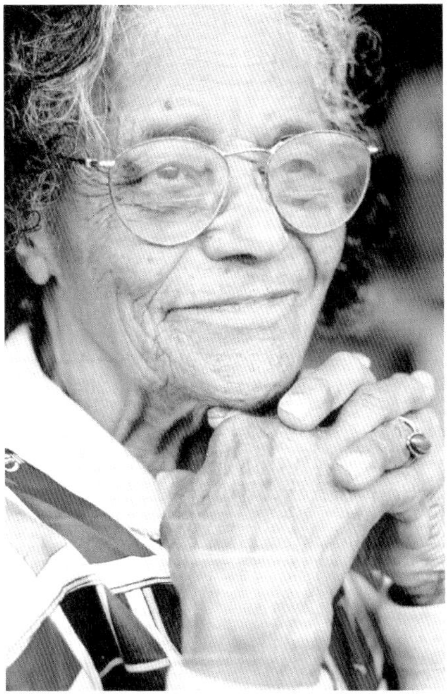

Melding Dedication and Faith

Most people are thinking about retirement when they head into their 60s, but "Mother" Mary Ann Wright was just getting started. In 1983, she started feeding the homeless in Jefferson Square Park once a week, supported only by her $236 Social Security check. Her efforts eventually grew into the Mother Mary Ann Wright Foundation, which feeds more than 450 people a day. When Wright died in 2009, her memorial service was so large that it was held at the Oakland Convention Center. (Courtesy *San Jose Mercury News*.)

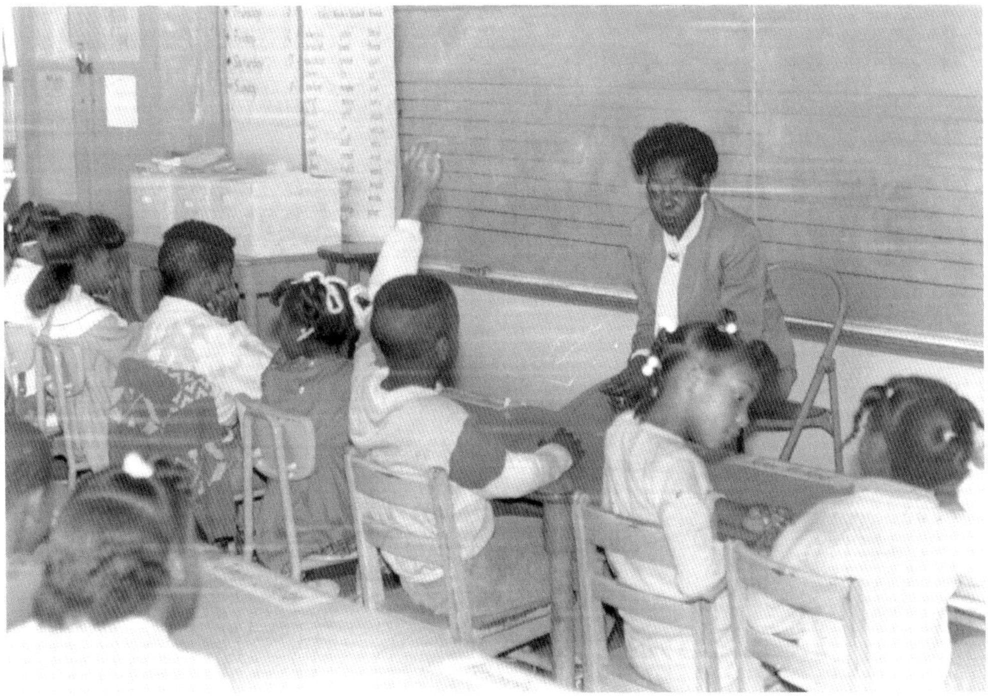

An Extraordinary Promise

In 1987, Oral Lee Brown made an extraordinary promise to the entire first grade glass at Brookfield Elementary School. If they stayed in school and graduated from high school, she would pay for them to go to college. The first phase saw 19 of the 23 original students go on to college. (Courtesy Oakland Post Photograph Collection, MS 169, African American Museum & Library at Oakland.)

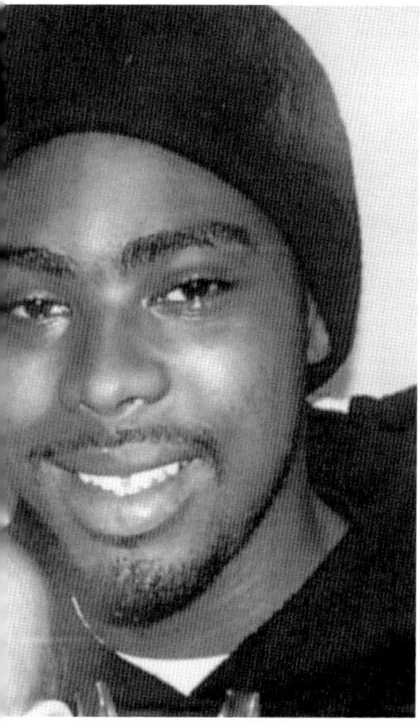

Murdered at Fruitvale Station

Oscar Grant did not live in Oakland, but he worked and died there. On his way home from New Year's celebrations in 2009, Grant and others were pulled off a BART train at the Fruitvale station, accused of fighting. Grant was unarmed and lying facedown on the platform when BART police officer Johannes Mehserle shot him in the back. Mehserle said Grant was resisting arrest, and he meant to use his Taser and accidentally pulled his gun instead. Numerous people witnessed the shooting and several caught it on cell phone videos.

After Mehserle resigned instead of attending an investigative interview, protests started in Oakland. In the evening, some of the protestors became violent and vandalized police cars, offices, and businesses. News stations broadcast images worldwide, and the circling helicopters and large police presence left the city on edge. A jury eventually found Mehserle guilty of involuntary manslaughter, but many people felt it should have been a more serious charge. The award-winning movie *Fruitvale Station* chronicled the last 24 hours of Grant's life. (Left, courtesy Johnson family; below, author's collection.)

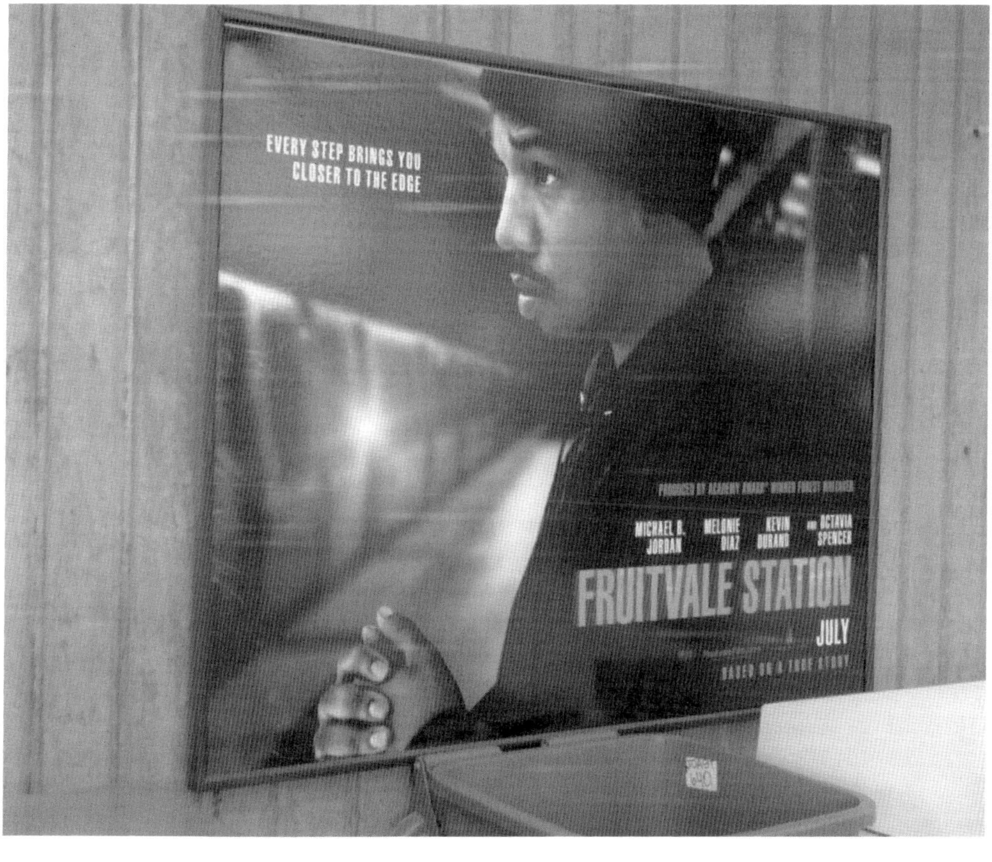

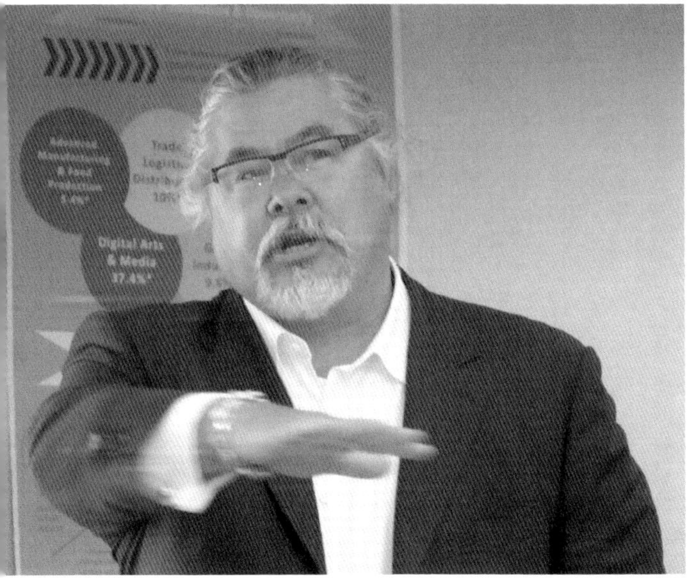

Shotgun Phil

A major developer in Oakland whose projects have included restoring the Fox Theatre and the Rotunda Building, Phil Tagami made national headlines during Occupy Oakland in 2011. "Black Bloc" protesters were smashing windows and starting fires, and Tagami faced them, armed with a shotgun from inside the Rotunda Building. Tagami is currently working on developing the former Oakland Army Base for new uses. (Author's collection.)

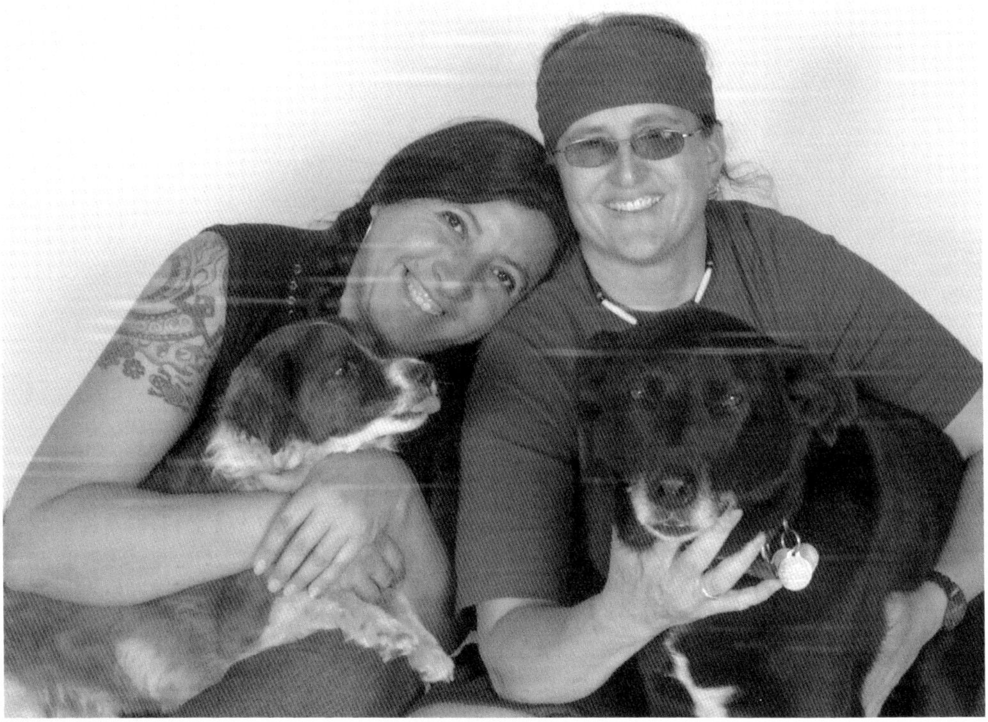

Anchors in the Dimond

Local small business owners Ruth Villasenor (left) and Diane Pfile (right) have planted deep roots. After careers at the Native American Health Center and in construction, they opened a natural pet food store, Paws and Claws, which has been an anchor in the Dimond district for more than a decade. They were married at Oakland City Hall in 2008 by mayor Ron Dellums, with US Representative Barbara Lee and city council member Jean Quan amongst the witnesses. (Photograph by Helga Sigvaldadóttir, courtesy Ruth Villasenor.)

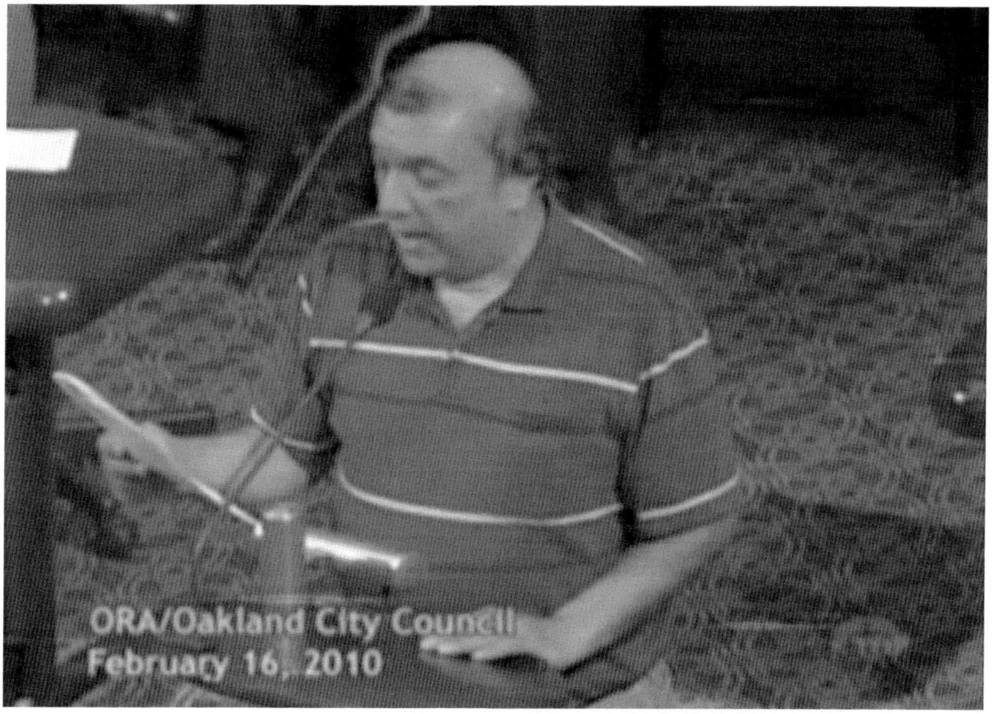

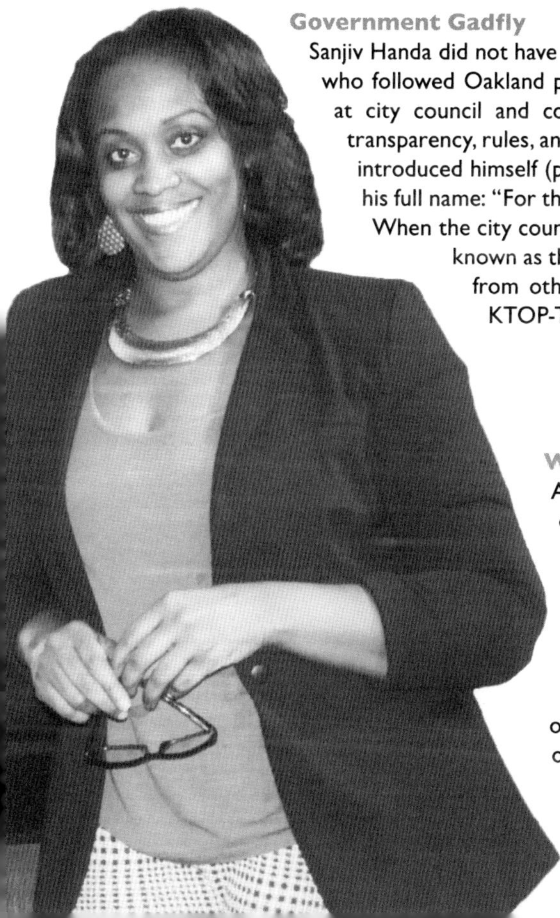

Government Gadfly

Sanjiv Handa did not have many friends in local government, but everyone who followed Oakland politics knew who he was. Handa was a fixture at city council and committee meetings, haranguing officials about transparency, rules, and ethics. Although everyone knew him, he always introduced himself (per the rules) with what some people joked was his full name: "For the record, Sanjiv Handa, East Bay News Service." When the city council limited the time for each speaker (informally known as the "Sanjiv Rule"), Handa collected speaker cards from others to maximize his speaking time. (Courtesy KTOP-TV10.)

Working for Open Government

At contentious city council meetings, fans of city clerk LaTonda Simmons can count on her to keep an even keel, and although she is not the official parliamentarian, council members often defer to her on the rules. Since being appointed in 2004, Simmons has worked to modernize the office of city clerk, making more information available electronically and thereby making the overall process of government in Oakland more open. (Author's collection.)

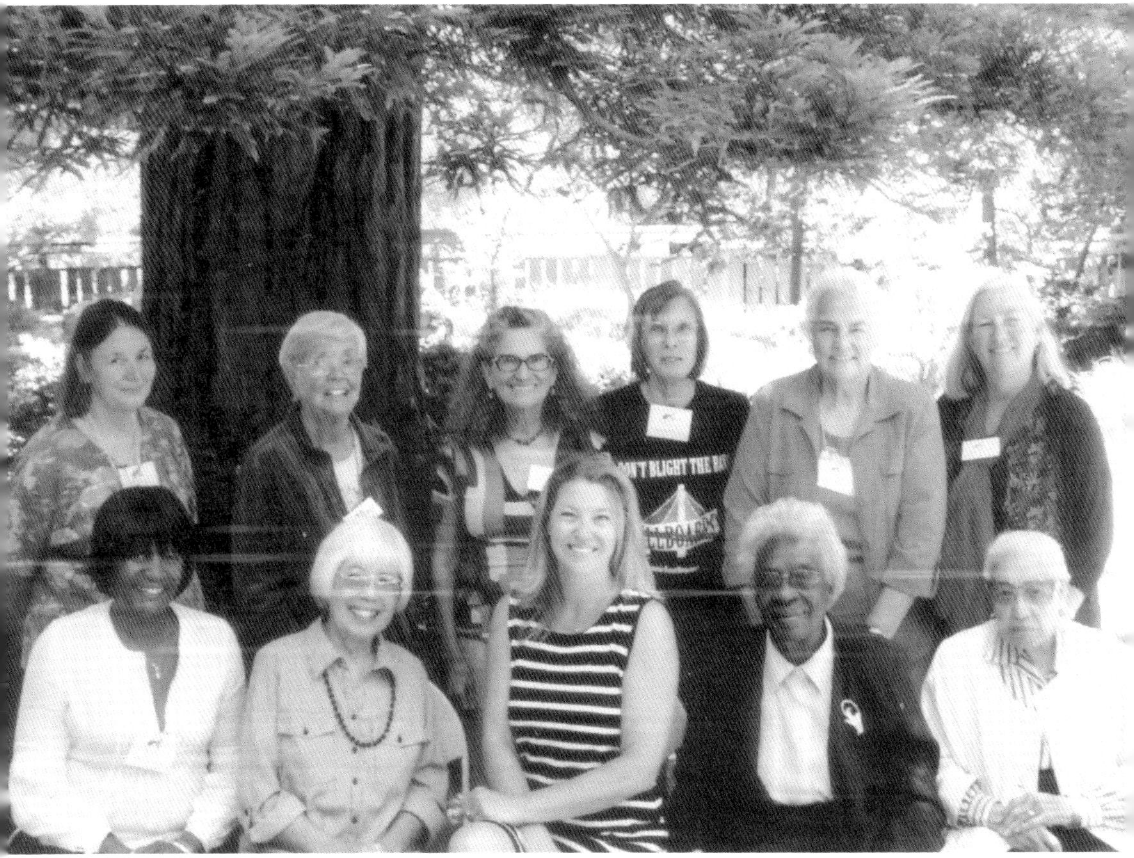

Mother of the Year

In a tradition that goes back to 1954, each year, a woman in Oakland is honored for her work to improve the quality of life for the people of Oakland. From left to right are (first row) Diane Burr (1994), Rose Luey (1972), Lisa Klein (2014), Mattie Jones (1997), and Ellen Wyrick-Parkinson (2008) (second row) Naomi Schiff (2005), Barbara Schaaf (1996), Lisa Lemus (2012), Caroline Kim (2002), Anne Woodell (2009) and Annalee Allen (2013).

Anne Woodell was the second woman on the Oakland Parks and Recreation Committee and founder of Friends of the Oakland Parks and Recreation in 1981. She also served on the boards of Children's Fairyland, the Dunsmuir Historic Estate, and the Alameda County Historical Society.

Naomi Schiff helped found the Oakland Heritage Alliance in 1980 to preserve Oakland's historic, architectural, and cultural resources. She has served as board president and on the board of directors numerous times and worked tirelessly to help preserve Oakland's history. (Courtesy Annalee Allen.)

A Passion for History

Dennis Evanosky has a passion for local history and teaching others about it. When he is not busy as editor of the *Alameda Sun*, Evanosky can usually be found leading history tours for the city of Oakland's walking tours program, the Oakland Heritage Alliance, Oakland Urban Paths, or Mountain View Cemetery. He is also the author of numerous local history books and was instrumental in the restoration of the cemetery's Civil War plot. (Author's collection.)

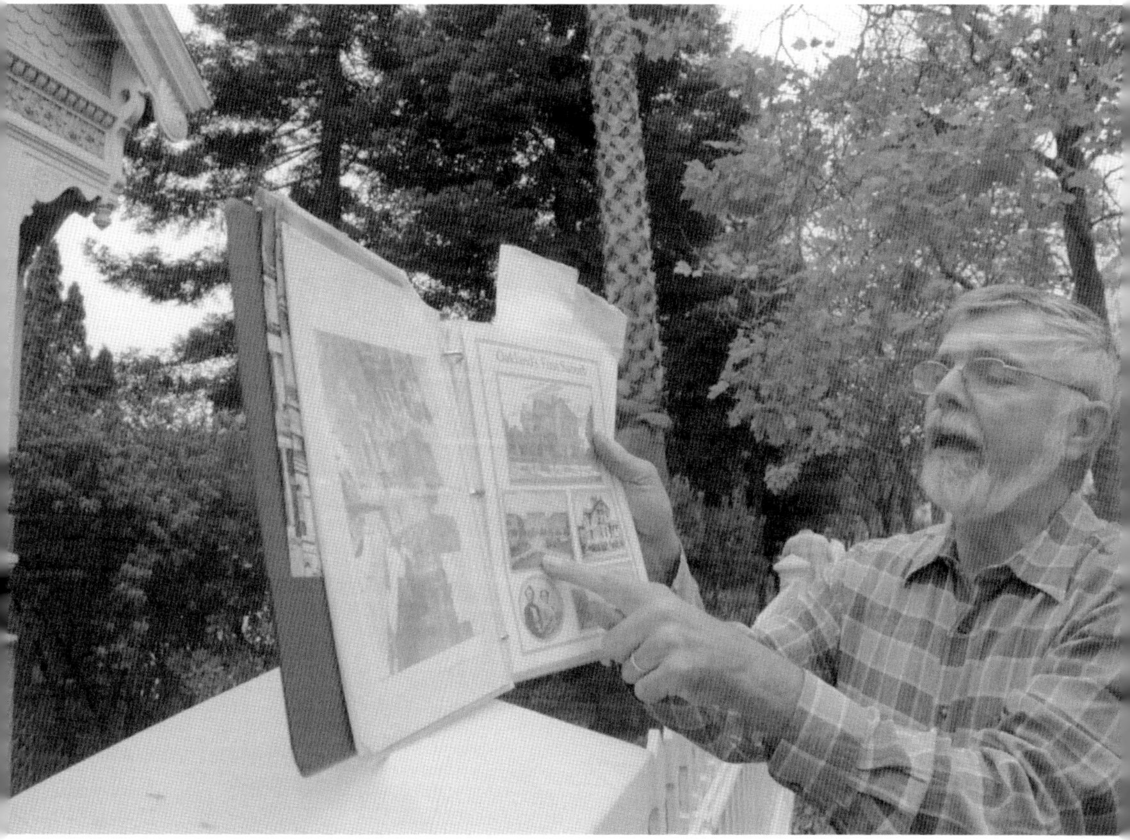

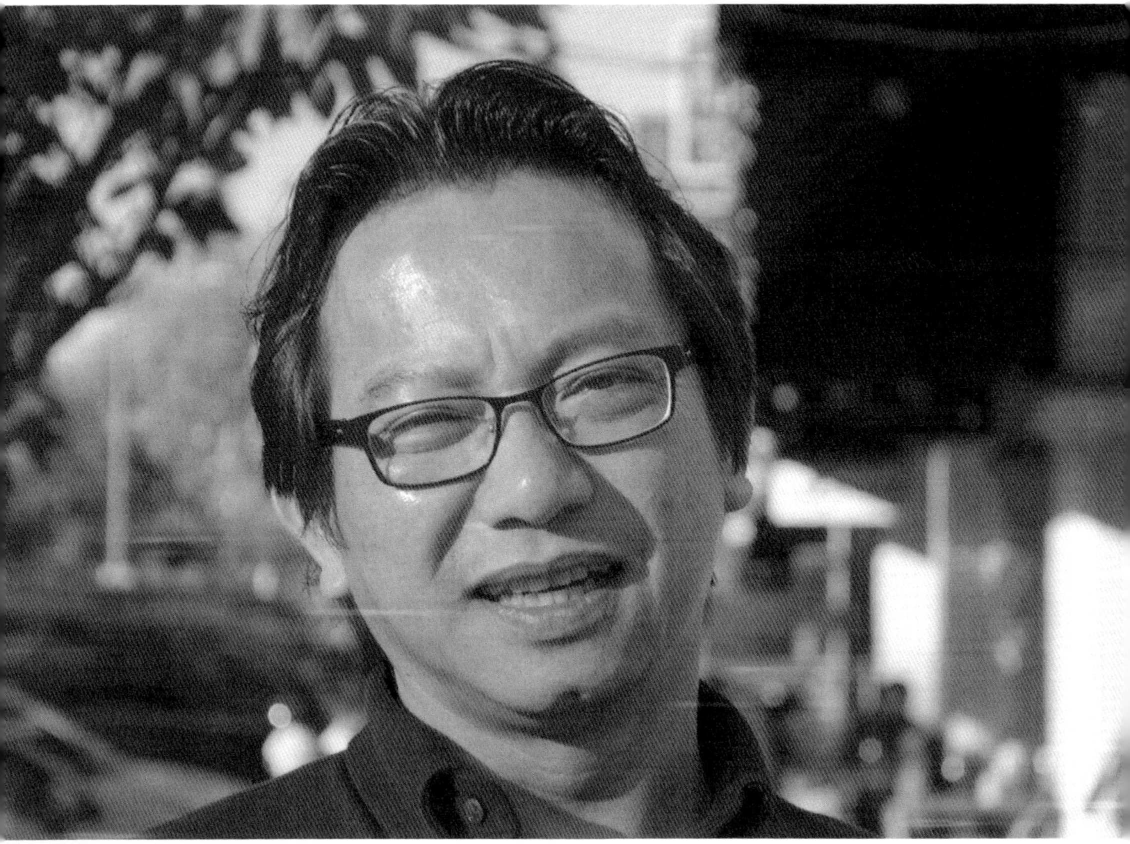

Immigrant to Advocate
Sonny Lê is a former Vietnamese refugee who arrived in Oakland without parents and unable to speak much English. He found acceptance within a pan-ethnic circle of former 1960s and 1970s student activists. Inspired by the Third World Student Strikes at Merritt College and San Francisco State University, Lê eventually found his voice in the arts community. A turning point in Lê's world view came while he was serving as a volunteer press aide during Nelson Mandela's speech in Oakland in 1990.

Lê managed the US Census Bureau's multilingual public relations campaign and served as its regional spokesperson, covering five Western Pacific states during the 2000 and 2010 censuses. Lê was also director of the former Ohana Cultural Center in Temescal, communications and development director for the Oakland Asian Cultural Center in Chinatown, and on the board for the Museum of Children's Art (MOCHA) and Pro Arts. He teaches courses on nonprofit management at San Francisco State University, works as a Vietnamese language medical interpreter, and is looking forward to the 2020 census. (Author's collection.)

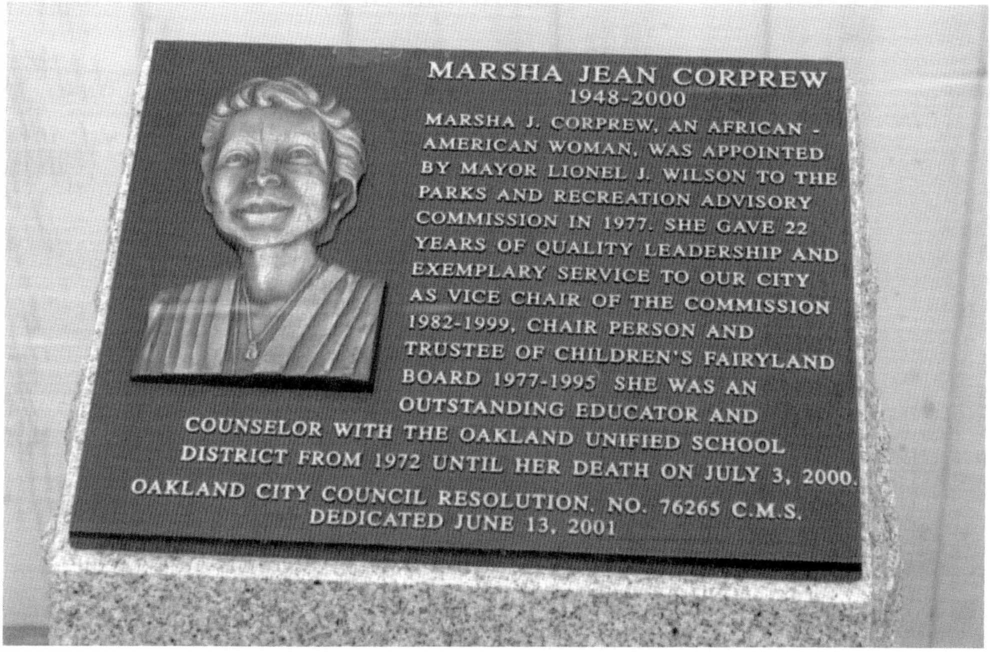

She Loved Parks and Children
Appointed by Mayor Lionel Wilson in 1977, Marsha Jean Corprew served on the Parks and Recreation Advisory Commission from 1977 until 1999 and was chair of the Children's Fairyland Board from 1977 until 1995. She was a teacher and counselor with the Oakland Unified School District from 1972 until her death in 2000. In 2001, the city council voted unanimously to rename the Lakeside Park Garden Center in her honor. (Author's collection.)

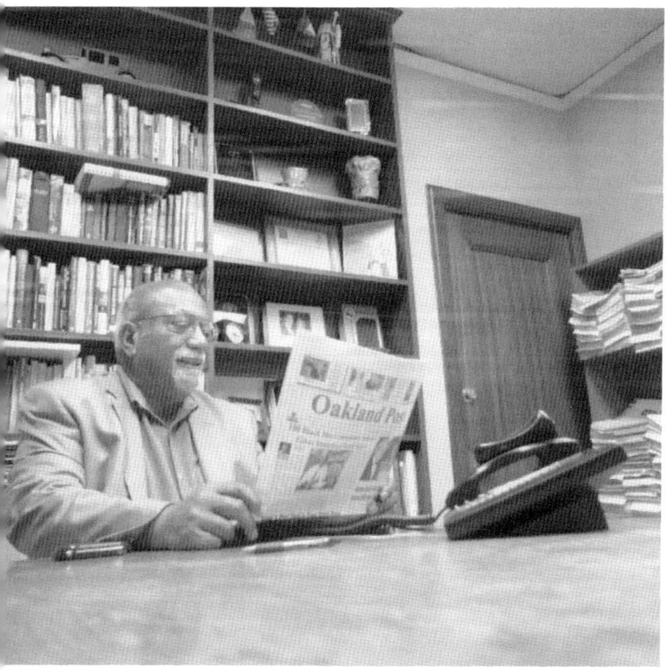

Publisher and Civil Rights Advocate
Named for poet, novelist, and playwright Paul Laurence Dunbar, Paul Cobb was destined to have writing in his future. His journey has taken him from shining the shoes of Pullman porters in front of his parents' West Oakland grocery to selling newspapers to interviewing and marching with Martin Luther King Jr. In 2004, Cobb purchased the *Oakland Post* from Thomas Berkley's widow (see page 67) and hired Chauncey Bailey (see page 109). (Courtesy Pendarvis Henshaw.)

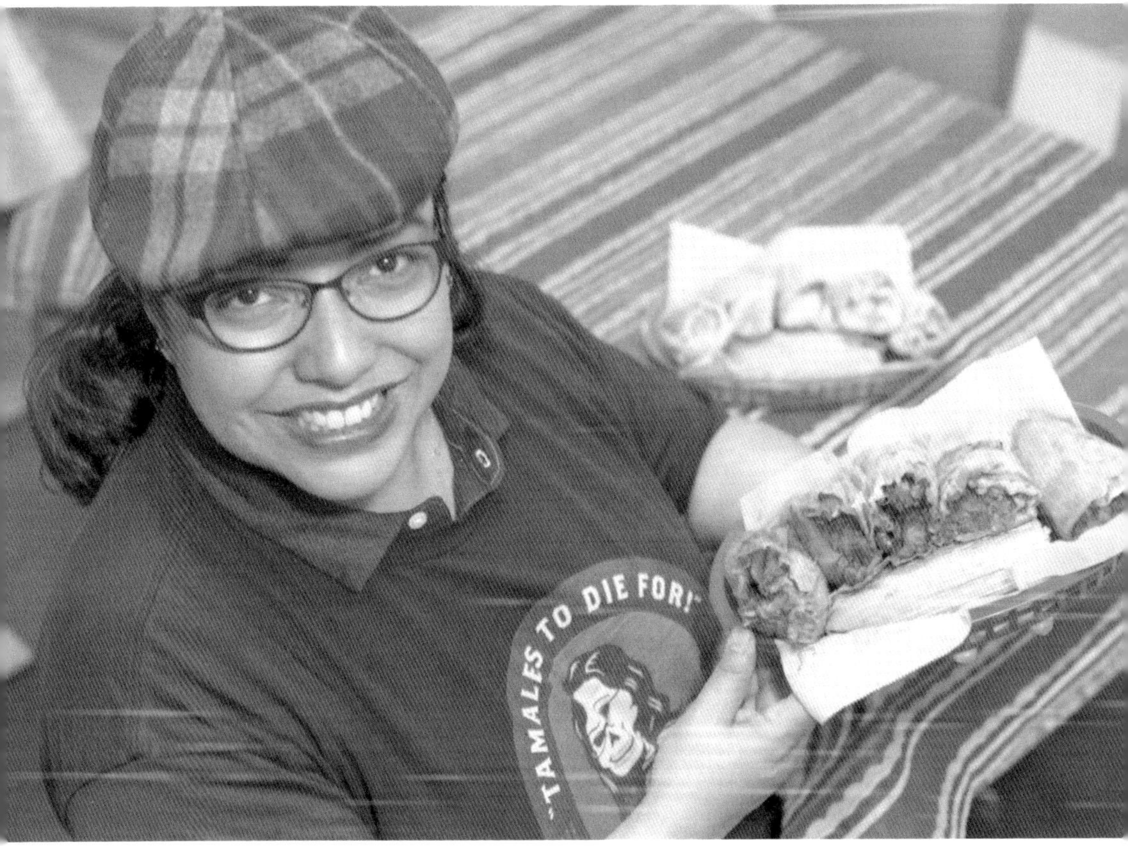

Third Generation Small Business Owner

Tina "Tamale" Ramos is a third generation Oaklander and small business owner who was born in Oakland and has lived there her whole life. She ran La Borinqueña Mexi-catessen in Old Oakland. Ramos's grandmother Rosa Lopez started La Borinqueña Mexi-catessen in 1944, borrowing $100 from each of her friends. Lopez was Mexican American, but the name La Borinqueña reflects her husband's Puerto Rican background. It translates to "Puerto Rican woman" and is also the name of the Puerto Rican national anthem. Lopez's daughter Natividad (Ramos's mother) started working at the shop when she was 12.

The family first opened the shop and grocery at Fifth and Brush Streets but was forced to move twice because of freeway construction. The land was taken by eminent domain, and thousands of residents had their homes and businesses uprooted, each time dividing and scattering the Latino community. In the late 1950s, the store was moved from Fifth and Brush Streets to Seventh and Castro Streets because of the construction of the Nimitz Freeway. In the late 1970s, the store was moved to 582 Seventh Street because of the construction of Interstate 980. (Courtesy Paula Wirth.)

BIBLIOGRAPHY

Allen, Annalee. *Selections from the Oakland Tribune Archives*. Charleston, SC: Arcadia Publishing, 2006.

Bagwell, Beth. *Oakland: The Story of a City* (second edition). Oakland, CA: Oakland Heritage Alliance, 2012.

Brekke-Miesner, Paul. *Home Field Advantage: Oakland: The City that Changed the Face of Sports*. Oakland, CA: Paul Brekke-Miesner, 2013.

Evanosky, Dennis. *Mountain View Cemetery*. Redondo Beach, CA: Stellar Media Group, 2007.

Hildebrand, George H. *Borax Pioneer: Francis Marion Smith*. Berkeley, CA: Howell-North Books, 1982.

Metz, Randal. *Storybook Strings: 50 Years of Puppetry at Children's Fairyland's Storybook Puppet Theater*. Oakland, CA: Rappid Rabbit Publishing, 2003.

Norman, Jeff. *Temescal Legacies: Narratives of Change from a North Oakland Neighborhood*. Oakland, CA: Shared Ground, 2006.

Oakland Wiki. www.oaklandwiki.org.

Reed, Ishmael. *Blues City: A Walk in Oakland*. New York, NY: Crown Journeys, 2003.

Self, Robert O. *American Babylon: Race and the Struggle for Postwar Oakland*. Princeton, NJ: Princeton University Press, 2005.

Thompson, Jerry, and Duane Deterville. *Black Artists in Oakland*. Charleston, SC: Arcadia Publishing, 2007.

Tramble, Thomas and Wilma. *The Pullman Porters and West Oakland*. Charleston, SC: Arcadia Publishing, 2007.

Wong, William Gee. *Oakland's Chinatown*. Charleston, SC: Arcadia Publishing, 2004.

INDEX

Adams, Edson, 11
Akiba, Yoshie, 104
Alden, Solomon, 30
Allen, Annalee, 108
Anderson, Harry S., 42
Aoki, Richard, 59
Bagwell, Beth, 63
Bailey, Chauncey, 109
Barndollar, Gladys, 41
Beasley, Bruce, 92
Beasley, Delilah, 38
Beckford, Ruth, 102
Bercovich, Sam, 77
Bergeron, Vic, 68
Berkley, Thomas, 67
Bey, Yusuf IV, 109
Blake, Millicent Kittredge, 26
Brown, Jerry, 113
Brown, Oral Lee, 116
Brubeck, Dave, 88
Buckel, Chloe, 18
Budge, Don, 75
Burckhalter, Charles, 16
Burke, Glenn, 79
Carlos, Guadalupe, 89
Carpentier, Horace, 11
Chabot, Anthony, 17
Chapman, Melvin, 26
Chase, Moses, 13
Chin, Carolyn, 106
Cobb, Paul, 123
Conners, Mollie, 48
Coolbrith, Ina, 84
Copes, Jim, 113
Corprew, Marsha Jean, 123
Cottrell, Frederick, 41
Courtney, Del, 88
Covel, Paul, 71
Dargie, William E., 31
Davie, John, 45
Davis, Al, 76
Davis, Belva 55
de Fremery, James and Virginie, 16
de la Fuente, Ignacio, 111
Dellums, C.L., 36
Dibble, Rod, 103
Dickey, C.W., 85
Dimond, Hugh, 22
Doty, Ernest, 93
Douglas, Emory, 60
Duncan, Isadora, 85
Durant, Henry, 13
Eagar, Thomas, 14
Escovedo, Juan and Pete, 100
Escovedo, Sheila, 100, 104
Evanosky, Dennis, 121
Everett, Dorothy Turner, 61
F.A.B., Mistah, 98
Fancher, Faith, 109
Feng, Ru, 36
Finley, Charlie O., 81
Flood, Curt, 77
Flood, Elizabeth, 18
Fong, Get Moo, 39
Foster, Marcus, 50
Frank, Rachel Ray, 28
Galvez, Daniel, 92
Gilbreth, Lillian Evelyn Moller, 47
Gilmore, Carter, 114
Gordon, Joyce, 96
Grant, Oscar, 117
Green, Cora, 115
Greenhood, Jacob, 74
Hamilton, Laurentine, 24
Hammer, MC, 98
Handa, Sanjiv, 119
Hays, Jack Coffee, 22
Henderson, Rickey, 80
Hoff, Sid, 90
Holdsworth, Anthony, 95
Hong Kingston, Maxine, 97
Huggins, Ericka, 60
Irish, John P., 23
Jackson, Ida Louise, 50
Jayne, Hannah, 12
Jenkins, Slim, 90

Johnson, Chuck, 63
Kaiser, Henry J., 42
King, Bill, 78
Kirkham, Kate, 24
Klinkner, Charles, 19
Knowland, William, 70
Korematsu, Fred, 51
Lamoreaux, Adam, 107
Landeza, Jayson 110
Laney, Joseph, 46
Latham, Henrietta, 21
Lawrence, Harold, 87
Lê, Sonny, 122
Lee, Barbara, 108
Lee, Janet Chan, 52
Lee, Joseph, 52, 82
Lemmon, Sara Plummer, 28
Levingston, Tobie Gene, 68
Lew, Hing, 46
Lewis, Tarika, 60
Liu, Hung, 95
London, Jack, 34
Luelling, Henderson, 12
Lutkey, William, 49
Lynch, Marshawn, 80
Mabry, Esther, 54
Mahlmann, Lewis, 91
Martinez, Xavier Timoteo Orozco, 101
Maynard, Robert, 66
McChesney, Joseph, 23
McCullum, Donald, 56
Merritt, Samuel, 29
Miller, Joaquin, 84
Mitchell, Felix, 58
Montoya, Malaquias, 89
Moon, Andrew, 11
Moore, Mary, 114
Moran, James, 74
Morcom, Fred, 40
Morgan, Julia, 86
Mott, Frank K., 40
Mott, William Penn, 72
Newton, Huey, 59
Ogawa, Frank, 57
Olney, Warren, 30
Oz, Frank, 91
Pardee, George, 19
Patten, Bebe, 54
Peralta, Antonio, 10
Petris, Nicholas, 65
Pittman, Tarea Hall, 72
Pleasant, Mary Ellen, 25
Pointer Sisters, 99
Quan, Jean, 112
Raimondi, Ernie, 79
Ramos, Tina, 124
Reed, Ishmael, 62
Remillard, Lillian, 47
Reyna, Hector, 62
Reynoso, Lena Verderano, 96
Robinson, Tom, 74
Rodriguez, Favianna, 94
Rumford, William Byron, 69
Schiff, Naomi, 120
Shoong, Joe, 44
Shorey, William, 32
Simmons, Calvin, 87
Simmons, LaTonda, 119
Smith, Francis Marion and Mary R., 33
Snow, Henry, 43
Stein, Gertrude, 20
Stinnett, Peggy, 111
Summers, Obediah, 27
Syhabout, James, 107
Tagami, Phil, 118
Towns, Royal, 49
Tubbs, Hiram 21
Turner, Morrie, 99
Van Haltren, George, 74
Villasenor, Ruth, 118
Wall, Fannie Franklin, 39
Warren, Earl, 56
Weed, Mabel, 37
Wightman, Kingsley, 106
Williams, Archie, 78
Williams, Ralph, 65
Wilson, Lionel, 64
Wong, William Gee, 97
Woodell, Anne, 120
Wright, Bertha, 37
Wright, Mary Ann, 116
Yoakum, Wilhelmine, 48

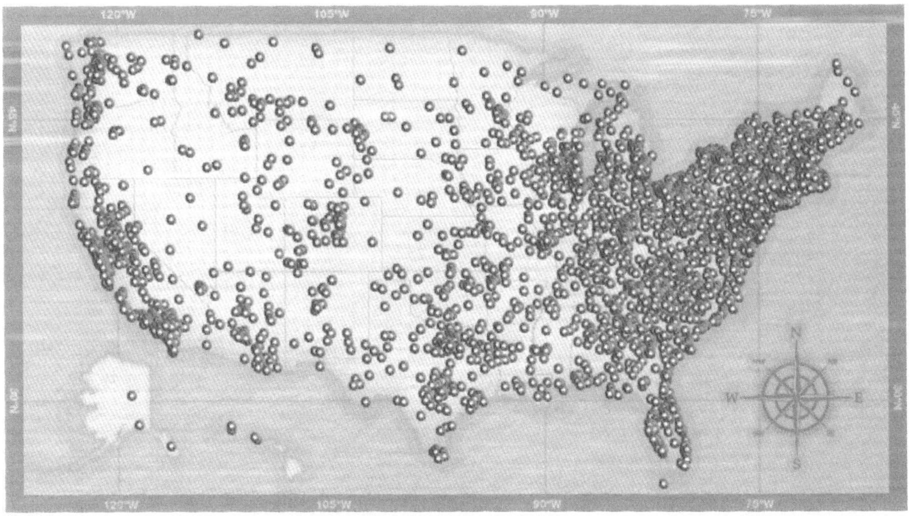